The Heart of Addiction

Mark E. Shaw

The Heart of Addiction
A Biblical Perspective

©2008, 2018

By Mark E. Shaw

ISBN 978-1-885904-68-3

Printed in the United States of America

Published by Focus Publishing
PO Box 665
Bemidji, MN 56619

Cover Design by Melanie Schmidt

Dedication

I do not cease to give thanks for you, remembering you in my prayers, that the God of our Lord Jesus Christ, the Father of glory, may give you a spirit of wisdom and of revelation in the knowledge of him, having the eyes of your hearts enlightened, that you may know what is the hope to which he has called you, what are the riches of his glorious inheritance in the saints, and what is the immeasurable greatness of his power toward us who believe, according to the working of his great might that he worked in Christ when he raised him from the dead and seated him at his right hand in the heavenly places, far above all rule and authority and power and dominion, and above every name that is named, not only in this age but also in the one to come. And he put all things under his feet and gave him as head over all things to the church, which is his body, the fullness of him who fills all in all. (Ephesians 1:16-23, ESV)

❀ In Memoriam ❧

Kenneth Hobbs Libby (1925-2005) and Don Bowen (1945-2007) two of my favorite Christians, who through their radical obedience to their Father in heaven, and by their demonstration of loving service in thanksgiving for eternal life, lived their final years as a living sacrifice of praise to their Savior, Jesus Christ.

Acknowledgments

I have attempted to diligently cite all the information I have learned from such great teachers as Jay Adams, Howard Eyrich, Stuart Scott, Lou Priolo, Aaron Fleming, Wayne Mack, and Harry Reeder. I have read so many of these men's books and listened to their preaching that it is often extremely difficult to differentiate from whom I learned which truth. However, I must particularly thank Lou Priolo, who opened the world of biblical counseling to me, and first instructed me in the crucial foundational concept that all of God's Word is profitable for doctrine, reproof, correction, and disciplined training in righteousness. All wisdom comes from God, and I am grateful for the faithful preaching and teaching of these and many other Christian men.

I thank my parents, Ronny and Sandra, for their love, support, admonishment, and encouragement.

A special thanks to my wife, Mary, who is my helper suitable, and from whom I have learned the most about my blessed Savior, the Lord Jesus Christ.

Contents

Appendixes

Introduction

My primary purpose for writing this book is to glorify God by pointing you to His Word that you may see how it sufficiently addresses the problems of "addiction" and substance abuse. Frankly, I find it troubling that, although God's Word lovingly tells us the truth about "the heart of addiction," it is a neglected resource for those who suffer from a variety of "addictions." Why would people disregard such a valuable resource as the Bible? Are some Christians limiting themselves by neglecting to consult God's Word and His powerful wisdom on this subject?

One of the reasons for failing to seek God's Word is that it does not fit with the world's ideas of addiction as a "disease." What a shame that Christians do not start with the Word of God but rather choose to start with the theories and ideas of mankind! Nearly every common behavioral problem is "diseased" in American culture: gambling, overeating, excessive time spent on the internet, excessive shopping and spending, stealing, and rebellious behavior. It all started less than one hundred years ago with the popularization of alcohol and drug abuse as a "disease concept" that is now widely accepted as "truth" rather than hypothesis and conjecture. The originators of this "disease concept" believed that the symptoms of "addiction" looked like a "disease" so they developed an *analogy* to describe the similarities. The symptoms were so frequently observed that the originators of this concept concluded that the heart of the problem had to be a "disease" that attacked the "addict". This of course would then relieve the addict of his guilt. The originators of this "disease concept" were not committed, evangelical, Bible-believers, therefore most of their ideas do not reflect foundational, biblical principles.

Consistent with this reasoning, non-Christians have no power to truly overcome an "addiction" so they really are "powerless." But can a Christian claim to be powerless if he or she has the indwelling power of the Holy Spirit to enable them to say "no" to a choice to excessively use a mood-altering substance? The answer is "no" since the power working in and through the Christian is the Holy Spirit. Because of the physical results of excessive consumption associated with "addiction," it is true to say that a Christian can be overtaken by a drug physically speaking; however, a Christian must not allow a drug to enslave him. The Bible calls this a "sin" problem.

Sin?

Sin is a misunderstood concept even in Christianity today so there is no wonder that it is misunderstood by unbelievers. If you watch television or listen to the radio, let me challenge you to a contest. Take a pen and paper and record how many times you hear the word "sin" used in a serious manner in a twenty-four hour period on any secular program. Do not count Christian television or radio (though some programs in that medium would be deficient!). If you hear the word "sin" used correctly just one time, I will be pleasantly surprised and you will win the contest (no prizes, of course).

Sadly, our culture has successfully removed this word from our everyday speech, and the concept of sin is nowhere to be found. So why did Jesus die? Did Jesus die for a "disease of addiction" that is not really our fault in the first place? No. Why would Jesus have to die for something that is not our fault? If God is fair, He would not unnecessarily punish His Son on the Cross. If one believes the "disease concept of addiction," there is no need for a Savior since the disease is not the addict's responsibility.

So, what did Jesus die for? "Our sins" is the obvious answer, but if sin is rarely mentioned in the culture, the Cross becomes less important in the minds of people. We need a larger understanding of sin so we can obtain a larger understanding of the Gospel message of the Cross. We need a solution for our sin problem and God has graciously provided the answer for sin in the atoning sacrifice of His Son Jesus and in the indwelling power of the Holy Spirit. You can overcome a sin problem but you will never overcome a "disease of addiction" problem. For this reason, I believe that purely biblical teachings provide hope for addicts.

We must establish a foundational principle about the use of the term "sin" when dealing with addiction. Since the Garden of Eden in Genesis 3, man has rejected the truth of God's Word, and the same rejection often holds true today in addiction counseling. I encourage you to embrace the idea of sin as the underlying cause for your addiction and you will gain more insights into how to overcome it.

The Specific Name of the Sin

Chemical addiction problems and excessive substance abuse really have two biblical names: one is a general name and the other is more specific. In general, "idolatry" is the proper biblical name for substance abuse problems whether you consider yourself a drunkard, binge drinker, drug addict, substance abuser, or whatever name you wish to call it. The problem is biblically labeled as the sin of idolatry and it is a heart problem from within one's sinful nature. Webster's Dictionary defines 'idol' as "a person or thing too much loved, admired or honored." The substance abuser seeks to please himself with his "god of choice" above pleasing God. The excessive user of alcohol and drugs is his own god; he is actively serving and pleasing the god of self by using drugs and alcohol. Ask yourself: "Am I serving God right now or seeking to please myself?"

In the Bible, God addresses addiction as a "sin nature" problem and everyone since Adam and Eve is born with a "sin nature" having the potential to become physically addicted to a chemical substance. Some mistakenly think that "drunkenness" only refers to alcohol, not drugs. The fact that many of us have been successfully indoctrinated into separating drugs and alcohol demonstrates the power of our culture upon our thinking. But, in fact, alcohol is a drug in liquid form!

Have you ever taken cough syrup for a cold or persistent cough? If so, then you *drank* a drug in liquid form. Likewise, alcohol contains mind-altering drugs in liquid form. Therefore, alcohol is a drug and "drunkenness" refers to the effect that a drug has on the one who consumes it. Whether someone drinks, snorts, shoots, inhales, smokes, dissolves, or imbibes a drug, the effects of the substance will be "drunkenness" which is what God has called the problem all along. The Bible is more relevant in addressing this "addiction" problem than you may have first imagined, but you will see God's wisdom magnificently displayed in His Word, and how it is relevant to your life. God's Word provides real hope and practical help to the problem of drunkenness when one is willing to redefine the problem God's way rather than mankind's way.

Who Should Read this Book?

In this book, a distinction is made between two words commonly used regarding this problem of drunkenness: "abuse" and "addiction." Addiction is best defined as the "persistent *habitual* use of a substance known by the user to be harmful" and often, but not always produces a physical dependency. Dependency depends upon the substance used. The other term used is "abuse" of an intoxicating substance which is defined as the "improper or excessive use, or misuse"[1] of that substance. Do not fool yourself. Abuse, addiction, occasional excessive use of a substance, and drunkenness might have consequences with varying degrees of severity, but they are all the result of the same inward problem of the sinful heart: idolatry. In the case of drunkenness, idolatry is manifested by the excessive consumption of alcohol or drugs to please self or escape the problems of life and avoid responsibilities; in essence, to feel pleasure and avoid pain or difficulty.

You may belong to either of the following two groups of people who qualify as "idolaters" and "drunkards" under this terminology:

- Those Christians who **occasionally yet excessively abuse** alcohol and drugs but do not consider themselves to be addicted to alcohol and drugs, or

- Those Christians who are **physically addicted** to alcohol and drugs.

Both groups are encouraged to read this book and apply the practical instruction to their lives. Regardless of the extent of the devastation in your life due to your substance abuse behaviors and sin, abuse and addiction both have the same root issues – the same sinful motives of the heart.

Excessive use of a substance is not just a simple sin problem. It is a life-dominating and life-devastating sin nature problem. This sin nature problem requires the Savior's forgiveness and the Holy Spirit's power to overcome it; not just an individual's "will power." It is the "will of God power" that overcomes addiction. The "perishing" mentality fueled by pride, selfishness, and self-pity must be put-off. The mind must be renewed by the Holy Spirit who works in conjunction with God's Word under the authority of the local church. A "joyful" and optimistic mentality fueled by serving and pleasing God (and others) must be 'put-on' to replace old attitudes, thoughts, and behaviors. It will require a change in thinking and acting called "repentance" to overcome your substance abuse problems.

If you are reading this book for a loved one who abuses drugs or alcohol, you must apply these principles to yourself first because you may have a desire for something in your life that would qualify as "idolatry." Ask the Lord to change your heart and enable you to grow in the grace of God in this area of your life. A great theologian

---

[1] Merriam-Webster, I. (1996, c1993). Merriam-Webster's collegiate dictionary. Includes index. (10th ed.). Springfield, Mass., U.S.A.: Merriam-Webster.

once said that each human being is an "idol factory" because we are all capable of producing new idols in mass quantities.[2]

If you are struggling right now with what the world calls an "addiction" to food, sex, gambling, video games, shopping, or anything else pleasurable, then this book should be a great source of hope and help to you. You will find biblical tools to help you examine your heart's motives at the root of the addiction. It is true that in some ways an "addiction" to food is different than an "addiction" to alcohol. Likewise, an "addiction" to sex manifests differently than an "addiction" to gambling and so on. The consequences of these various "addiction" categories can be vastly different, too. Nevertheless, these differences do not change at the heart level of the problem: a focus upon pleasing and worshiping oneself (idolatry) rather than pleasing and worshiping the Lord Jesus Christ. "Addiction" is a "worship disorder" and not a man-made, theoretical "disease." The principles found in God's Word are simple yet profound, and have a variety of applications for a variety of "addiction categories" and sin patterns.

What You Will Be Learning

This book is divided into four sections that follow the pattern described in II Timothy 3:16-17: **"All Scripture is breathed out by God and profitable for <u>teaching</u>, for <u>reproof</u>, for <u>correction</u>, and for <u>training in righteousness</u>, that the man of God may be competent, equipped for every good work"** (Emphasis mine).

- Section One will provide biblical "teaching" and insights about addictive thinking.

- Section Two will provide a "reproof," or a "rebuke." A "reproof" is defined as a "criticism for a fault."[3] The Lord wants to turn you from walking down the wrong path of serving yourself to serving Him.

- Section Three will provide "correction" so you will learn how to renew your mind to think more biblically about addiction.

- Section Four will provide "training for righteousness" so that you can successfully practice doing what is right to overcome addiction permanently.

---

[2] Taken from several sermons and teachings of Pastor Harry Reeder at Briarwood Presbyterian Church.

[3] Merriam-Webster, op. cit.

Prayer of Heart Change and Application

My Father in Heaven, you alone are holy. Thank you for sending Your Son, Jesus, to save your children from their sins. Please save me from my sins and place Jesus' righteousness upon me. I do not deserve your forgiveness nor have I earned it. Empower me to begin living for you, Lord. Enable me to overcome my addictions and idolatrous heart desires by replacing them with righteous desires. Help me to be teachable, intentional, and open-minded to your Word of Truth. Give me a hunger to read, study, and memorize the Bible so that I can know you more, Father God. I ask that you would send someone to disciple me to help me better understand biblical truths. Amen.

Section One

Teaching

Chapter 1
A Spiritual Problem

Interestingly, the world's approach and God's approach to the problem of drunkenness are very similar. Both approaches agree on the categorization of the problem. Both approaches agree on the symptoms of the problem. Both approaches even agree on the fact that the root cause of the problem is "spiritual!" Though many Christian ministry workers or counselors try to marry these two approaches because of these commonalities, the two systems of thinking are diametrically opposed at the heart level. At its core, the main issue is whether "addiction" is a "disease concept" or a "sin nature" problem of idolatry and drunkenness. At this heart level, you cannot merge the world's approach with God's approach to addiction.

Any approach that combines worldly, man-centered ideas with biblical truths is a "mixture approach" that often leads to utter confusion for all, Christians and non-Christians alike. Persons suffering from the problem of substance abuse are already confused and often desperate souls in need of real answers. The Bible provides these answers from Genesis to Revelation. In this book, I will present some of the relevant, biblical truths applied to "addiction" without "mixing in" many of the confusing ideas of mankind's worldly wisdom. The majority of recent books written on the subject of "addiction" are "mixture approaches" that confuse Christians.

Providing biblical principles for overcoming all types of addictions, especially chemical addictions, is another goal of this book. God wrote the greatest Book of all time, and He addresses this serious problem more effectively than any other book you will ever read. It is my desire that His Word of Truth will be opened to you by His power provided by the Holy Spirit because you cannot overcome your addictions and the idolatrous desires of your heart without Him.

What I purposely avoid in this book is the temptation to give ten, twenty, or fifty steps to overcoming addiction. Instead, I want to point you to a healthy spiritual relationship with the unique and incredible God of the Bible. The only steps to follow for cultivating a relationship with God is to humble yourself, confess your sins and sinful nature, place your trust in Christ alone, and ask the Holy Spirit to lead you so you can live a life pleasing unto the Lord. If you desire some helpful structure for your transformation process, then I strongly encourage you to turn to Appendix K and implement those guidelines.

The biblical approach to addiction offers hope and opportunity for success if you will strive to be open-minded and teachable. You may have to lay aside some of your old ideas in favor of what the Lord says in His Word regarding this issue, but He promises that it will be worth it when you do. You are encouraged to get a trusted, Christian friend who can disciple you by using this book together with the Bible so you can grow in your relationship with Christ. I pray that God will provide more insight, power, and grace to overcome your addiction in a biblical manner.

A Testimony of the Power of God's Word

Several years ago, I conceived of the idea to start a residential "Bible Program" for substance abusers at the counseling center where I worked as clinical director. I was granted permission by the executive director to launch this new, pilot program. The Bible Program was planned to mirror the "mixture approach" program that had existed there for over a decade. For example, if the "mixture" program required self-help meetings; the Bible Program required interactive Bible study discussion meetings. If the "mixture" program required a group meeting on anger from a secular perspective, then the Bible Program required a group meeting on anger from a biblical perspective and so on. I wanted to demonstrate that the Bible dealt with every topic the "mixture" program addressed but with more effectiveness and power. The Bible Program was a purely biblical approach to addiction.

Prior to admission, the coordinator for the entire facility would screen men to determine their appropriateness for treatment. I instructed the coordinator to give the incoming persons a choice using this statement and following question: "We have two options for you to consider: you can choose to go into our traditional, self-help program we have used to help addicts for over a decade, or you can choose to enter a newly developed, pilot program that only teaches what the Bible says about addiction, anger, depression, and the problems of life. Which program would you prefer to enter?" The incoming counselee had the opportunity to choose his program's approach to his problems![4] Obviously, there were times that an incoming person desired more information about the Bible Program and it was provided to them. One person was told that the Bible and Bible studies were substituted for secular books and that church fellowships, services, and mentoring were substituted for secular, self-help meetings.

During the brief six months that the program existed, twelve men voluntarily entered the Bible Program. I asked my friend and co-worker, Don Bowen, to be the primary counselor in the Bible Program. Don did a great job of teaching those men the Bible. I helped by teaching Bible groups and asking members of churches in the local area to help us disciple and mentor these young men. Truly, it was a team effort of united Christians from several different denominations who wanted to uplift the Lord Jesus Christ by speaking the truth of God's Word to these men in the love of the Holy Spirit.

It was easy to identify several contrasts between the two approaches existing side-by-side under the same roof. First, the Bible Program men were required to eat meals together, which fostered a sense of community unlike the other program which was "every man for himself." Second, the men were asked to pray for each other both privately and corporately. Again, a genuine, brotherly love for one another was developed. Third, the focus of the Bible Program was not about "getting off drugs" or "staying clean and sober." Instead, the focus was on Christ and Him alone. When the proper focus upon Christ was in place, men in the Bible Program stayed clean and sober because their sin disorder was diagnosed and treated properly.

One observable difference between the two programs was that the Bible Program men kept their grounds beautiful. Both programs had cigarette smokers but you would be hard-pressed to find a cigarette butt on the Bible Program grounds whereas they were frequently found on the "mixture approach" grounds. In fact, men in the Bible Program beautified their grounds by planting flowers, mowing, and landscaping their living areas. Overall, there was an atmosphere of love, warmth, acceptance, support, and respect for their living quarters and environment that the men of the Bible Program displayed that I have not seen at any secular drug and alcohol treatment program I have ever visited.

The most important difference between the two programs was

---

[4] An interesting note is that most men we were trying to help chose the "mixture" approach over the Bible Program.

evident in the quality of the changed lives of the majority of men
in the Bible Program. The Lord's amazing power working through
those men inspired me to write this book. I do not pretend to know
everything about the Word of God, yet I do believe that when
Christians honor God's Word, God is pleased that we are listening
to Him tell us the truth about addiction and the real needs of our
human hearts. You deserve real answers that are only found in the
Word of God. Do not sell yourself short by believing the lies of Satan
and worldly wisdom that merely want you to "stay clean and sober"
while on this earth with no hope for eternal life. God wants you
to have a higher goal of worshiping Him alone because when you
succeed in that goal, you will receive both heaven and earth.

A Spiritual Answer

Substance abuse and addiction[5] manifest as a physical problem
but the root issues are in the spiritual realm of one's own heart.
Even many unbelievers and secular programs treat addiction as a
"spiritual" problem of the heart though their "spiritual" approach is
often not Christian or based upon a biblical foundation. Unbelievers
view addiction as a "disease" that attacks addicts, who need a
"higher power" because they are "powerless" to overcome it. They
are free to choose their "higher power", but who really is the "higher
power"? It is the person doing the choosing of his "god." Does that
"higher power" really have more power than the person choosing it
to be a "higher power"? This may be a "spiritual" approach, but is it
Christian? Is it biblical?

Is it safe for Christians to turn to any "spiritual" approach for
help? What "spirits" are Christians turning to in this type of "mixture
approach"? It may agree with the Bible in some ways but strongly
oppose the Bible on other, foundational points. These are strong
questions that every believer must contemplate with an open mind
to the God of the Bible. Thankfully, the deep, spiritual problem of
the heart is sufficiently addressed by the Bible. The terms for this
problem of the heart may be different than what you usually hear,
since the Bible labels this problem as "idolatry" and "drunkenness."

---

[5] I have redefined the world's term 'addiction' and extensively explained
my new definition eliminating the idea of compulsive behavior and
addressing the sin issues involved in the chapter entitled, "Redefining
the World's Terminology."

In the following pages, the terms "substance abuse" and "substance abuser" are utilized at times as well as the words "addict" and "addiction" because this is the terminology that most people understand. However, as a Christian who possesses a new heart and new identity in Christ, understand that "addiction" is a *physical symptom* of a *deeper, spiritual problem of the attitudes of the heart* generally called *"idolatry"* in the *Bible*. Specific to substance abuse, the Bible labels the effects of "addiction" as *"drunkenness."*

A Worship Disorder

Some people understand the word "worship" to be limited to something that can only occur at church during a church service. However, nothing could be further from the truth. "Worship" is "reverence offered a divine being or supernatural power"[6] and any thought, word, and act is worship. For example, if you work as an accountant and you do your best work unto the glory of God, then your daily work involves acts of worship. This definition of "worship" is understood in the Bible as I Corinthians 10:31 states: **"So, whether you eat or drink, or whatever you do, do all to the glory of God."**

"Idolatry" is defined as "the worship of a physical object as a god or immoderate attachment or devotion to something."[7] It is "immoderate"; meaning it leads to extreme thinking and behaving. It is an "attachment" to a "physical object" for the purpose of "worship." For the Christian, it is a sin to worship a physical object. It is also a sin to worship self. Christians are designed by their Creator to worship Him. All human beings worship. Everyone worships either a physical object, themselves as "god," a false religion's god, or the one true God: the Lord Jesus Christ.

The word "idolatry" can be applied to any pleasure that becomes so excessively desired that it replaces the desire to worship God. This may include drugs, alcohol, sex, food, gambling, sleep, television, internet, exercise, sports, and video games, just to name a few! II Timothy 3:4 identifies persons who desire an idolatrous pleasure more than they desire to honor God as **"lovers of pleasure rather than lovers of God."** Loving pleasure may include avoiding pain; the two ideas are different sides of the same coin. Both the love of pleasure and the avoidance of pain (or escape) fuel any "addiction."

---

[6] Merriam-Webster, op.cit.
[7] Merriam-Webster, op.cit.

The idolatry of drunkenness, substance abuse, and addiction is not a new problem to the Lord. This book will specifically address the sins related to substance abuse and a physical addiction to drugs and alcohol. However, the biblical principles for overcoming a substance abuse problem also apply to the various idolatrous pleasures listed above, since those pleasures can be experienced excessively, can cause one to neglect his or her responsibilities, and can lead to devastating problems and consequences.

Defining the "Heart"

The English language has a literal and figurative meaning of the word "heart." Literally, the heart is the physical organ that pumps blood throughout your body to all of your extremities. We would all agree that the heart is an essential component in the physical body.

Figuratively, the heart is the spiritual, innermost part of a human being. The Greek word the Bible often uses for "heart" is "kardia", figuratively defined as "the *soul or mind*, as it is the fountain and seat of the thoughts, passions, desires, appetites, affections, purposes, endeavors."[8] The Bible teaches that the spiritual heart of a person is the essence of that person and will live forever in eternity.[9]

When I mention your "heart" in this book, I mean your inner, spiritual person consisting of your mind, spirit, and soul. You are a wonderful mixture of a physical body and a spiritual body. While your physical body consists of many intricate parts such as your brain, spinal cord and nervous system, your spiritual body has intricate "parts," too as mentioned above: "thoughts, passions, desires, appetites, affections, purposes, and endeavors."[10] Your mind, will, and emotions are contained in your spiritual person.

My desire is to deal with your spiritual person in this book. There is an interaction of the physical person and spiritual person; however, the "will, soul, attitude, and thoughts (or mind)" are all terms that are distinctly spiritual. It is your spiritual heart that matters most to God. I Samuel 13:14 describes David as **"a man after"** God's own heart when it says: **"The Lord has sought out a man after his own**

---

[8] Strong, J. 1996. The exhaustive concordance of the Bible : Showing every word of the text of the common English version of the canonical books, and every occurrence of each word in regular order (electronic ed.). Woodside Bible Fellowship: Ontario.

[9] I Peter 1:9. John 10:28 & 6:58. Titus 1:2 & 3:7.

[10] Strong, J. 1996, op.cit.

heart." The Lord must perform spiritual heart surgery for every one of us so that our hearts of selfishness become transformed by the Holy Spirit to become hearts that seek and serve God. Psalm 119:36 asks of the Lord: **"Incline my heart to your testimonies, and not to selfish gain!"**

Keeping It Simple

Throughout this book, simply keep in mind that there are two paths for us to travel in life. The first path is to follow the flesh and its desires to seek pleasure and avoid pain. In other words, one who walks down this road is living to please self. Theologians would call this type of lifestyle "idolatry" and the "worship of self." The second path is to follow the leading of the Holy Spirit. One who travels down this road is living to please the Lord. Theologians would call this type of lifestyle "Christianity" and a proper understanding of "worship." If you will remember these two paths throughout the book, you will have greater insight and enhanced understanding of the content. Try not to make things more complicated than they already are!

God's wisdom is both simple and profound at the same time. Only God can truly manage that feat successfully. It may surprise you that God has given His people the answers for addiction in the Bible. The Christian substance abuser and addict can find tremendous hope and practical advice in the Word of God. It is my desire that this book will help point the way to God's Way.

Prayer of Heart Change and Application

Dear Heavenly Father, I have been confused about addiction. It is a confusing subject. Therefore, I need your wisdom to answer my questions. Help me to believe you when I read your Word, knowing that you alone can be trusted. I cannot even trust myself in what I already think about addiction because I have not searched your Word diligently to find out the truth about idolatry and addiction. Father, as I read this book, teach me not only what you say about addiction, but teach me to identify my heart's motives when I excessively use alcohol or drugs. Help me not to seek pleasure but to seek to glorify you first in all I do. Transform my heart by making me more like Jesus Christ by the power of the Holy Spirit working through your Word of Truth. Oh God, enable me to become what you intended me to be. Forgive me for living independently of you. Let my actions match these words of repentance. Create in me a clean heart that wants to do what you want first and wants to know you more deeply. I need You, Lord, to guide me, teach me, and reveal yourself to me. Open my eyes so that I may see you when I read the Bible and go to church. Thank you for being patient, kind, and loving to me when I have been impatient, unkind, and unloving to you. Amen.

Chapter 2
Man's Theories and God's Truth

While there may be many approaches to addiction, at the heart level there are really only two approaches: God's biblical approach and mankind's worldly "wisdom" approach. Most of mankind's approaches are what I call "mixtures" because they mix Christian truths with worldly lies. Nearly every modern writer on addiction uses a worldly mindset to deal with addictive thoughts and behaviors. While it is impossible to critique every program and its approach, I will address three critical foundational theories of man that oppose the Bible in this chapter.

The world's approach differs from the biblical approach in three important, foundational ways. It is important that you understand how these approaches differ fundamentally so that your thinking can become more biblical. These distinctions can be most easily understood by recognizing that the world's way is primarily "man-centered" while God's way is primarily "God-centered." God has commanded His creatures to be God-centered: **"See to it that no one takes you captive by philosophy and empty deceit, according to human tradition, according to the elemental spirits of the world, and not according to Christ."[11]**

Man-centered ideas focus upon pleasing man first. God-centered ideas focus upon pleasing God first, and when that occurs, the secondary result is that man will find his pleasure in God. Man-centered ideas can be seen in the prevalence of such unbiblical ideas as "self-help groups," addiction as a "disease," and the idea of a "recovery process." The lies behind these concepts must be exposed with biblical truths prior to understanding the biblical approach to addiction. Sadly, some of today's churches are preaching and promoting these unbiblical concepts as biblical truth or mixed with biblical truth. It is the "oil and water approach" and everyone knows that oil and water do not mix. They may be placed together into one container, but they remain separate because they are totally different substances. Likewise, biblical truths do not mix well with man-centered concepts and theories. Many of the modern, secular concepts have little biblical support, but because they are popular

---

[11] Colossians 2:8.

and supposedly "work,"[12] some churches embrace them.

Self-Help Groups vs. Christ's Church

How many ideas and phrases have we believed in the past, thinking they were Christian when they were not? For example, where in the Bible does it say, "God helps those who help themselves"? Give up? It is not in the Bible, yet people quote it as a biblical idea. The phrase is not entirely erroneous because God does hold us responsible for our thoughts and actions and He expects us to grow spiritually. However, God has made us dependent upon Him and others, and He has given us resources so that we do not have to rely only upon our own efforts to successfully overcome substance abuse and addiction. God has provided every Christian with:

- a Savior in Jesus Christ
- the indwelling of the Holy Spirit
- the Bible
- the evangelical church
- prayer
- fellowship with believers in Christ in your local church

There is no such thing as "self-help" for a Christian. God does not expect you to "pull yourself up by your bootstraps" without His help or the help of other believers in Christ. Repeatedly, the Bible warns believers about traveling down their own path rather than walking God's path.[13] Proverbs 12:15 states: **"The way of a fool is right in his own eyes, but a wise man listens to advice."** Proverbs 28:26 says: **"Whoever trusts in his own mind is a fool, but he who walks in wisdom will be delivered."** In a group setting, "self-help" meetings, which are often devoid of the Word of God and the leading of the Holy Spirit, are like the blind leading the blind. Eventually, you are going to fall into a ditch or walk off a cliff.

Turn to your pastor, deacons, elders, biblical counselors, and

---

[12] I caution you to investigate how "scientifically" most programs report their "successes." What is the criteria used to define a success? Total abstinence, heart change, mere completion of a program, 6 months of sobriety?

[13] Judges 17:6, Psalms 81:12, Proverb 3:5 and 3:7, Philippians 2:21, and II Timothy 3:2, to name a few!

trusted Christian friends for support, help, accountability, and counseling. God ordained the church to do His work, and helping you to overcome addiction is included. Matthew 16:18b quotes Jesus who says that He is the foundational rock for God's church: **"I will build my church, and the gates of hell shall not prevail against it."** Addiction feels like hell on earth. You must utilize God's church in overcoming addiction because it is an integral part of His plan.

Referral to the "Experts"

Whether churches believe that Christians can become physically addicted or not, they generally refer their members to secular modalities for help in coping with substance abuse. The physically addicted Christian must then submit to worldly wisdom devoid of Christianity in order "to get clean and sober." Some pastors, elders, and deacons believe the lie that the church and its leaders are inadequate to help the suffering Christian addict. God has commanded His church to shepherd, protect, help, serve, and minister to Christian addicts.

It may be necessary to refer a Christian addict to a medical facility or detoxification unit temporarily if there is the possibility of life-threatening withdrawal symptoms. However, there are numerous drawbacks for Christians who attend secular treatment programs for alcohol and drug addiction. *Christians who spend weeks or months in secular treatment facilities are programming their minds with humanistic, man-centered, and anti-Christian teachings.* While learning these worldly perspectives that deny the very truth of the Bible, it becomes much more difficult for a Christian who is enslaved to an addiction to come to know the God of the Bible. And it becomes nearly impossible for an unbeliever to hear the Gospel and be saved. Biblical teachings are the only answer because the Bible

- is the truth
- is sufficient to teach the man of God all things (II Timothy 3:16-17)
- reveals God's character in an accurate and balanced manner

Most secular modalities cannot or do not teach the biblical principles of addiction *accurately*. In fact, basic concepts about mankind propagated by these secular modalities are in direct opposition to the Holy Scriptures. Here are four examples of unbiblical ideas that are promoted in many "Christian programs":

- Man is born without a sinful nature
- Man is inherently good and has a "clean slate" at birth
- Man goes "bad" due to an "addiction" and must "recover" the old person who was really "good" prior to the "addiction" problem
- Addiction is not a sin – it's a disease

Turn to Appendix A for a comparison and contrast of the biblical church and self-help groups.

Disease Concept of Addiction vs. Sin Nature

Although the idea is less than one hundred years old, the theory of addiction as a "disease" is so prevalent today that it is being preached in some churches! When a lie is repeated many times over, it is often perceived to be true. Such is the case with addiction. While the purpose of this book is to demonstrate the transforming power of the biblical approach to addiction, the prevalence of the disease idea makes it necessary to briefly acknowledge it.[14] Initially, the idea of addiction being compared to a medical disease was conceptualized to help people understand the dynamics of addiction. By comparing it to a medical disease, theorists hypothesized that addiction could be better understood. The idea was not originally intended to make addiction into a disease of its own, but regrettably, that is exactly what has happened.[15]

The humanistic idea that addiction is a "disease" implies that some sickness outside of the addict overtakes them once they've tried a mood-altering substance. This "disease" has either penetrated them somehow from the outside, or it is a genetic "disease" passed down by parents. When addicts accept the "disease" idea, they believe they must wrestle with this cancer-like illness for the rest of their lives. The "disease concept" gives the worldly approach more credibility as people often consider the idea to be "real science" and a "medical problem." This lie offers *no hope* that the addict will ever completely overcome the "disease". It is a flawed, humanistic theory on addiction.[16]

---

[14] The Useful Lie by W. Playfair and Addicted to Recovery by Almy and Almy give much more insight into the flaws of the disease concept.

[15] Ideas presented at a lecture taught by Don Bowen at Eastwood Presbyterian Church in 2004.

[16] Again, read The Useful Lie by Playfair for a better understanding of the treatment industry and its ideas.

This worldly advice is the best that mankind has to offer. Non-Christians are hopelessly lost, however, whether addicted to drugs or not because they are not trusting Christ with a faith in Him that produces repentance. However, this lie tells Christians that they are *hopeless victims* of a false "disease" which is not true for the believer in Jesus Christ.

Addiction is not a disease. Addiction is a "sin nature" problem and the body responds to the substances in natural ways. Then, in time, the actions associated with addiction become habitual and extremely difficult to overcome. The "symptoms" of the problem are observable and common in most addicts. However, the similarities between the biblical approach and the secular, man-centered approach end there.

How can these mixture approaches (mixing some truth with lies) help you attack addiction God's way when these humanistic lies are in direct opposition to the Holy Scriptures? They can help someone overcome the addiction in the short-term but they do not offer long-term, sustaining help. They do not help an addict clearly understand the heart of addiction and the mixture often confuses those who desire to study God's Word. God does not consider addiction a "disease," but a "sin nature" problem. Biblical concepts are truly life-giving to those who profess to love and to trust in Jesus Christ.

Trust God's Word More than Your Ideas and Feelings

If you, the Christian addict, have established sinful habit patterns in the flesh, then you must replace them with godly habits. You have made small decisions in the beginning of your usage of the substance that has now led you to a *seemingly* hopeless situation in which you *feel* as if you have no choice. Thankfully, Christians are "born again" and receive a new heart and new nature. The Holy Spirit takes up residence inside you and works in conjunction with God's Word. You still experience struggles against sin because the sinful nature does not automatically vanish when you are born again. Some of the habits you have learned are not just physical habits but are habitual patterns of *thinking and responding* to life's hardships. Your responsibility as a Christian is to cultivate Godly ways of habitually thinking, speaking, behaving, and feeling. This is to be thoroughly explained in the chapters on "Renewing Your Mind."

Again, the idea that your struggle with an addiction is an "incurable, lifelong disease" is a half-truth of humanistic and mixture approaches. The Bible tells you the truth: you will struggle with sinful thoughts, words, and behaviors related to addiction even after you have initially overcome the physical portion of addiction. A biblical, Christian counselor will acknowledge that:

- Physically, you may experience real cravings.

- Mentally, you may always battle to take your thoughts captive in this life.

- Emotionally, you may struggle with feelings of depression, despair, anger, and guilt that will tempt you to want to use drugs and alcohol for an "escape."

- Spiritually, there may be days when you think God has forgotten you and you believe yourself to be separated from Him.

A biblical counselor will point you to John 14:16-17 which states: **"And I will ask the Father, and he will give you another Helper, to be with you forever, even the Spirit of truth, whom the world cannot receive, because it neither sees him nor knows him. You know him, for he dwells with you and will be in you."** The Holy Spirit lives <u>within you</u> even when you feel as if God is far away so do not trust your *feelings*.

To battle your substance abuse problem and addiction requires your best efforts to work at overcoming the powerful grip of the physical, mental, emotional, and spiritual components of the sin involved. However, the good news is that your struggles with your "sin nature" will lessen in time as you build a sober and obedient lifestyle while applying the practical tools given in God's Word, some of which are outlined in this book. In addition, you are not ill-equipped if you are a Christian – you have the power of the Holy Spirit working in you. It is hard work, but worth both the temporal and eternal benefits from God. This is called the process of sanctification in the life of a believer. We will address more on this cooperation of the believer and the Holy Spirit in later chapters. I John 4:4 has some good news for God's people: **"Little children, you are from God and have overcome them, for he who is in you is greater than he who is in the world."** Therefore, you cannot say that you are "powerless" to overcome your addiction because Christ within you provides you with the power you need.

"Recovery" vs. "Transforming"

A final distinction between the secular and mixture approaches as opposed to the biblical approach to addiction is in basic terminology. Instead of the secular word "recovery,"[17] a Christian addict who is truly willing yet struggling to maintain sobriety is in a process called a "transformation" according to Romans 12:2: **"Do not be conformed to this world, but be transformed by the renewal of your mind, that by testing you may discern what is the will of God, what is good and acceptable and perfect."** Let's distinguish between the two terms and their underlying, foundational meanings.

The verb "recover" is defined as "to bring back to normal position or condition" as though you have "stumbled, then *recovered* yourself."[18] The idea of stumbling and then recovering yourself is rooted in the idea that we are born as "good" people without a sin nature. This idea is a comfortable, humanistic concept akin to the idea of "self-help." Its popularity stems from our desire to believe that we are inherently good rather than inherently sinful. Also, it is a popular idea that we can stumble along life's path and pick ourselves up "by our bootstraps." Who needs God when we can "recover our self?" No one needs God if they have the power to "recover" without Him.

Furthermore, in the definition for "recover," you do not need to return "back to" a "normal position" because you were not "normal" before. You were born with a "sin nature" and must become "a new creation" in Christ Jesus.[19] There is nothing normal to regain other than returning to your normal, selfish, addicted person. Again, the foundational principle of this definition for "recovery" is the humanistic idea that man is inherently good. Humanists wrongly believe there are good people and there are bad people, but everyone starts out "good" with a "clean slate." Regrettably, many treatment

---

[17] Some Christian programs like "Celebrate Recovery" use the term "recovery" sometimes in an acceptable manner that closely resembles a transformation. I much prefer the word "transformation" because it is a life-giving, biblical word that provides hope more than "recovery." I understand the desire of programs like CR to help lead people to Christ so I do not fault them for that. I just prefer that they use biblical words and principles rather than mixing man's ideas with God's wisdom.

[18] Merriam-Webster, I. (1996, c1993). Merriam-Webster's collegiate dictionary. Includes index. (10th ed.). Springfield, Mass., U.S.A.: Merriam-Webster.

[19] II Corinthians 5:17

centers, locked facilities, and self-help groups propagate these humanistic lies and sometimes do so under the guise of Christianity as a so- called "Christian program"!

In stark contrast, the Bible does not view man as born "good." The Bible shows all persons to be born with a selfish "sin nature." The focus of the sin nature is to please self. The verb "transform" is defined as having "to change in character or condition."[20] Addicts must have the nature of their hearts changed. Addicts cannot change their own hearts. Family members cannot change the addict's heart. Biblical counselors cannot change the addict's heart. Only God has the power to change someone's heart; He changes the heart of a Christian addict *by making that heart want* to do the right things. *Willingness* is the essential starting point for a Christian addict. When God changes your heart, then you can begin to replace your flawed, "perishing thinking" with the perfect, joyful, and righteous thinking of God Himself.

If you identify yourself as a Christian substance abuser or addict who has had a heart change yet you find yourself struggling with an addiction, then you are in need of a complete "transformation" and not just a "recovery" of your "old self." Let your old self die and let the new creation in Christ Jesus live! In fact, all Christians want to *avoid* yielding to their old selves as much as possible. All Christians have three primary responsibilities in the "transformation" process:

1) Put off the old habit patterns of the flesh
2) Renew the mind with God's Word
3) Put on godly habits of the Holy Spirit.[21]

Ephesians 4:22-24 is the basis of these three responsibilities that can be applied to the Christian addict: **"to put off your old self, which belongs to your former manner of life and is corrupt through deceitful desires, and to be renewed in the spirit of your minds, and to put on the new self, created after the likeness of God in true righteousness and holiness."** These three aspects of "transformation" will be covered in more detail in later chapters.

One more note about the secular word "recover." An alternate meaning for "recover" is "to cover again"[22] and unfortunately, this is

---

[20] Merriam-Webster, op.cit.
[21] Berg, Jim, Changed Into His Image: God's Plan for Transforming Your Life, Greenville, SC: Bob Jones University Press, p. 9.
[22] Merriam-Webster, op. cit.

precisely what most addicts do on a continual basis. Here are some heart searching questions to ponder:

- Are you willing to give up your mood-altering, addictive substance for a life of submission and sobriety, or does God still need to change your desires to be more pleasing to Him?

- Have you been trying to cover the consequences of your addiction by lying and deceiving those who love you? If so, maybe your heart has not yet changed, and you are not interested in becoming sober any more than a rich man desires to become poor.

- Have you gone to treatment centers in an effort to appease your wearied loved ones, but not been able to stay sober for long once you left the facility?

- Have you gotten off drugs and alcohol but then turned your addiction to sex, food, or other temporary pleasures? This concept is commonly called "cross-addicted" and occurs frequently because no real heart change was made.

- Are you willing to submit yourself fully to the process of change that will occur in you as you repent, are forgiven, put off the old manner, renew your mind, and put on the new manner of living for Jesus?

Rather than change temporary addictions, you, the Christian substance abuser and addict, require a complete "transformation" from your old self, old way of thinking, addictive habits, and old manner of speaking. Your "new self" must now live in a way that pleases and glorifies God. It is not a "recovering" process of forever grappling with a more powerful foe with no real hope of overcoming it. Instead, it is a "transformation" process by God's grace and you become a new creation in Christ. It cannot be done apart from the Lord Jesus Christ.

One Approach with Authority

If you are still not convinced that addiction *is not* a "spiritual *disease* with a lifelong process of *recovery* and *self-help groups*," then I challenge you right now to stop reading and go research all *truly scientific* journals for one shred of scientific proof that addiction is a "disease." It cannot be done because there is no *scientific evidence* to support the notion that addiction is a "disease." It is a man-made theory and it is wrong. Secularists accept the idea of a "disease concept" because it makes sense to them, but their foundation is wrongly based upon the idea that man decides truth. God decides truth, not man. Addiction looks like a disease, but it is a sin nature problem in the heart rather than a disease coming from the outside to the inside. The heart of mankind is not inherently good at birth and does not become corrupted through the traumatic events of life. Instead, the heart of mankind is corrupt at birth and stays corrupt until God intervenes because of His love.

The biblical approach agrees with the world's observations about the symptoms of addiction. But the heart of addiction and the root cause are not the same because the biblical approach deals with a sinful, selfish heart. We are about to examine the same thoughts, words, emotions, and behaviors that humanistic, secular addiction counselors examine when "treating" an addict. This book will observe the same facts, evidence, or "symptoms" of the addiction as the secular world. However, a major difference will emerge in the following pages: you will view these "symptoms" from a biblical foundation of truth that will shed light upon this common problem of addiction. When that occurs, you will be better able to discern the half-truths of the world, and you will distinguish the lies from the truth. You must first learn God's truth to be able to identify the lies of Satan.

Do not try to merge the world's best ideas with God's truth or you will get confused. Allow God to speak the truth in love to you about your addiction and you will find peace, joy, comfort, wisdom, and blessing. *Read with an open mind realizing that your foundational thinking is probably a mixture of worldly half-truths rather than the purity of God's Word of Truth that is life-giving and freeing.* As you read, consider yourself a "transforming" substance abuser or addict rather than a "recovering" one if you are truly willing to maintain a sober lifestyle that pleases God.

Prayer of Heart Change and Application

Dear Heavenly Father, I want to face my addiction your way: not in my own strength, not in my own best ideas, not in mankind's best ideas, and not in a selfish way. I want to submit my knowledge of addiction to you so that you can transform my understanding of it and I can become wise. I need your wisdom, Lord. Please give me knowledge, wisdom, understanding, insight, and discernment so that I will no longer suffer from this addiction and so that I will honor you. Amen.

Chapter 3
Redefining the World's Terminology

Words are tricky in the English language. There are hidden meanings to some words and alternate meanings to many words. I believe that words are important because God refers to Jesus as the Word that became flesh in John 1:14. Furthermore, with the exception of the formation of mankind, God *spoke* much of His creation into existence in the first two chapters of Genesis. For example, in Genesis 1:3: **"And God said, 'Let there be light,' and there was light."** Repeatedly, God spoke and it was created. Words are important to God. In this chapter, I will redefine some secular words in the field of addiction with meanings that are biblical.

Secular Definition of Addiction

The world broadly defines "addiction" as the "persistent *compulsive* use of a substance known by the user to be harmful.[23] This definition should be problematic for Christians. Why? To label addictive behavior as *purely* "compulsive" is wrong because the Bible teaches that each person is individually responsible. Acts of drunkenness or over-indulgence are often carefully planned prior to the actual usage of the substance. Something that is planned cannot be described as "compulsive" because a compulsive behavior is defined as "an *irresistible* impulse to perform an irrational act."[24] We can agree that *the act is irrational* because it

- does not make sense
- gives only temporary pleasure
- often results in heartache once the pleasure disappears

However, the impulse to perform *the act is not "irresistible."* *Irrational, yes; irresistible, no.* The use of the word *"compulsive"* implies that you cannot control the behavior at all. In the early stages of addiction, wrong choices are often made with a planned purpose to escape from the sorrows of life. According to the definition of the

---

[23] Merriam Webster, op.cit.
[24] Ibid.

world, you are hopelessly out of control in your addiction because you cannot stop yourself. That is not true for a Christian filled with the Holy Spirit. Early in the addiction process, you have made a deliberate choice to use a harmful substance. You are responsible.

This worldly definition of compulsive behavior wrongly allows you to be free from responsibility for your actions, because your addiction is "irresistible." Simply put, you cannot ever resist the temptation to use the addictive substance. The word *"compulsive" implies that even God Himself cannot stop the addict from using.* The helpless addict, who has the unfortunate circumstance of being created with this compulsive nature, is without recourse. By this definition, not only is the compulsive addicted person free from accepting responsibility for his actions, but in addition, God can be blamed for the addictive behavior. Since God created the compulsive addict to live in an uncontrollable manner due to the "irresistible impulses" to act "irrationally," then *God Himself is responsible for the "compulsive" addict's sinful behavior according to society's inaccurate definition!* This is not a biblical view of addiction.

The word "compulsive" wrongly allows the addicted person, to

- deny responsibility
- deny God's power to change them
- blame their parents' genetic make-up
- blame parents for poor upbringing as a child
- blame God for making you in this manner

These ideas are not true! They cannot be derived from God's Word. In fact, if you believe these worldly ideas, you are hindering the forgiveness God can bestow on you. These lies prevent you from taking full responsibility for your actions and allow you to remain a victim of your addiction and to continue living a self-destructive lifestyle. Secular treatment modalities and even some "Christian" mixture programs embrace and perpetuate these lies that are contrary to the Word of God. Do you believe some of these lies right now?

The addict, as defined by society's terms, is similar to the ungodly and unrighteous persons the apostle Paul wrote about in Romans 1:18-23:

> **For the wrath of God is revealed from heaven against all ungodliness and unrighteousness of men, who by their unrighteousness suppress the truth. For what can be known about God is plain**

to them, because God has shown it to them. For his invisible attributes, namely, his eternal power and divine nature, have been clearly perceived, ever since the creation of the world, in the things that have been made. So they are without excuse. For although they knew God, they did not honor him as God or give thanks to him, but they became futile in their thinking, and their foolish hearts were darkened. Claiming to be wise, they became fools, and exchanged the glory of the immortal God for images resembling mortal man and birds and animals and reptiles.

Do you know the truth about a Sovereign Creator yet deny and **"suppress the truth"** according to Romans 1:18 above? Are you deceiving yourself into thinking that you are a helpless victim of your own harmful and "compulsive" behaviors and that you are being victimized by parents, spouse, society, or even God Himself? If you have been in a secular treatment program, you have been indoctrinated with these lies that propagate addiction as purely "compulsive" and uncontrollable. If you have embraced these lies, then you are like those whose **"foolish hearts become darkened"** according to Romans 1:21 above. Only the truth can bring light into your darkened heart. Only your willingness to embrace the truth will bring victory over the addiction.

Is it Really Compulsive Behavior?

The truth of the matter is that you are responsible and accountable to God for every thought, word, and behavior. Furthermore, behaviors the world labels as "compulsive" are rooted in your old sinful thoughts and habit patterns. The "compulsive" label makes it easy for you to blame-shift and to refuse to take responsibility for your own actions. Do not be deceived by the worldly label of "compulsive" behavior by wrongly thinking that you are not responsible for your sinful actions and habit patterns. The behavior is habitual sin that is so *automatic* that it appears to be "compulsive," but the behavior is really *planned in advance and rooted in your own thought-life.*

To change your thoughts and behaviors, a distinction must be drawn between the words "compulsive" and "habitual." They are similar to each other; however, one word conveys a lack of hope while the other gives hope. "Habitual" is a more accurate word used in the definition of addiction because it gives you hope. At first glance, because of a wrong view of habits, you may think that habits give you no hope for change. For example, if you have smoked cigarettes and have tried to quit, you have probably experienced much difficulty in quitting and not just for physical reasons.

Certainly there is a physical component to any substance addiction, including nicotine, caffeine, and alcohol. However, thousands of people have *completely* overcome the physical withdrawal symptoms of a substance, only to find themselves enslaved to the very same substance again later in their lives. Detoxification from a substance alone is not enough. Habits are not designed to be "broken" as the world believes. Instead, according to God's Truth, habits must be replaced. Poor habits must be and can be replaced by good habits. It is not sufficient for the cigarette smoker to simply "break the habit" after "detoxing" from the physical dependence of nicotine. You must replace smoking cigarettes with something constructive. In the Bible, this is called "putting off" and "putting on" and it can be applied to many areas of your life.

A Word about "Breaking Habits"

You are a creature of habit. You may think of habits in a negative way; however, habits are not always a bad thing. For example, when you drive your car, it is possible to be five blocks down the road before you even consciously think about being in the car and driving. You started your car, pressed on the brake, put the car into reverse, looked both ways (hopefully), slowly backed out of the driveway, put your foot back on the brake, put the car into drive, and pressed the gas to go on your way.[25] If it were not for God's wisdom to create people as creatures of habit, then every time you decided to go for a drive, you would have to remember every step of the process. Imagine how long it would take you to do anything. Even brushing your teeth would take forever!

Habits save you one of your most precious resources: time. However, we all know that we can develop destructive bad habits. God instructs us to replace sinful habits with godly habits. In His Word, God gives specific examples in Ephesians 4-5 and Colossians 3 of how you are to "put-off" and to "put-on" specific habit patterns of behavior. God knows how you are "wired" because you have

---

[25] Adams, Jay, Godliness through Discipline, Grand Rapids, MI: Baker Book House, 1977, p. 8-10.

been "fearfully and wonderfully made"[26] by a loving Creator. Every Christian addict is capable of replacing sinful habits of thinking and behaving with godly habits. In the chapters on practical change, you will learn how to apply these powerful principles more fully.

The secular world's definition of the word "addiction" is not the best term to describe what the Bible calls "drunkenness." This is a term of man and not God's Word. You are warned and commanded to be wary of worldly words and philosophies in Colossians 2:8: **"See to it that no one takes you captive by philosophy and empty deceit, according to human tradition, according to the elemental spirits of the world, and not according to Christ."** Nowhere in the Bible will you find the word "addiction," but God has plenty to say about addictive thoughts, habits, and behaviors. God knows all about it. He has designed you and created you to be a creature of habit, but it is not His design for you to go to extremes when attempting to satisfy your natural appetites and desires.

Quite simply, physical addiction occurs when you repeatedly satisfy a natural appetite and desire with a temporary pleasure until you become the servant of the temporary object of pleasure rather than its master. Addiction is likened to slavery and idolatry in the Bible. You use the temporarily pleasurable substance to escape, but in reality you find that you are physically enslaved rather than free. Human beings love a pleasurable "escape" because it seems so freeing, but addiction is a trap that lets you think that you will be "free" when you really become a "slave." God created you to have liberty in Christ, but that freedom from the slavery of sin was not without cost. It cost the Son of God His life on the cross.

Romans 6:16-19 tells the Christian that one is either a slave to sin or a slave to righteousness unto God:

> **"Do you not know that if you present yourselves to anyone as obedient slaves, you are slaves of the one whom you obey, either of sin, which leads to death, or of obedience, which leads to righteousness? But thanks be to God, that you who were once slaves of sin have become obedient from the heart to the standard of teaching to which you were committed, and, having been set free from sin, have become slaves of righteousness. I am speaking in human terms, because of your natural limitations. For just**

---

[26] Psalm 139:14.

> **as you once presented your members as slaves to impurity and to lawlessness leading to more lawlessness, so now present your members as slaves to righteousness leading to sanctification."**

You are to present your body as a slave that does what is right in God's eyes which is the practice of godly habits in the sanctification process of "putting on."[27] You are to work at becoming "godly" so that your good, righteous habits become second nature to you.

For example, actions of love must become automatic to you. Maybe you have learned to spend time talking with your wife each evening after dinner rather than watching television. You have <u>put off</u> time watching TV and have <u>put on</u> spending time with your wife. As you practice this loving act of listening to your wife, it should become habitual in a good way. Most Christians do not think of godliness as something to be practiced but it most certainly is practiced as I Timothy 4:7b-8 states: **"Rather train yourself for godliness; for while bodily training is of some value, godliness is of value in every way, as it holds promise for the present life and also for the life to come."** In other words, godliness (exemplified in the loving actions of a husband toward a wife, for example) is not natural; it requires training, and must be practiced so that good habits are developed.

For addicts, ungodliness and selfishness have been practiced for so long that godliness almost seems like an unattainable goal. It may seem just as unattainable as running a marathon would be for a "couch potato." Nonetheless, just like running a marathon requires self-denial and training, godliness requires self-denial and training. The prize is well worth the training as it profits both in this life and in the eternal life to come according to I Timothy 4:8.

Addiction Redefined

If you eliminate the word "compulsive" from the worldly definition for "addiction" and replace it with "habitual," then you can better use this word, "addiction." When you make this change, addiction is redefined as the **"persistent _habitual_ use of a substance known by the user to be harmful."** Once this new definition is in place, addiction becomes a word more closely resembling the life-

---

[27] Ephesians 4:24.

devastating sin of drunkenness described in the Bible. *When the word "addiction" is used in the remainder of this book, it will refer to this redefined and new definition since it is biblically more accurate.* The new definition of addiction also brings more hope to the suffering Christian addict. Because ungodly, destructive habits can be replaced by godly, productive habits, there is hope. Real and lasting change can and will occur in your life.

Prayer of Heart Change and Application

Dear Heavenly Father, I want real hope in my life. Help me to understand your terminology for my addiction. Help me to become willing to embrace your thoughts and Your Word, knowing that you alone can be trusted. Help my habits to become godly and not-self serving. Help me to think of others and not just myself. Teach me about your love and your power. Help me to trust in you by faith. Amen.

Chapter 4
Who are You?

Having met and counseled over a thousand addicts during the past fifteen years, there are many observations I want to share with you that I pray will be beneficial to your process of transformation. Some of these ideas are biblically-derived from Scripture but not biblically-directed. Biblically-directed principles are clear statements from Scripture such as "thou shalt not murder." Biblically-derived principles are not clearly stated but can clearly be implied from the Bible as a whole. Some of the observations and metaphors in this unit are not biblically based at all. When that is the case, I will endeavor to make that clear to you.

God Ponders the Heart

Examine your own heart in this matter of substance abuse and addiction. Understand that only God really knows what resides in the heart of any man. You and I do not know what is in another person's heart, and sometimes we don't realize what is in our own hearts; therefore, we can deceive ourselves.[28] Secular modalities believe that man is inherently good and that truth comes from within each person's heart. This is a lie. According to the Bible, mankind is born in sin. The sinful nature of mankind desires to please self; therefore, at times, man cannot examine his own heart without the help of God's Word and another person because most of the things he does are selfish and self-serving.

Man is blind and needs the truth of God found *outside the heart of man – in* the pages of the Bible – in order to illuminate his heart and motives. Man needs to put God's truth *within* his heart by studying, memorizing, and meditating upon the Holy Scriptures. To examine the motives and desires of his heart, the addict must believe the truth found in Hebrews 4:12-13:

> **For the word of God is living and active, sharper than any two-edged sword, piercing to the division of soul and of spirit, of joints and of marrow, and discerning the thoughts and intentions of the heart.**

---

[28] Jeremiah 17:9-10

> **And no creature is hidden from his sight but all are naked and exposed to the eyes of him to whom we must give account.**

The Being to whom we must give account is God alone according to Hebrews 4:13. God knows every creature's heart since He is the Creator and is all-knowing. God is merciful to us by giving us His Word that is alive, active, and able to discern the thoughts, intentions, and motives of our heart. For this reason, we must let God's Word guide us in any self-examination. God's Word is the standard by which we are to measure the motives of the heart.

Creation, the Fall, and Redemption

The best understanding of addiction is derived from a biblical framework. Let's start at the book of beginnings – Genesis. A perfect world was created by God in the beginning, and man did *not* have a sinful nature and a sinful heart. Mankind was holy and righteous but created with the capacity to make a *willful choice* to disobey God. Genesis chapters 1 and 2 give you a glimpse of the beauty of God's creation, but what happened in Genesis 3 changed the world forever.

In Genesis 3, all of mankind represented by the perfect man named Adam willfully chose to disobey God. This is known as "The Fall." As a result of the disobedient choice Adam made, every person is now born with a sinful nature and sinful heart. In other words, mankind is born with a self-centered nature that *wills* to think, speak, and act selfishly and *independently* from God. For example, no one has to teach a one year old baby to cry and throw a temper tantrum when he does not get what he wants! Selfishness does not have to be taught to children! They automatically respond in a self-centered manner driven by their sinful nature and sinful heart.

Do you believe you were born with a fallen, sinful nature and sinful heart? Genesis 5:1-3 states:

> **...When God created man, he made him in the likeness of God. Male and female he created them, and he blessed them and named them Man when they were created. When Adam had lived 130 years, he fathered a son _in his own likeness, after his image,_ and named him Seth** (Emphasis mine).

Genesis 5:3 says that Adam's son, Seth, is born in *Adam's image* which is now corrupted by sin: defiled, frail, miserable, and mortal. Seth and everyone born after him are now born in the image and likeness of sinful Adam with a marred and fallen nature. Sinners produce more sinners. Human beings are still like God in many respects but they are unlike God in that they have a natural desire toward evil. It is a strange mixture indeed.

God does not know evil experientially. You and I are born into this selfish state of wanting to be independent of God. In essence, we say, "God, You do your thing and let me do mine. I don't need you. I can do better on my own." We think we know better than God!

Most people do not see the "bigness" of sin. They underestimate sin's power. Sin is a big and powerful foe that resides in your heart! Your sinful nature is much more powerful than you realize. Even if you have the Holy Spirit living within you, you have the "old man"[29] full of self-serving, sinful thoughts and habits that you will contend with for the remainder of your life. By God's power and grace, you will gradually learn how to overcome your old nature (or "old man"), but it is a lifelong process called sanctification. God is a redeeming Person who desires to give back to you what was lost, but you are responsible for giving your best effort during this battle. It is called a "battle" and "spiritual warfare" in the Bible because you will struggle.

Regardless of how we have served or failed to serve God, He deals with sinful man in a loving, merciful, patient, and gracious manner. From Genesis 3 to the end of the Bible, God reveals His Plan of Redemption to us: God sends a new "Adam," His only begotten Son, Jesus, in the form of a man. *Jesus represented mankind in paying the penalty for sin with His death on the cross just as Adam represented mankind in committing sin.*[30] Because of God's justice, He could not allow sin to go unpunished; therefore, someone had to pay the penalty of sin by the shedding of blood and the loss of life. That Person is Jesus and because He died, sinners were "redeemed," which means "bought back" from the penalty, position, and practice of their sinful ways.[31] God purchased you if you are trusting in Jesus.

---

[29] Ephesians 4:22.

[30] Romans 5:12-17.

[31] Reeder, Harry, "Genesis in Biblical Perspective: The Gospel of Christ from Genesis," sermon series preached at Briarwood Presbyterian Church, Birmingham, AL, on May 15, 2005.

In fact, God not only owns you, but He adopted you into His family and is your Heavenly Father.

Do not underestimate and miss the significance of what God did. God not only redeems and adopts His people, but God *empowers* His people by giving them a measure of the Holy Spirit to dwell within them and to battle the sin nature. II Corinthians 5:16-17 states: **"From now on, therefore, we regard no one according to the flesh. Even though we once regarded Christ according to the flesh, we regard him thus no longer. Therefore, if anyone is in Christ, he is a new creation. The old has passed away; behold, the new has come."** Born again Christians have a new, Spirit-filled nature that indwells their sinful bodies of flesh.[32] They must contend with their "old self"[33] and the habits of the flesh for the rest of their lives until they receive new, glorified bodies in everlasting life. The indwelling of the Holy Spirit gives Christians the ability and power to say "no" to sin habits. The Holy Spirit enables a Christian to change, repent, and overcome addiction. No longer do you have to say you are "powerless" to battle addictions because you are empowered by your Sovereign, Almighty Creator and Lord. It is God's power and not your own power that can conquer any addiction. In time, you will think, speak, and act like a new creation in Christ Jesus and the difference will be evident to everyone you know.

The Importance of the Word of God

As a result of the Fall of mankind in Genesis 3, you now have a capacity for addiction in your flesh; however, you must take responsibility for your actions, walk according to the leading of the Holy Spirit, and learn how to think, speak, and act according to God's Word. How do we get a proper understanding of God's commandments? God alone gives wisdom and understanding.[34] Ask Him to give you insight and understanding about your problem of addiction. James 1:5-6 states: **"If any of you lacks wisdom, let him ask God, who gives generously to all without reproach, and it will be given him. But let him ask in faith, with no doubting..."**

Your understanding will increase as you learn His commandments in the Bible. God will open your eyes so you can learn to relate

---

[32] John 3:3, Romans 6:4, and Ephesians 3:17.
[33] Ephesians 4:22 - some versions say "old self" or "old man" referring to the sin nature.
[34] James 1:5.

properly to Him. God has created His people to have a relationship with Him and He reveals His character to His people through His Word of Truth. Throughout the Bible, God communicates to us who we are, how much He loves us, how He made us, what He wants us to do with our life, and where we are going to be in our final destination! With all of this essential information contained in the Bible, isn't it amazing how often Christians neglect reading, studying, memorizing, and meditating upon the Word of God?

God does not want you to be ignorant.[35] God's Word is an essential resource for the Christian.[36] Satan knows it is true, too, and that is why he will interfere greatly when people plan to read and study their Bibles in their quiet times devoted to God. Satan does not want you to know how good God really is!

In counseling, I often ask people: "What have you done about your problem?" The usual response is that the counselee has prayed, talked to friends, talked to family, and attended some fellowship groups. Rarely does a counselee respond by saying: "I have really been digging into my Bible to find the answer to my problem. I read and study it so much that I forget to eat sometimes!" If you have not yet turned to the Bible for answers, how can you experience the transforming power of God's Word applied to your life?

Are you reading this book in order to find the answer to your problem of substance abuse and addiction? If you are born again and still addicted to something, then you must become "addicted to Jesus." You have a worship disorder that makes you prone to worship (or serve) yourself rather than to worship and serve the Lord your Creator. Put on the Lord Jesus Christ! You must switch your addiction from something that temporarily pleases you into something that eternally pleases God and therefore pleases you! Put God first and everything else will take care of itself.[37] When I say that you must "get addicted to learning about Jesus," I simply mean that you must re-focus your heart's desires upon cultivating a relationship with Jesus. Your heart must learn to desire to know Jesus more intimately than it wants any temporary pleasure.

---

[35] Ephesians 4:18.

[36] This is a reminder to always have your Bible handy so that you can read the Bible verses that are referenced. The Bible is the only book you are required to read and it is far better than any book written by any man.

[37] Matthew 6:33.

Now you know that God *desires* to reveal His awesome character to you! It is your responsibility to seek after Him, and He will reveal Himself to you. ***Turn to God now by reading His Words to you.***

Believers and Unbelievers

The Bible categorizes people into two important and different groups: believers in Jesus Christ as their personal Savior and non-believers. It is really that simple according to the Bible.

It is important for you to determine whether or not you are trusting in the Lord Jesus Christ for your eternal life. In other words, are you a Christian? Are you a believer? Ask yourself: Am I a Christian who is physically addicted and enslaved to a mood-altering pleasure? Or am I what the Bible calls an "unbeliever" because I am trusting in my good deeds to outnumber my bad deeds to get me into heaven rather than Christ? Biblically speaking, you have to be in one of these two categories.

Satan tries to convince sinners that they are saints.[38] Satan wants unrepentant sinners (unbelievers) to think they are naturally good and do not need a Savior. Our sinful flesh willingly participates in this lie because we don't want to believe we possess a single undesirable quality. If the enemy can convince us to buy this secular lie, we will not believe the Gospel message of Christianity. The gospel message is foolishness to those who wrongly think they are saints. I Corinthians 1:18 states: **"For the word of the cross is folly to those who are perishing, but to us who are being saved it is the power of God."** The truth is that **"all have sinned and fall short of the glory of God"**[39] so everyone is in need of a Savior when compared to a perfectly holy God.

If you are an unbeliever, I urge you to go to Appendix B and read it immediately. The unbeliever does not have the resources to make lasting changes in regard to addiction. The unbeliever does not have:

- a Savior to trust
- the indwelling Holy Spirit to empower him
- a loving relationship with God the Father
- an ability to properly understand the biblical principles in the Word of God

[38] Evans, Tony, <u>Free at Last</u>, Chicago: Moody Press, 2001.
[39] Romans 3:23.

36

- probably does not have a membership in a Bible-teaching church.

Guilt: A Call to Repentance

The continued struggle with sin in this area causes more guilt in a believer than an unbeliever who is doing the same things! One of the Holy Spirit's functions is to convict people of sin.[40] For a believer who has the indwelling of the Holy Spirit, this lifestyle of continual sin and disobedience is a constantly painful state of being. You must repent of (turn from) your sin and become obedient to Christ in your thoughts and actions.

If you are a Christian who is living to please only yourself, then you are also acting as your own god, which is the sin of idolatry in the Bible (I Corinthians 10:1-14). You are created to serve God. Submit to God by confessing and then repenting of your selfish thoughts, words, and deeds of addiction. When you have a sense of guilt over your behavior it is a sign that God is speaking to you through the Holy Spirit. You can only do this with the help of the Holy Spirit. Apply the principles and practical wisdom in the following pages of this book.

Mistaken Identity?

A third category of persons in the church of the Lord Jesus Christ are those who are confused and deceived. They believe they are Christians when they are not truly born again. These persons mistakenly think they are Christians because they possess knowledge, but their hearts have truly not yet been changed by God. They are basing their heart change on some faulty, unbiblical assumptions.[41]

Jesus taught the parable of wheat and tares (weeds) in Matthew 13:24-30 and then explained its meaning in Matthew 13:36-43. Wheat and weeds grow together in the visible church according to the parable in Matthew 13:24-30. In other words, in the visible and local church body, there are those who are truly born again – called the "wheat" – and those who are not born again and yet belong to the church – called the "weeds."[42] Open and read this passage of Scripture in your Bible now. The parable is found in Matthew 13:24-

---

[40] John 16:8-11.
[41] The heart change by God is called "regeneration." See Titus 3:5-6.
[42] "Weeds" are also known as "tares" in some translations of the Bible.

30 and the meaning of the parable explained by Jesus is found in Matthew 13:36-43.

Sincerely Deceived

Those who are not truly "born again" of the Holy Spirit may still experience the benefits and blessings of being around true believers. This third category of persons who are not truly saved may be the toughest category to counsel because of the deception—they think they will ultimately be in heaven. They are sincere, but they are sincerely deceived. The Apostle Paul called them "false brothers" in II Corinthians 11:26b and nearly every church has members who are false brothers and sisters.

Desperately Sick

Jeremiah 17:9-10 warns that you cannot understand your own heart if you are an unbeliever: **"The heart is deceitful above all things, and desperately sick; who can understand it? I the Lord search the heart and test the mind, to give every man according to his ways, according to the fruit of his deeds."** Self-deception is a major element of addiction and will be addressed in more detail in later chapters. For now, understand that self-evaluations are not entirely accurate because of a selfish bias. A trusted Christian friend may be needed to help you gain an accurate picture of your weaknesses because everyone has blind spots. Again, we are all created to be dependent creatures so we need God, and God has given us other people to help us as well.

Do You Know the Lord Jesus Christ? Are you Born Again?

Even though self-evaluations can often be imperfect, begin to examine your own heart and your behaviors right now to determine if you need the saving grace of the Lord Jesus Christ. Jesus plainly states to Nicodemus in John 3:3-8:

> **Jesus answered him, "Truly, truly, I say to you, unless one is born again he cannot see the kingdom of God." Nicodemus said to him, "How can a man be born when he is old? Can he enter a second time into his mother's womb and be born?" Jesus answered, "Truly, truly, I say to you, unless one is born of water and the Spirit, he cannot enter the**

> kingdom of God. That which is born of the flesh is
> flesh, and that which is born of the Spirit is spirit.
> Do not marvel that I said to you, 'You must be born
> again.' The wind blows where it wishes, and you
> hear its sound, but you do not know where it comes
> from or where it goes. So it is with everyone who is
> born of the Spirit."

Salvation is of the Lord, meaning that eternal life is a gift from God and the Holy Spirit is the agent who stirs and works in your spirit and causes you to trust in Jesus Christ.[43] If you have any uncertainty about your eternal destination, I strongly encourage you to ask for someone to help you to understand the gospel message of grace now.

Honestly answer the following question: "If I asked ten of the people who know you the best, would those people say that you are a godly, Christian person or that you are a selfish person, a drunkard, or an idolater?" List those ten people on a sheet of paper and write your answer beside each name.[44] If you are not sure what each person would say, call them and ask them to tell you the truth without holding back. Since they might not want to answer you honestly, you may need to have a spouse or close, trusted Christian friend call the ten people. You must be serious about this issue because God is serious about it. Galatians 5:19-21 states:

> Now the works of the flesh are evident: sexual
> immorality, impurity, sensuality, idolatry, sorcery,
> enmity, strife, jealousy, fits of anger, rivalries,
> dissensions, divisions, envy, drunkenness, orgies,
> and things like these. I warn you, as I warned you
> before, that those who do such things will not inherit
> the kingdom of God.

Do not think that any practicing drunkards will inherit the kingdom of God. Remember that you are only deceiving yourself—not God—if you continue to pretend to be a Christian.

---

[43] Ephesians 2:8-9.
[44] Idea originated from Tim Brown at His Steps Ministries in Atlanta, GA, a residential men's program for addiction.

God says the same thing in I Corinthians 6:9-10: **Do you not know that the unrighteous will not inherit the kingdom of God? Do not be deceived: neither the sexually immoral, nor idolaters, nor adulterers, nor men who practice homosexuality, nor thieves, nor the greedy, nor drunkards, nor revilers, nor swindlers will inherit the kingdom of God.** God is serious about sin and the sin of drunkenness in particular.

Intimate Fellowship

God is serious about requiring us to have a relationship with Him. In Matthew 7:21-23, Jesus states:

> **Not everyone who says to me, 'Lord, Lord,' will enter the kingdom of heaven, but the one who does the will of my Father who is in heaven. On that day many will say to me, 'Lord, Lord, did we not prophesy in your name, and cast out demons in your name, and do many mighty works in your name?' And then will I declare to them, 'I never knew you; depart from me, you workers of lawlessness.'**

Do not take your relationship with the Lord for granted, but be diligent in your pursuit of intimate fellowship and knowledge of Him. You are robbing yourself if you do not get to know your Creator more intimately!

Life-Dominated Abusers vs. Occasional Abusers

After you identify by the Lord's grace whether you are an unbeliever or a believer who is enslaved to an addiction, the next issue is to determine the extent to which the addiction problem has infected and dominated your life. When a sin begins to dominate your life the Bible gives you a label. You actually begin to be personified by the sin that so dominates you. Some examples of this are liar, thief, adulterer, glutton, rebel, fool, proud person, drunkard, sluggard, lover of money, lover of pleasure, and idolater. To be identified and personified as one of these is a serious problem.

A drunkard is a person whose life is so dominated by the sin of drunkenness that he is properly labeled as a "drunkard." If you are an occasional excessive abuser of a desired intoxicant, you could be labeled as a "sinner" or an "idolater" according to biblical standards.

Whether you are a drunkard or an occasional excessive user of a drug, there is still a sin problem in your heart.

The world refers to these two groups of drunkards and addicts as "chemically dependent" or "chemically abusive." Both groups of people are manifesting a heart problem of idolatry and drunkenness. The only difference is that one group is at an earlier stage of physical control. Remember that people usually only look at the result of a drunkard's life when it is spiraling out of control. Therefore, those people think thoughts like:

- "That could never happen to me"
- "Boy, that drunkard really can't control himself but I can"
- "I'll never end up like her."

The drunkard had those same thoughts earlier in life, too! The thoughts of escape and behaviors of avoidance seem innocent and harmless in the beginning. Then an addict (drunkard) becomes trapped and wonders: "How did I get this way?" The drunkard is losing control of nearly everything due to the invasion of the problem into every area of his life. Drunkenness manifests itself in marital, economic, social, physical, emotional, familial, occupational, and spiritual problems.

Whether you are a believer or an unbeliever, a life-dominated abuser or an occasional abuser, you are in need of a radical heart change. You can do it with God's power so you must not try it alone. You need other people, you need the Holy Sprit's power, you need Jesus to forgive you and sustain you. Call upon the Lord who hears you! **"In my distress I called upon the Lord; to my God I called. From his temple he heard my voice, and my cry came to his ears.**[45]

---

[45] 2 Samuel 22:7.

Prayer of Heart Change and Application

Dear Heavenly Father, as you look into my heart, tell me what it is about myself that I must know in order to overcome this addiction. Thank you for saving me by grace through faith in you. You alone are worthy of praise as you have taken this hard-hearted person and are beginning to transform me by your truth. Reveal to me the extent of my addictive problem so that I may [begin] [continue] the transformation process knowing that you are guiding me every step of the way. Amen.

Chapter 5
Frequently Asked Questions

If you could ask God anything about your struggles with substance abuse, what would your question be?[46] Maybe yours would be one of the following questions: "Lord,

- "Why would you create something as destructive as alcohol and drugs for a people whom you love?"
- "Why do I like alcohol and/or my drug of choice so much?"
- "Are my addictive thoughts and behaviors genetic or learned?"
- "Is it a sin to drink alcohol?"
- "Is it a sin for me to drink alcohol?"
- "Is it a sin for me to take prescription medications?
- "Lord God, why did you create me this way?"
- "Why did you create this substance to feel as good as this?"
- "I pray everyday to you, Lord, but what else do I need to do to overcome this addiction?"
- "Lord, will you just take away my desire for this addictive behavior so that I will have victory?"

Have you ever thought that moving to a remote part of the world, living in a monastery, or even going to jail would be helpful to keep you physically removed from the substance that you love to abuse? If so, you were probably looking for an easy way to escape the grip of the addictive substance hoping you would no longer be able to freely engage in the addictive behavior. Unfortunately, many times the Christian person hoping to get away from the enticing drug is looking for a quick fix, magic dust, or an easy answer to the problem of addiction.

There is no quick fix that will solve the problem of substance abuse because it is a heart problem that only God can heal. The problem is not the substance itself; that is external. Your problem

---

[46] If you are utilizing the workbook that accompanies <u>The Heart of Addiction</u> to help you through your transformation process, pull out the list of questions that you wanted answered from this book.

lies within yourself – *in your heart*. You cannot run from your own heart! We will soon discuss how God has a good purpose for alcohol and drugs. However, it is your selfish heart attitudes that lead you to problems with alcohol and drugs.

No treatment program on earth has the ability to change your heart. There are many secular modalities available but they are designed for the unwilling, unrepentant, and unbelieving person. Most are not designed for Christians! Have you ever been forced to enter a treatment program against your will, cleaned up from drugs and alcohol for awhile, only to return to your lifestyle of active addiction? If so, then there never was a change of heart, or genuine repentance, because your attempts at "recovery" were in your own strength rather than in the mighty power of God. *The God of the Bible, who is your Creator, Redeemer, and Sustainer, knows all and has all of the power you need to change – to "transform" you into the image of Christ.* Do you believe this?

These frequently asked questions (and any others you may have on your list) do not catch God off-guard. He is not surprised by them; He has all of the answers. It may surprise you to know that God has <u>already given you</u> the answers to these questions in the Bible. You are going to find many of His solutions to your problem of substance abuse as you read further and as you begin to search your Bible. *God uses different names to identify these problems. Mankind often invents new words to explain, minimize, and sometimes cover up his sin.* God's people err because they do not know the Scriptures nor the power of God contained in the Scriptures![47]

While it is true you will not find the words "substance abuse" and "addiction" in the Bible, the Word of God has the answers for overcoming these common problems. Man's word "addiction" emphasizes the physical component of addiction – cravings, appetites, withdrawal, and physical dependence – and all of these physical elements are truly involved in addiction. However, the permanent solution to a physical addiction is a spiritual answer. Again, even the secular, humanistic counseling approaches for substance abuse attack the problem of physical addiction with a so-called "spiritual," non-religious program with steps, self-help group meetings, fellowship, and therapy devoid of the Christian God.

God has answers and God has power. He has given you both if you are a Christian. So you can put your trust and hope in the God of

---

[47] Matthew 22:29

the Bible who has already revealed Himself and His loving character to you and has provided you with all of the answers you need to lead a victorious life. II Timothy 3:16-17 states: **"All Scripture is breathed out by God and profitable for teaching, for reproof, for correction, and for training in righteousness, that the man of God may be competent, equipped for every good work."** God's Word is sufficient and complete in addressing the enslaving yet increasingly common problem of substance abuse.

Hope for You

The problem of substance abuse and physical addiction is not new to modern day society. The Lord addressed the subject of substance abuse in the days of Noah approximately 6,000 years ago in Genesis 9. The Lord has clearly spoken on substance abuse many times in Scripture. Addicts and substance abusers, however, face two problems when trying to understand what God has said about their abuse.

Problem #1: Inability to See Clearly Without Help from Above

The first problem is that you cannot rightly understand God's Word without God's help. People are created to be dependent upon God and others to survive and thrive. A newborn baby depends upon someone else to do everything for it. A newborn cannot navigate, go to the bathroom, or eat without someone's help. Someone else must nourish the newborn or death will be certain. Likewise, Christians need other Christians to disciple and nourish them with God's wisdom; that is God's design. You need other people to help you overcome this substance abuse or alcohol problem, so don't try to do it yourself. Remember, there is no such thing as "self-help" when trying to have victory over a substance abuse problem. You cannot "recover" by your own power because you must be "transformed" by God's power.

Ask yourself the following questions and see if you can identify the lies believed by addicts when they are enslaved to an addiction of any type:

1. Do you believe you only need yourself?
2. Do you only trust yourself?

3. Do you see other people as "controlling" and "hindrances" to your happiness and plans to use drugs?

4. Do you see other people as objects to serve, please, and help you rather than as people whom you can serve, please, and help?

5. Are you self-centered rather than God-centered?

6. Are you the master of God in your own mind rather than God's servant?

7. Are you willing to do everything in your power to begin the transformation process?

If you answered 'yes' to most of these questions, you are probably enslaved to your substance abuse and addiction. But if you answered 'yes' to Question 7, there is hope to be found in Jesus Christ's forgiveness. Turn to Appendix B now to learn more about the good news of forgiveness found in the Gospel message of Christ Jesus.

Christians are dependent upon the Holy Spirit. No one can rely completely upon his own abilities when confronting substance abuse. To properly interpret God's Word, the Christian addict's eyes have to be opened to the Truth of God by the Spirit of Truth.[48] This may sound like a contradiction at first. All persons are born in sin and "all have sinned and fall short of the glory of God."[49] Because of this, your eyes first see things through your sin nature; thus, you are darkened and blinded to the truth even if you are already a Christian. Your nature must change which is a work of God's redemptive power. Then you must "be transformed by the renewal of your mind."[50] This transformation indicates that there is a growth process for a Christian who is trying to abide in Christ. You are "born again"[51] as a baby in Christ who must grow, learn to crawl, and then learn to walk as an adult believer in the faith. You are dependent upon other people to teach and disciple you with sound doctrine from God's Word which provides the nourishment to help you grow in your faith. God's character, thoughts, and ways must be revealed to you through His Word by the power of the Holy Spirit. The only true way to find the solution to your heart problem of substance abuse

[48] II Corinthians 4:1-4.
[49] Romans 3:23.
[50] Romans 12:2
[51] John 3:3.

is to view the problem as God does. You need the help of the Holy Spirit to do so.

Solution to Problem #1:   Seeing Things God's Way

How can you view the problem from God's perspective when you have a sin nature and a natural tendency to see things through your own selfish, man-centered view? If you are already a Christian, the answer is that you trust Him by faith realizing that His Word is infallible Truth. Then when you read the Bible, God Himself will speak the truth in love[52] into your situation of being a Christian who struggles with addictive behavior.

Once you rightly understand God's Word about addiction, the solution to the problem does not come from within yourself, the solution must come from God. Jesus taught His disciples in John 14:25-26: **"These things I have spoken to you while I am still with you. But the Helper, the Holy Spirit, whom the Father will send in my name, he will teach you all things and bring to your remembrance all that I have said to you."** It is encouraging to know that one of the tasks of the Holy Spirit is to teach you all things. He does this in conjunction with your diligent reading of the Bible.

In these same verses of John 14, another task of the Holy Spirit is to bring to your remembrance all that Jesus has taught. Of course, you must first have some of the Word of God in your memory in order for the Holy Spirit to bring it back to your remembrance and to be applied and used. If nothing exists in your memory banks, then how will the Holy Spirit bring God's Word back to your remembrance? You must put God's Word into your heart and memory bank by reading it and listening to preaching and teaching. You need to know the truth about abusing substances or getting drunk with wine, and the truth is the Word of God.

Psalm 119:11-16 talks about God's Word in the following manner: **"I have stored up your word in my heart, that I might not sin against you. Blessed are you, O Lord; teach me your statutes! With my lips I declare all the rules of your mouth. In the way of your testimonies I delight as much as in all riches. I will meditate on your precepts and fix my eyes on your ways. I will delight in your statutes; I will not forget your word."** Will you commit this day to storing up God's Word in your heart, declaring God's Word with

---

[52] Ephesians 4:15

your mouth, and fixing your eyes upon His ways? If you will do so, then you will mature rapidly.

Problem #2: Lack of Will Power to Change Yourself

As a Christian addict or substance abuser, the second problem you face is that you, individually, lack the ability and "will power" to change your thoughts and behaviors. God alone possesses the power to change your heart and your addictive behaviors. God alone can impart this power to you by the Holy Spirit who lives inside a Christian. You need the "will of God power" to change your life. If you desire true answers to the questions posed earlier, if you truly want to change your heart, and if you truly want to change your behaviors, *then seek after God's Truth alone and forsake the best wisdom of man.* When the best wisdom of man contradicts God's wisdom, you especially need the truth of God. God states in Proverbs 8:17: **"I love those who love me, and those who seek me diligently find me."** By seeking His Truth and allowing it to **"dwell richly in your heart,"**[53] then and only then, will you begin to experience victory over your addictive behaviors as God releases His power by the Holy Spirit who dwells within you.

Do not be discouraged because, at times, you will fall short in your pursuit of truth. It is very easy to get sidetracked by temporary pleasures, deceitful lies, or your own prideful heart. Do not let the enemy prevent you from believing God's Word. Just as Satan deceived Eve and that led to Adam and Eve's sinful fall in the Garden of Eden,[54] you can be deceived, too. Both of these problems for the Christian addict have already been overcome by the power of Jesus Christ with His death on the cross and resurrection. *You no longer have to be a slave to sin,[55] but the power living inside you can either be hindered by or activated by you.* The choice is yours to make.

Think of yourself as the light switch on the wall in your kitchen. Think of the Holy Spirit as the generating plant that produces the power that runs from the outside power lines into the wiring of your house and into the kitchen light switch. There are millions of volts of electrical energy available to you, the light switch. Whether the light is illuminating the room or not depends upon whether the switch is turned "on" or "off." God's power is abundantly available to you.

---

[53] Colossians 3:16.
[54] Genesis 3:4; II Corinthians 11:3; I Timothy 2:14.
[55] John 8:34; Romans 6:16-20; II Peter 2:19.

Just as the light switch is a circuit breaker, you are a circuit breaker for God's Power. The switch is turned off by your own sinful choices and actions of disobedience to God. When you do what you learn is right, according to God's Word, you will be "turning the light switch on" for God. The result will be an energizing empowerment from God allowing you to overcome the addictive behavior.[56]

Active addiction is like a spiral staircase. When you give in to your addiction just one time, you begin to spiral downward and separate from God and His power. After that euphoric feeling provided by the high, you feel guilty about what you have done, knowing that it was a wrong decision. In addition, you do not feel close to God because your sin has separated you from the close fellowship you experienced with Him. Next time, it becomes easier to continue to give in to your addiction as God seems farther away, and you feel worse as more guilt piles upon you every time you use your drug of choice. Thereafter, the cycle continues as you walk farther and farther down that spiral staircase.[57]

To give you hope, the same spiral staircase that goes down also goes up with acts of obedience! In other words, by acting obediently to God and choosing to act righteously, you can begin to be led by the Holy Spirit back up the spiral staircase and into intimate fellowship with your Creator, the Lord Jesus Christ. Just as your disobedient and rebellious addictive choices led you down the spiral staircase, your obedient and God-centered choices will lead you up that same spiral staircase, but you must "turn on the light switch of your heart" for God. Choose to live your life for Him both in this life and in the eternal life to come.

Solution to Problem #2: The Power of God's Word

"For this is the will of God, your sanctification."[58] Real hope for the Christian who is an "alcoholic, substance abuser, addict, drunkard, idolater, and sinner" is found only in the pages of the Bible, the inerrant and sufficient Word of God. Who wrote the Bible? The Bible is a book written by men who were inspired by the Holy Spirit. These men wrote only what God wanted to be written. To whom did

---

[56] Sanchez, George, Changing Your Thought Patterns, Denver, CO: International Association of Biblical Counselors, pgs. 14-15.

[57] Adams, Jay, Competent to Counsel, Grand Rapids, MI: Zondervan Publishing House, p. 144-148.

[58] I Thessalonians 4:3.

these men write? The Bible is written primarily to Christians who believe in the Lord Jesus Christ and is not written only to evangelize non-Christians! Again, II Timothy 3:16-17 tells us that: **"All Scripture is breathed out by God and profitable for teaching, for reproof, for correction, and for training in righteousness, that the man of God may be competent, equipped for every good work."** The man of God in verse 17 above is the Christian. The Christian who struggles with drinking to excess or any type of addiction needs the Word of God. *The Word of God is not only the means God uses to get people saved. The Word of God is the means God uses to sanctify saved people.* As one who already possesses the gift of salvation, the Christian addict must now depend upon God's Word for his sanctification, or growth in Christ. A saved Christian must continue to read, memorize, study, and meditate upon God's Word.

Prayer of Heart Change and Application

Dear Heavenly Father, Open my eyes so that I may see how wonderful your ways are. Reveal your character to me and mold me into someone who looks more like Jesus. Transform me with your truth in the Bible and help me to live according to biblical principles rather than according to my feelings. Give me hope in you to change me and to empower me to overcome this addiction and to glorify your Name. Amen.

Chapter 6
The Good Purpose of Drugs and Alcohol

Have you ever asked: "Lord God, Creator of the Universe, why did you create a substance to feel as good as this?" Why would God create something as destructive as alcohol and drugs for people He loves? Could He not see this problem coming, especially for people who have an "addictive personality" (as the secular world calls it) toward mood-altering substances? Is there any good purpose for alcohol and drugs? Scripture gives us some evidence that God intended a good purpose for alcohol and drugs.

A Medicinal Purpose: Pain Relief

In I Timothy 5:23, the Apostle Paul instructed Timothy regarding the therapeutic and medicinal use for "wine" in the following way: **"No longer drink only water, but use a little wine for the sake of your stomach and your frequent ailments."** It is possible that Timothy took a strong vow not to touch wine for any reason similar to the vows that a Nazirite took in the Old Testament.[59] Because Christians are to avoid even the appearance of evil,[60] Timothy probably abstained from any type of wine; even the wine that was commonly used in that culture to purify drinking water.[61] For this reason, Paul commands Timothy to "use a little wine" for medicinal purposes. The "little wine" would also act as a purifier for Timothy's drinking water.

This command by Paul is in no way a contradiction to the qualification of a bishop that Paul gave to Timothy just a few chapters earlier in I Timothy 3:3 that a bishop must "not" be "a drunkard." A drunkard is someone who drinks wine to excess, which is different

---

[59] Judges 13:3-5. Again, it is *possible* that Timothy took this vow but not stated clearly from Scripture.

[60] Proverbs 3:7; I Thessalonians 5:22.

[61] MacArthur, John F. Jr., "Not Addicted to Wine," transcribed by Tony Capoccia from a sermon recorded on tape in 1993 at Grace Community Church. Tape #GC 56-8, titled "The Qualifications for a Pastor" Part 4, Noble Character Part 2, Titus 1:7-8, is the original source.

than what Paul tells Timothy in I Timothy 5:23 to drink "a little wine" in moderation for the purpose of treating his infirmities. There is both moderation and purpose for Timothy's use of "wine," or medicine.

Medicating physical pain is an acceptable purpose of drugs according to the Bible. In Proverbs 31:6-7: **"Give strong drink to the one who is perishing, and wine to those in bitter distress; let them drink and forget their poverty and remember their misery no more."** In this proverb, God states the good purpose of alcohol; namely, that it is to be utilized for someone who is "perishing." In the original Hebrew language, the word "perishing" was used for someone who was being "destroyed, annihilated, or obliterated." In other words, there was no hope of survival. In a situation where someone has little to no hope of survival due to a terminal illness, God gave people drugs and alcohol as an acceptable means for dealing with legitimate physical pain. However, Christians have used drugs and alcohol to deal with emotional pain – as a pleasurable means to escape and avoid this fallen world. When that happens, often the Christian becomes irresponsible in many ways and begins to fail God and others by sinning.

The problem for the Christian addict is that the use of "wine," or any drug, for medicinal purposes can get out of control in a hurry. Great caution must be exercised whenever a Christian addict uses a prescription medication for pain relief.

One Christian Man's Experience

A Christian addict who was continuing to transform from his addictive lifestyle had eight years of sobriety. He was to have a minor, out-patient surgery utilizing Valium, to produce a calmative effect before and during surgery. He stated that he had to be extremely careful during the three months following the procedure because the Valium® had reminded his body and mind *experientially* how he used to feel when drunk. His thought life during that time period after the surgery was filled with many more temptations as he shopped at the grocery store and went near the wine and beer aisle. He had never imagined the challenges in his own flesh and the thoughts that he would have to take captive[62] after that simple procedure.

Is this to say that you should never have surgery if you are an addict? No, certainly the answer is not to deny ever having a surgical

---

[62] II Corinthians 10:5.

procedure if your doctor deems it necessary. The solution is to be careful to explore alternatives for pain relief and to be upfront with the doctor about why you would like to avoid the narcotic pain medication. Be authentic with the doctor by telling him that you do not want to get addicted to any substance and that you would prefer a non-opioid pain reliever. Do not lie, but it is not always necessary to tell the doctor that you have been an "addict" because it is a harmful label to some doctors. However, you should be very open and honest with your doctor about your goal to insulate yourself from the temptation of becoming addicted.

It is true that non-narcotic (or non-opioid) medications do not "work" as well as narcotic medications but that is a sacrifice you may have to make. Remember that the sacrifice Jesus made on the cross on your behalf is greater than any pain you will ever experience in your life. The issue of being responsible regarding your propensity for addiction does not always produce an easy way out so you need to think the issue through prior to taking any medication whatsoever. This decision should be accompanied by much prayer, personal Bible study, and advice from trusted Christian friends.

Another Christian's Radical Approach

Another approach taken by a Christian addict to avoid temptation was the refusal to take any pill, even an aspirin, for the first three years of her "transformation" following her active addiction. Because she was concerned that taking a couple of aspirin every now and then could lead to the return of her habit of "popping pills," she would abstain from taking any medication in pill form. Her view was that she needed to find out the root physical cause of her headache rather than trying to medicate every ache or pain. What she discovered is that her headaches were due to allowing herself to become too "stressed out" at work, skipping a meal, handling a conflict incorrectly, or not drinking enough water. The emotional stress impacted her physical health in the form of a headache.

Rather than take a pill for the headache, she would deal with one of these root causes and the headache would subside every time. Eventually, she did begin to be more moderate in her approach, as she would allow her husband to help regulate her taking of non-narcotic pain medications appropriately when needed for legitimate pain. Until she had learned moderation, however, she abstained from the habit-forming behavior and the "quick fix" mentality of relieving the symptoms without dealing with her heart. Later, she recognized that "feeling stressed out" was really a problem of worrying and not trusting in God. Yes, worrying is a sin.[63]

Radical Obedience

Is this radical? Yes, it is radical and sometimes necessary. Does God call us to radical obedience? Yes, Jesus Himself lived radical obedience by giving His life to die upon the cross. He also taught a principle called "radical amputation" regarding adultery that can be applied to drug addiction.[64] In Matthew 5:27-30, Jesus said: **You have heard that it was said, 'You shall not commit adultery.' But I say to you that everyone who looks at a woman with lustful intent has already committed adultery with her in his heart. If your right eye causes you to sin, tear it out and throw it away. For it is better that you lose one of your members than that your whole body be thrown into hell. And if your right hand causes you to sin, cut it off and throw it away. For it is better that you lose one of your members than that your whole body go into hell.**

Does Jesus want you to literally pluck out your eye and cut off your hand every time you sin? No, He is not teaching you to do so literally. But the point is that you must be serious about sin; what thoughts, words, and behaviors lead to sin, and how you deal with the many temptations to sin. You need to think radically about what people, places, and things you need to eliminate from your life so that you are not tempted to sin or give place to the Devil. This is "radical amputation" and is referred to as "putting off" in Ephesians 4:22. Use Appendix C to make a list of those persons, places, items, and other temptations you must "put off" immediately because they entice you to sin. Once you finish the list, make a diligent effort to eliminate them or remove yourself from everything and everyone on that list. Radically amputate them from your life.

What about My Friends?

- Can *people* remind you of sin and lead you to sin? Yes, certain people you formerly considered to be your friends were truly "using buddies" who cared nothing for you except that they could use and have a good time with you.

---

[63] Matthew 6:25-34.
[64] Adams, Jay, The Christian Counselor's New Testament, Hackettstown, NJ: Timeless Texts, p. 13.

- Can *places* tempt you to sin? Yes, certain places you frequented can certainly bring back old patterns of thinking leading to "romancing" the drug and the drug-induced lifestyle, leading to utter ruin.

- Can certain *things* lead you to be more tempted to use? Yes, certainly something like an old cooler that was always filled with beer can be something that you associate with drinking and easily lead you astray.

- Can certain *songs* you hear lead you to further temptation to sin? Yes, certain songs you listened to while using alcohol or drugs may bring back that "romancing" mentality leading you to strongly desire a "pick me up" drink or drug.

Yes, there is a lot to amputate, or put off, from your former life. Many drugs can actually cause a physiological reaction in your body when certain people, places, things, and songs are experienced. For example, a crack cocaine addict reported to me that she smoked crack in a certain, brand-named empty soft drink can. After she had sobered up for six months, she went to work one day and saw that same brand-named drink can sitting on a window ledge outside of her building. When she saw this specific soft drink can and how it looked sitting on that ledge, she was immediately reminded of how she used to smoke crack with her "friends." Next, physiologically, she began to taste the drug in the back of her throat. She could even smell the drug as though she were using it again. Her mind remembered, and her body manifested these real physiological symptoms. Thankfully, she went inside and called a Christian girlfriend who met her for lunch later that day and stayed with her that night until she went to sleep. People, places, things, and songs can produce the same type of physiological reaction of craving in the early stages of the <u>transformation</u> process.

Start Now

Although God has a medicinal purpose for drugs, you must examine your thoughts and heart carefully regarding anything and everything with which you associated drugs and alcohol in your past so that it does not adversely affect your transformation. Then after you have completed your "put off" list, God wants you to develop a "put on" list of new persons, places, hobbies, and other things with which you can associate because it pleases God first. Take a sheet of paper and write down both lists right now. Use Appendix C to help you. Start contacting those persons on the "put on" list to build your support system. Make a diligent effort to immediately "put on" the items on your list. Today is the day of salvation![65] You are being saved from the practice of this sin. Do not wait any longer to begin doing the right things because God has a plan and purpose for your life.

Prayer of Heart Change and Application

Dear Heavenly Father, I want to start only utilizing drugs for your intended purpose of pain relief rather than escaping from my emotional pain. When I have physical pain, provide me with physical pain relief and with loved ones who can help me to deny fulfilling my temporary cravings, appetites, and emotional desires to escape. Help me find a support system of godly and loving people to put on. Protect me from myself, Lord, and help me replace any of my ungodly desires with your good desires. Amen.

---

[65] II Corinthians 6:2.

Chapter 7
Drunkenness

Noah is best known for building the ark God used to save him and his family from drowning in the historical event of The Flood. In Genesis 9, however, you discover that Noah was not a perfect man when he sinned by drinking strong wine to excess and became intoxicated. What made it even worse was that Noah was a *preacher* and a man committed to his God. In fact, the Bible refers to him as "righteous" and "blameless."[66]

Noah walked with God and God saved Noah and his family from what would have been a certain death in The Flood.[67] After saving his life here on earth, God saved his eternal life by establishing a covenant with Noah and his descendants. Despite this, Noah got drunk with wine and sinned against his Lord. Therefore, it is certainly possible for Christians to sin in the area of substance abuse even *after* experiencing great blessings from the Lord!

A Familiar Problem to God

Perhaps you find yourself in one of these categories: an admitted, full blown drunkard, an addict, or maybe an occasional alcohol and drug user who partakes to excess. Well, God is so merciful to drunks and abusers of addictive substances that He addresses this problem very near the beginning of the Bible—in the ninth chapter of the book of Genesis! Think about it in this way: since God knows how dangerous the problem of addiction is and how devastating the consequences, He chooses to lovingly introduce you to the problem in the first book of the Bible. The book of Genesis is the book of beginnings and God wastes no time in dealing with the significant problem of substance abuse and physical addiction. God even demonstrates how drunkenness has negative consequences for the family members of the drunkard! Genesis 9:20-27 states:

> **Noah began to be a man of the soil, and he planted a vineyard. He drank of the wine and became drunk and lay uncovered in his tent. And Ham, the father of Canaan, saw the nakedness of his father and told**

---

[66] Genesis 6:9.
[67] Genesis 7 gives the account of The Flood.

> his two brothers outside. Then Shem and Japheth took a garment, laid it on both their shoulders, and walked backward and covered the nakedness of their father. Their faces were turned backward, and they did not see their father's nakedness. When Noah awoke from his wine and knew what his youngest son had done to him, he said, "Cursed be Canaan; a servant of servants shall he be to his brothers." He also said, "Blessed be the Lord, the God of Shem; and let Canaan be his servant. May God enlarge Japheth, and let him dwell in the tents of Shem, and let Canaan be his servant.

Prior to this passage, the Bible speaks of Noah as righteous. Genesis 6:9 states: "...**Noah was a righteous man, blameless in his generation. Noah walked with God.**" Noah's righteousness means he was saved by grace through faith in the Messiah to come[68] and *does not* mean that God chose to use Noah because he was a perfect man. God made Noah righteous just as He makes all Christians righteous. We still have a sin nature affecting our thoughts, words, and actions, even though we are born again and filled continually by the Holy Spirit. In other words, the habits of our old nature (the flesh) in our sinful thinking and acting are not completely eradicated when we become a Christian. Instead, the Holy Spirit is given to dwell in us so we are empowered to overcome sin by being changed in our thoughts, words, and actions. In John 14:15-17, Jesus encouraged His disciples by saying,

> "If you love me, you will keep my commandments. And I will ask the Father, and he will give you another Helper, to be with you forever, even the Spirit of truth, whom the world cannot receive, because it neither sees him nor knows him. You know him, for he dwells with you and will be in you."

If you truly love Jesus more than yourself, there will be a change of heart after studying the Scriptures that will result in a change of behavior. One changed behavior immediately evident is more obedience to God's commands because of the power of the Holy

---

[68] Ephesians 2:8-9 and Hebrews 11:7.

Spirit working through you. A second changed behavior is evidenced when a Christian sins. The Holy Spirit brings conviction (guilt) for the Christian who realizes that this is sin against a Holy God and wants to confess it to God and ask for forgiveness. It is when your heart is broken in repentance over your sin that God draws near to you (Psalm 34:18).

Noah was a believer. He had a close relationship with God, and he walked with God, but Noah was not perfect. We are shown in the passage above that on at least one occasion, he gave in to the sin of drunkenness. Likewise, if you drink to excess or abuse prescription medications occasionally or even just once, you have sinned and you need to repent. It is a matter of your heart. *"The heart of your problem is a problem with your heart."*[69] Examine your heart. What is motivating you when you drink to excess? Is it a desire for excessive pleasure, avoidance of pain, loneliness, despair, depression, guilt, people-pleasing, escape, pride, selfishness, or other ungodly desires? Often these momentary reasons for drinking reveal a more serious problem of the heart that needs to be addressed quickly before it becomes even more problematic.

Comparative Morality

Someone who is an occasional, excessive substance abuser is just as guilty of committing sin as an addict or a drunkard. Often, the alcohol or drug abuser deceives himself by thinking he is really not as bad as an addict or drunkard. Comparative morality, which thinks "there's always a worse sin than mine," is exemplified by the following examples of thought:

- "I'm sure glad my problem isn't as bad as theirs." This is often the mentality at "self-help" group meetings. "At least I'm not as bad as that guy over there! I never drank that much."

- The person taking 15 hydrocodone pills a day says, "I have a legal prescription for my pills. I have legitimate pain. I even have a diagnosis. I'm not like those people who are buying and selling their drugs on the street and using illegal substances. My drugs are legal."

- "Once I get to the point of selling my body or stealing so I can get drugs, then I will know I've got a problem. At least I'm not that bad off...yet."

---

[69] Statement provided by Pastor Harry Reeder during a sermon at Briarwood Presbyterian Church in 2005.

- The nicotine addict says, "I just smoke cigarettes. At least I don't drink alcohol."
- The marijuana addict says, "At least I don't go out and drive under the influence of alcohol. I smoke at home and don't hurt anybody but myself."
- The cocaine addict says, "I'm snorting my drug. At least I don't use the needle like a heroin addict."
- The Friday night drunk says, "At least I only get drunk once a week. Some people are drunk every night of the week."
- The heroin addict says, "I'm only hurting myself. I don't get in the car to drive when I use drugs. At least, I don't rob people or shoot people like a methamphetamine addict."
- The self-help industry in the United States feeds this same mentality: "We don't call ourselves 'addicts' at these meetings because we are not 'addicts.' We are 'alcoholics.' We abused alcohol not drugs," they say.

Comparative morality is a primary reason for the large variety of "self-help group meetings". This categorizing of our sin is often prideful. Abusing drugs in any form is a sin called drunkenness in the Bible.[70] Alcohol is a drug in liquid form.

It doesn't matter if you inject it, snort it, drink it, pop it, or inhale it; whatever means you use to get the substance into your body excessively is the sin of drunkenness. It is a sin in God's eyes, and it will destroy you according to Ephesians 5:18. When you minimize your sin, blame-shift, or rationalize your behavior it is easy to continue in your sin by using your substance of choice excessively. By comparing your life to others that you consider "worse," you are justifying your sinful actions. You can always find another sinner who is "worse" than you, but *by minimizing and comparing your morality to others, you will never come to full repentance* – to full acknowledgement of the truth of your life.

The Bible says, **"God may perhaps grant them [you] repentance leading to a knowledge of the truth, and they [you] may escape from the snare of the devil, after being captured by him to do his will."**[71] The prerequisite indicated in this verse of Scripture is that God grants you repentance to acknowledge your sin before Him. You can give your sin as many various labels and diagnoses as you

---

[70] Ephesians 5:18.
[71] 2 Timothy 2:25-26

wish, but unless you fully acknowledge the truth of your sin, you have not been granted repentance from God. Think of it. *You can repent because God can grant it to you. It's not your own strength.* You can receive forgiveness because your behavior is a sin. It's not a disease that has attacked you. You can change because the Power of God working in you through the Holy Spirit can give you the ability to do it. He works in you to will and do His good pleasure. You must obey, but your success is a result of His power in Christ Jesus, the Hope of Glory. That's hope for lasting change!

God does not want you to compare your behavior to that of other people. God wants you to compare your behavior to His laws, standards, and commands in the Bible. When compared to the Word of God, you realize your occasional, excessive drug and alcohol usage is a sin issue according to Ephesians 5:18: **"And do not be drunk with wine, for that is debauchery, but be filled with the Holy Spirit."**

The occasional substance abuser on prescription medications also needs to examine his heart frequently and apply the same biblical principles, laws, standards, and commands in order to change his life. So you ask, "What if I *only* drink or use prescription medications to excess *occasionally*?" Even though this question minimizes the severity of the drug usage and abuse, the Bible still considers it to be a sin. You do not have to be a life-dominated drunkard to commit the sin of drunkenness. In fact, if you are one who sometimes gets drunk with alcohol or occasionally uses too much of a prescription drug, you may be in a worse spiritual condition than a drunkard! You may be deceiving yourself.

Genesis 19:30-36 records what happened to Lot after he and his family left the burning cities of Sodom and Gomorrah. Because Lot was righteous in the sight of God, he and his family were spared. We all know what happened to Lot's wife when she disobeyed and looked back to see the cities, so that only Lot and his two daughters remained alive.

> **Now Lot went up out of Zoar and lived in the hills with his two daughters, for he was afraid to live in Zoar. So he lived in a cave with his two daughters. And the firstborn said to the younger, "Our father is old, and there is not a man on earth to come in to us after the manner of all the earth. Come, let us make our father drink wine, and we will lie with him, that we may preserve offspring from our father." So they**

> made their father drink wine that night. And the
> firstborn went in and lay with her father. He did not
> know when she lay down or when she arose. The
> next day, the firstborn said to the younger, "Behold I
> lay last night with my father. Let us make him drink
> wine tonight also. Then you go in and lie with him,
> that we may preserve offspring from our father." So
> they made their father drink wine that night also.
> And the younger arose and lay with him, and he did
> not know when she lay down or when she arose.
> Thus both the daughters of Lot became pregnant by
> their father.

Here is another example of a man considered to be righteous
before God who suffered great sin and shame at the hand of his
daughters because of the wine he drank. Lot and Noah are just two
biblical examples of men who were not life-dominated drunkards,
yet the Bible records one sinful instance for each man when he
became drunk with wine. As a result, both men experienced terrible
consequences from their one time sinful choice.

Apart from the temporary, earthly consequences of the sin of
drunkenness, there is the eternal consequence for the unbeliever
of unconfessed, unrepentant sin—eternal separation from God,
in an eternal, physical (bodily) punishment of fire. You must take
responsibility for your sin – no matter how big or how small it may
seem in your eyes. This is a big deal! Jesus gave His life for your sin.
It does matter. Abusing substances and alcohol for your pleasure or
for your escape is a sin. But the good news is that Christ died for
sinners, and you *can* be forgiven. Romans 5:8-11 states:

> ...but God shows his love for us in that while we
> were still sinners, Christ died for us. Since,
> therefore, we have now been justified by his blood,
> much more shall we be saved by him from the
> wrath of God. For if while we were enemies we
> were reconciled to God by the death of his Son,
> much more, now that we are reconciled, shall we
> be saved by his life. More than that, we also rejoice
> in God through our Lord Jesus Christ, through
> whom we have now received reconciliation.

I urge you to confess any and all of your sins of drunkenness, idolatry, lying, selfishness, or addiction to God now. The hopeful message of the Bible in I John 1:9-10 states: **"If we confess our sins, he is faithful and just to forgive us our sins and to cleanse us from all unrighteousness. If we say we have not sinned, we make him a liar, and his word is not in us."** Know this: if you are a Christian struggling with an addiction, occasional substance abuse, or drunkenness, you will always be God's son or daughter; however, your relationship with God is hindered by your chemical use. Imagine that you moved to Africa and your father lives in Kansas. You are still your father's child but your relationship with him would be severely limited in terms of the closeness and opportunities to communicate. Drug and alcohol use make you feel even more distant from those who love you most: God the Father and your loved ones.[72]

Drunkenness is the Name: Your Heart is to Blame

In the Bible, God does not separate those who get drunk with wine and those who get intoxicated with drugs. Substance abusers are not viewed differently than physically addicted Christians. You may be thinking, "I'm addicted to pain pills or marijuana or cocaine but the Bible does not say anything about any of those drugs *specifically*. So does God say anything about my specific problem?" The answer is "yes." In reality, alcohol is a *drug* just like marijuana, cocaine, opiates, benzodiazepine, methamphetamine, nicotine, and even caffeine. God in His Word describes your drug problem (or drinking to excess) as "drunkenness," whether it is alcohol or any other drug, legal or illegal, that you are using to get high or low. Drunkenness is the name of your condition, and it is really a condition of your heart.

You may ask, "Am I really sinning if I just feel a little out of control?" If you try to split hairs about whether you are feeling the effects of a "buzz" from the intoxicant or that you are drunk and out of control, then you are missing the point and allowing pride to get in the way of obeying God. Your attempts to do this are minimizing your heart's motives in the matter. In reality this is an effort to justify your using behaviors.

Is it a sin to drink alcohol? No. Alcohol, by itself, is the amount of tiny, fermented microbes in the liquid that produces the intoxicating results. Does God want you to count the number of microscopic

---

[72] Luke 15:11-32 is an excellent example of how sin can lead one to become distant from the Father.

fermented molecules that are in your drink? No, because the bigger question here is "what is the motivating desire in your heart when you want to drink or use the intoxicant?" This question applies to the use and misuse of prescription drugs as well as alcohol and illicit drugs.

Should I take prescription medications? Yes, if you have a medical need for pain medications, then submit yourself to the advice and care of your physician. God has a good purpose for drugs and alcohol: pain relief. Take your prescription as directed by the instructions on the bottle for physical pain. You could also ask a friend or loved one to keep the medication from you if you think you will be tempted to abuse it.

If substance abuse is your area of struggle, you must look into your heart for the real reason for your abuse of prescription medications. Are you taking the drug to escape from emotional pain such as depression, sadness, bitterness, anger, and hurt? Prescription medications have a godly purpose when used as God intended, but we are considering here the motives of the heart for taking the medication and the resulting failure to be responsible.

Here is a simple tool to use the next time you desire to do something sinful but struggle as to whether you really should do it or not. Before you commit the action, bow down on your knees, close your eyes, and pray to God saying these words: "Lord, I am planning to do _____ right now *to your glory*. I am going to do this *unto You, Father God,* because I know it will please you." If what you are about to do will *not* fit properly in the blank line above because that action cannot be done to glorify God, then you must not commit the action. Do something in place of that action that does glorify God!

It is really that simple. For example, if you are going to drink a couple of beers, then do this technique with "drink these beers" in the blank line above. *Can you do that behavior to God's glory?* Can you put "drink a six pack of beer," "bottle of wine," or even "one shot of tequila" in that blank line and make that statement to God's glory? Speak that sentence out loud using one of the above examples and hear how ridiculous it sounds. Do not concern yourself with a comparison of anyone else who does that same behavior. You must evaluate whether or not *you* should commit the action. Can you do it unto the Lord? If not, then don't do it. Do it only when you know it will please God.

When your actions start to please God, it is called obedience and it leads to blessings. Turning away from sin and becoming obedient to Christ leads to spiritual, physical, mental, and emotional blessings according to I Peter 3:10-13: **"For 'Whoever desires to love life and see good days, let him keep his tongue from evil and his lips from speaking deceit; let him turn away from evil and do good; let him seek peace and pursue it. For the eyes of the Lord are on the righteous, and his ears are open to their prayer. But the face of the Lord is against those who do evil.' Now who is there to harm you if you are zealous for what is good?"** The truth is that you can begin obeying God today and the blessings of obedience will begin immediately. Honor God right now with your actions of obedience.

Prayer of Heart Change and Application

Dear Heavenly Father, Thank you for revealing the truth that Christians can become physically addicted and enslaved to various substances. I repent and ask you to forgive me for allowing myself to become enslaved by my sinful choices. Thank you that you forgive my sins based upon the work of Jesus. When I confess my sins, you are faithful and just and will forgive my sins and cleanse me from all unrighteousness. Thank you for the Spirit of Truth, the Holy Spirit, who is with me and is in me. Strengthen me, be my help, cause me to stand on your truth. Uphold me, my Loving Father. Amen.

Chapter 8

The Depiction of Substance Abuse from Proverbs 23

In addition to Noah and Lot, the Lord gives another biblical example of the tragic experience of a person who drinks to excess in Proverb 23:29-35:

> ²⁹**Who has woe? Who has sorrow? Who has strife? Who has complaining? Who has wounds without cause? Who has redness of eyes? ³⁰Those who tarry long over wine; those who go to try mixed wine. ³¹Do not look at wine when it is red, when it sparkles in the cup and goes down smoothly. ³²In the end it bites like a serpent and stings like an adder. ³³Your eyes will see strange things, and your heart utter perverse things. ³⁴You will be like one who lies down in the midst of the sea, like one who lies on the top of a mast. ³⁵"They struck me," you will say, "but I was not hurt; they beat me, but I did not feel it. When shall I awake? I must have another drink.**

Unlike most proverbs, this one begins by asking questions similar to a riddle. The answer to the riddle comes in verse 30. Clearly, this situation results from the specific sin of drinking wine to excess. Interestingly, God does not assign the specific name of "drunkard" to the person in this proverb. Not using the label of "drunkard" suggests that this proverb is directed toward *anyone* who *occasionally* abuses alcohol, prescription drugs, or the like, in an *excessive manner.* There is a tendency for Christian abusers to deceive themselves into thinking that the problem of using alcohol or drugs to excess as addressed in the Bible only applies to the "drunkard" whose life is dominated by the addiction. God knows that any excessive use of a substance is a heart attitude of selfishness and self-worship.

Proverbs 23

Typically, as verse 29 states, someone who uses an intoxicant to excess has **"woe, sorrow, strife, and complaining."** Most people drink and drug to excess to cover emotional pain with something temporarily pleasurable, but the proverb tells us that drinking behavior leads to more pain and problems. The **"wounds without cause"** come from awakening from a drunken stupor and realizing you have aches, pains, bruises, cuts, and even broken bones of unknown cause. While you were intoxicated, you were clumsy with an unsteady gait causing your sense of reality to have been altered. As a result of your intoxicated state, you do not remember clearly.

The **"redness of eyes"** describes the physical manifestation of redness but also may be referring to the look of despair that accompanies and follows the drunken stupor. Many addicts have a hopeless look whether they are intoxicated or sober. Verse 30 refers to **"tarrying long"** at the wine. Drinking for an extended period of time like this is obviously drinking to excess.

Apply verse 31, **"Do not look at wine when it is red, when it sparkles in the cup and goes down smoothly."** to your own thought life and allow it to be a challenge for you. Similar to the command that Jesus gave His disciples in Matthew 5:27-29 to guard their eyes and hearts, God commands you not to gaze at the wine when it is "red" and when it "sparkles in the cup" because of its inviting appearance of temporarily fulfilling an appetite. Jesus taught that your heart's desire is the problem, not the object that you desire. Jesus knew that the eyes are like windows that open up and what your eyes dwell on will be what your thoughts dwell on.[73] The problem for you in verse 31 is that by staring at the substance with your eyes, your thoughts are those of glorifying, "romancing the substance" so to speak, and remembering what it did and can do for you.

Your eyes lead you to think on the alcohol or drug as if it is your friend. God explains in this verse that the wine has the temporal power to look and feel good as it **"goes down smoothly"** yet partaking of the wine in this manner will lead to potentially harmful and deadly consequences as it **"stings like an adder"** (verse 32). The Bible never says that sin does not feel good, temporarily speaking. Instead, the Bible warns that temporarily, good-feeling sins will lead to devastating consequences and complicating problems.

If you do not die physically, your spiritual vitality suffers as you become more separated from God by your continued drinking. Abusive alcohol and drug use also separates you from your family and close friends. You are no longer controlled by the Holy Spirit but

---

[73] See also Matthew 6:22-23 and Luke 11:34-36.

are controlled by the "spirit" of the intoxicating substance. Evidence of your being controlled by the intoxicating substance is found in verse 33 of Proverbs 23: you begin to **"see strange things"** and out of your mouth you begin to **"utter perverse things"** revealing your wicked heart. Obviously, the Holy Spirit does not cause you to do these sinful things; it is the "spirit" of the substance that "frees" you by bringing out some of the worst, sinful thoughts and deeds from within your self-centered heart.

Next, your entire body – eyes, mouth, and heart – is further out of control. This feels as if you are lying down in the middle of the **"sea"** on the most unstable, wavy, and 'tossed about' part of the boat: the **"mast"** (verse 34). Finally, in verse 35, you are so out of it that you do not feel pain from such things as a striking or beating from someone else and you are oblivious to the reality around you. That is the goal for most Christian addicts: escape from the pain by feeling extreme pleasure. Verse 35 ends by saying, **"when shall I awake?"** You are in your own, self-absorbed dream world of make-believe where you cease to have meaningful relationships with anyone else and nothing seems real. It's as though you are asleep.

Obviously, the person in this proverb prefers to be alone, in a pain-free state, enjoying selfish pleasure of his drunken state as evidenced by the final statement that he **"must have another drink."** God tells it like it is, doesn't He, in Proverbs 23? The tragedy of this picture is that in spite of all the consequences and problems that drunkenness brings into the person's life, the person still desires another drink at the end of the proverb in verse 35. Remember that this person could be an occasional drug abuser, addict, or drunkard, but regardless, when will this insanity end?

Sin is Deceptive and Powerful

When some people think of sin, they imagine horrible and extreme acts of murder, violence, sexual abuse, rape, and the like. But to God, the sin of *thinking* about committing adultery is the same as committing the actual act of adultery.[74] Obviously, the temporary, or earthly, consequences of the sins are very different. However, do not *minimize* your sin actions or sinful attitudes in your heart and mind before God who gave His Son to pay the penalty for sin.

Sin simply means "to miss the mark or standard set by God."

---

[74] Matthew 5:27-28.

Think of an archer who shoots his bow and arrow at a target. If his aim is slightly off the mark, he will shoot the arrow wide of the bull's eye. If his aim is off just a little more, he may miss the entire target altogether. Sin does not have to be a large or extreme act. It is often very insidious and may have the appearance of being "no big deal." But be warned, it will surely lead one down the path resulting in a huge deal!

To demonstrate how powerful sin is, consider this flight analogy. You want to fly from Birmingham, Alabama, to San Diego, California. You get on the plane in Birmingham. During the flight, the pilot does not realize that the plane's compass is off one degree. You wouldn't think one degree would make much difference, but when the pilot lands the plane, he realizes that he has ended up in Canada near Seattle, Washington. He is over one thousand miles north of where he wanted to land the plane. He is very far from his planned destination!

Acts and even thoughts of sin can be represented by the compass that is one tiny degree off the mark. The compass is inaccurate by only one degree! Sin can be defined as missing the perfect target that God requires. If not corrected, the sin of one degree leads to traveling away from the original destination. Over time, "little" sins cause Christians to land far from the intended destination. Therefore, you can see there is no such thing as a "little" sin. All sin has the power to lead someone astray in a big way. Sin is walking down the pathway of self rather than the pathway of the Lord and His best for your life.

Prayer of Heart Change and Application

*Dear Heavenly Father, I have minimized my sin, but I can see that it did not and does not please you to do so. Therefore, I ask you to forgive me and to enable me to forsake my sin so that I can end up in the place that you have called me to be. I do not want to live for me, but I want to live for you alone. Help me to not drink or take drugs if it means that I am **not** going to glorify you when I do so. By faith, Lord, I trust in you to work in my heart by the Holy Spirit working through Your Word. Amen.*

Chapter 9
The Physical Components of Addiction

God has created our bodies with incredible adaptability to even some of the most harmful of substances. The world's use of the term "dependent" is accurate, and involves a very real, observable set of circumstances and symptoms. It's true that a person's body may become physically "dependent" upon certain drugs if the substance is used excessively over time. One who is "dependent" is one who will experience definitive, physical withdrawal symptoms that vary according to the specific drug being used if the person were to completely and abruptly stop taking the medication or substance. For this reason, I urge you to submit yourself to the care of a medical doctor for any substance you have been using and have become "dependent" upon.

God-given Appetites

Appetites are "any of the instinctive desires necessary to keep up organic life."[75] These "instinctive desires" are placed in every human being God created. Appetites are internal alarm clocks to remind us that we must do such things as eat, drink, and sleep. When an appetite is satisfied, the satisfaction is only temporary as the appetite will reappear in a short amount of time. Appetites are designed to be satisfied at regular intervals and in moderation to help sustain your life.

Appetites should remind us that we are finite, limited, and dependent upon God for our sustenance. We are created to have our **batteries recharged** regularly so to speak. Appetites are not the cause of the problem for the addict; everyone has appetites and not everyone is addicted. The heart attitudes that drive the habitual, destructive manner in which the addict fulfills instinctive desires are the root of the problem. The addict fulfills appetites by drinking alcohol or taking mood-altering drugs excessively, causing an addiction to develop. Again, addiction is not a "disease" but learned behavior.

---

[75] Merriam-Webster, op. cit.

What is The Purpose of Appetites?

The question, "Is it a sin to drink?" is akin to the questions: "Is it a sin to have sex?" or "Is it a sin to eat?" or "Is it a sin to work?" or "Is it a sin to sleep?" Your "flesh" has been 'hardwired' by God with five basic, natural appetites that He created for our good and His glory. He intended for sleep, work, food, drink, and sexual intercourse to be pleasurable.[76] These appetites, in and of themselves, are not right or wrong. They are neutral appetites and natural desires. When these appetites are satisfied in moderation and under the right 'biblically-mandated' boundaries, there is no sin and therein is the blessing: pleasure.

Appetites are blessings from God intended for regular and moderate, God-glorifying pleasure. It is not a sin for a married couple to have sexual relations every day; however, it *is* a sin for two **unmarried** persons to have sexual relations **any** day according to the Bible.[77] God has given us *protective* parameters in the Bible for fulfilling our natural, God-given desires because He loves us and requires this from us. When we satisfy an appetite in an extreme manner and fail to meet our responsibilities to God, we are committing sin. God sets parameters for our own good to protect us; therefore, if we fulfill an appetite in a manner that is outside of God's protective parameter, there is always danger of physical addiction and its consequences.

Made to Worship

One more God-given, spiritual appetite is the desire to worship something or someone. "Worship" as a noun is defined as "extravagant respect or admiration for or devotion to an object of esteem."[78] What is the object that pleasurably fulfills your natural appetites, for which you have "extravagant respect and admiration"? What are you prone to devote your thoughts, words, and actions to obtaining? Is it the Lord Jesus Christ or is it an object of temporal value?

Christian substance abusers and addicts have a worship problem

---

[76] Notes from a private teaching by Pastor Harry Reeder at Briarwood Presbyterian Church, Birmingham, AL, in August of 2004.

[77] I Corinthians 5, I Timothy 1:10, Hebrews 13:4, and Galatians 5:19.

[78] Merriam-Webster, op. cit.

(called idolatry) in that they seek to fulfill temporary appetites with temporary pleasures rather than disciplining themselves for godliness and eternal rewards. The Apostle Paul told Timothy in I Timothy 4:7b-8: **"Rather train yourself for godliness; for while bodily training is of some value, godliness is of value in every way, as it holds promise for the present life and also for the life to come."** We must train ourselves to produce godly habits of worshiping our Creator and Sustainer.

Instincts

Instincts are God-given impulses that are automatic and are not learned. For example, if you skip lunch, then by evening when it is time for dinner, your stomach begins to function as if food is truly there. If food is not there, your blood sugar drops and you may feel as if you are starving. God gave us these "instinctive" mechanisms to make our bodies aware of our need for food. Hunger is an instinct.

How you choose to fill that instinctive appetite of hunger is "inherent" and learned. For example, it is dinnertime, and you are "instinctively" hungry, and you "inherently" desire to eat a meat and two vegetables because that is what you have always eaten at dinnertime since you were a child. Throughout your lifetime, you have learned to "inherently" desire the meat and two vegetables at dinnertime; therefore, your "instinctive" appetite for food in general has been "inherently" learned to be satisfied specifically by a meat and two vegetables. Now when you are hungry, you think specifically about a meat and two vegetables and that is what you are craving. Appetites trigger learned behavior called "inherent" desires; desires that you learn to fulfill in a certain way.

A person can learn to eat any type of food to satisfy the appetite. Some people eat only vegetables and do not eat meat. Some people eat "junk food" rather than a vegetable, so when hunger is experienced, they crave "junk food." *What you feed your appetite will become a learned, or "inherent," desire.* Alcohol and drug abuse are learned (or inherent) behaviors. Substance abusers have learned to satisfy their "instinctive appetites" with "inherent substances" and their bodies respond to the physical impact of the chemical use.

How is the appetite of thirst related to alcohol? Addictions to drugs and alcohol are "inherent" not "instinctive." The distinction is that the abuser of alcohol chooses to satisfy his "instinctive" appetite of thirst with a beverage that has a high content of alcohol in it so that he will get inebriated. He is not satisfying his thirst with water but willfully *choosing* to satisfy it with alcohol. His thirst could have easily been satiated by drinking water. Again, what you feed your appetite will become a learned, or "inherent," desire.

What Are Cravings?

Cravings are real, physiological experiences of desire for a substance that has been used excessively. The body adapts to the majority of conditions to which it is exposed. Drug addiction is no different. "Tolerance" to alcohol and drugs increases as the substance is increasingly used. This means it takes more and more of the substance to get the same original effect. In particular, the alcohol-addicted person must drink a certain amount of alcohol just to avoid the "shakes," which is a "street name" for withdrawal symptoms. The addicted ones have often declared, "Now, I merely drink alcohol to feel normal." They are telling the truth. This is the physical component of tolerance and cravings, and for this reason, a physician's care is necessary.

For an opiate addict,[79] cravings manifest soon after the effects of the drug ceases. Before long, the opiate addict is physically craving the drug again as his or her body has become dependent upon it. Tolerance can be illustrated in the following example: Suzie takes two or three opiate pills as prescribed by her physician each day for her lower back pain. Over time, the pain in her back still persists after she takes two or three pills, but she finds that by taking five or six pills, the pain disappears. Suzie's body is increasing its tolerance. Suzie's body says to itself, "Wow, Suzie keeps getting these opiates in such a great quantity that I (her body) do not have to make any natural endorphins for her anymore. This is great because I can make other things that Suzie needs since she obviously does not need any natural, pain relievers that I can make." Suzie now has a problem called "dependence" as she now requires these opiates that come from outside of her body in order to feel "normal."

Cravings are legitimate, diagnostic, and physical phenomena that come from the *excessive* fulfilling of natural appetites. If you are experiencing cravings, you have developed a more serious problem than you realize. Whether you believe you are a "hard core" substance

---

[79] Opiates are in the opium family of drugs commonly known as heroin, morphine, dilaudid, hydrocodone, and oxycontin, among many others.

abuser, or drug addict, or an "occasional user who sometimes goes to excess," you need God's guidance for living your life in a way that pleases Him. This comes from being self-controlled.

The final fruit of the Spirit discussed in Galatians 5:23 is **"self-control."** Notice that the object under control is "self." Self is <u>not</u> the *source* of control. Rather, it is the *object* of control. Self is the object that must be controlled.[80] Self must continually remain under the control of the Holy Spirit, not itself.

If you continue to sin by satisfying your natural appetites in excessive and uncontrolled ways, you will develop tolerance, dependence, and cravings. These will become an "inherent" and essential component of your being. Even if it seems difficult, you must conform your will to God's will. God is not *as* interested in your happiness <u>as</u> He is in your holiness. When you become "holy," you will likely become more joyful. The Bible teaches that your holiness, or obedience, will lead to more joy, happiness, and contentment.[81]

By remaining obedient to Him, you will avoid developing insatiable and powerful cravings for your drug of choice. Obedience will enable you to avoid problems of cravings, dependence, and tolerance. Your biggest problem is not your appetites for alcohol, drugs, sex, sleep, or food. It is your sinful heart attitudes that indicate you prefer satisfying temporary pleasures with drugs and alcohol rather than fulfilling them with a thriving relationship with an eternal God. Excessive satisfaction of temporary appetites leads to sinful ways of acting, thinking, and speaking along with tolerance, cravings, and dependence upon the drug. In this sense, your flesh and its lusts and desires are your primary problem and your own worst enemy. God's grace will empower you to overcome your addictive tendencies of your heart. His grace is your primary solution!

---

[80] This idea was taught to me by Pastor-Teacher Harry Reeder. His sermon series at Briarwood Presbyterian Church, Birmingham, AL (2005) is a great study on the fruit of the Spirit. You may obtain it at www.briarwood.org

[81] I Peter 3:10-13

Prayer of Heart Change and Application

Dear Heavenly Father, Thank you for revealing your approach to my addiction problem. Thank you for redefining the world's definition of addiction because it gives me real hope for change. I know that Jesus died for sin and He died for my sins of addiction, drunkenness, selfishness, lying, and other sins. Reveal the truth to me. Help me to live by eternal principles found in the Bible rather than by feelings, cravings, appetites, and temporary desires. I realize that my appetites are not under the moderate control of your Holy Spirit. You have given me a body to glorify you and I have abused it for the temporary pleasures of _____ and _____ and to escape from the pain of my life. Cause my mind to hear and understand these new definitions of cravings, appetites, and addiction. Stir in me a desire to conform my will to yours, Lord God. Thank you that you are patient with me and that you are telling me the truth about addiction because you love me and want what is best for me. Amen.

Chapter 10
Idolatry

The current fad in secular addiction counseling is that addiction is a "brain disease." It is apparently no longer good enough to label addiction as a "disease" but to add that it is a "brain disease." In twenty years, it will very likely change again. The secular world thinks it is discovering new, "scientific" information that points to addiction being a "brain disease" due to all of the genetic research of the current day. It is somewhat comical to me that the addiction counselors I know personally say this new "discovery" is "revolutionary" yet they still treat this supposed "brain disease" in the exact same manner that they did last year, ten years ago, and even twenty years ago!

Secular counselors can only "treat" the symptoms of addiction because the heart of addiction is a spiritual problem requiring the power of Christ to transform an idolater into a true worshiper of God. God "treats" the heart of the addict by completely changing it. Are there genes that indicate one is prone to addiction? Research is inconclusive at the time of this book's writing. Even if a specific gene is found that "predisposes" someone to a chemical addiction, the person will still be responsible before God for feeding that addiction. Scientists may never identify such a gene and it really doesn't matter if they do since we know what is at the heart of addiction: "idolatry." It's not new.

What is Idolatry?

"Idolatry" is defined as "the worship of a physical object as a god or immoderate attachment or devotion to something."[82] Idolatry is the preoccupation in one's thinking that leads to *demanding* any temporarily pleasurable desire that gratifies self. Addicted idolaters think and say, "I must have" this pleasurable substance. Idolatry can manifest in the form of drugs, alcohol, sex, sleep, work, gambling, shopping, eating, and living to please someone else more than God. These temporary pleasures are short-lived and do not permanently satisfy. The pleasures feel good for a time, but they bring with them

---

[82] Merriam-Webster, I. 1996, c1993. *Merriam-Webster's collegiate dictionary.* Includes index. (10th ed.). Merriam-Webster: Springfield, Mass., U.S.A.

many problematic consequences when responsibilities are neglected. The pleasures often bring feelings of guilt, shame, depression, and anger because one is seeking to satisfy an eternal appetite for God (called worship) with a temporary fix. Idolatrous desires seek to please self above pleasing God and others. Idolatry quite simply is the worship, or pleasing, of self.

Christians can allow themselves to become idolaters. I Corinthians 10:7 is written to believers in Christ and says: **"Do not be idolaters as some of them were..."** Christians should not give themselves over to the worship of an idol, but many do and must repent once they realize the problem. Idolatry is not an unforgivable sin, but it is devastating as it separates idolaters from God and the people who love them most.

Most people are blind to their idolatrous desires and need someone else to help them see idolatry. In order for an addict to overcome an addiction, other people need to point out their sinful, selfish heart attitudes, and these will become even more obvious when the alcohol or drug is taken away! Stopping the abuse of the mood-altering substance does not "fix" the idolatrous heart. Many addicts quit using their drug of choice only to become sober and even more selfish than ever before. It is a sad commentary on the human heart and is the primary reason why alcohol and drug usage are merely symptoms of a deeper, spiritual heart problem.

By "heart," I do not mean the organ that pumps blood throughout the body to all extremities. By "heart," I mean the inner, spiritual person consisting of the mind, spirit, and soul. God created us to be a wonderful mixture of a physical body and a spiritual body. Your physical body consists of many intricate parts such as your brain. Your spiritual body is the "heart" of mankind and consists of your attitudes, will, soul, and thoughts (or mind). When secular addiction counselors deal with the brain, they are only addressing the physical person. The spiritual person consists of the mind, thoughts, and heart attitudes that interact with the physical person yet are distinctly spiritual.

Genetics

God says in Ephesians 2:10: **"For we are his workmanship, created in Christ Jesus for good works, which God prepared beforehand, that we should walk in them."** God is your Creator; you are His workmanship. The world believes that people have a "genetic predisposition" to addiction or an "addictive personality." The truth is that every human being on planet Earth is capable of becoming "addicted" to any pleasurable activity because of the capacity for idolatry in the human heart. Do not underestimate the power of sin and the wickedness of the human heart.

The world's definitions and terms for substance abuse are often man-made, half-truths, and often hopeless. If you believe you have an "addictive personality," the world would explain that you have a "genetic predisposition" to substance abuse, drunkenness, or addiction. Essentially, the best the world can offer you is an excuse to blame the substance abuse problems in your life on your Creator for your "genetic predisposition" and "addictive personality." The lie the world is promoting is that you are not responsible for your choices because you did not choose to be created with an "addictive personality" with genes that cannot be reversed.

"Are my addictive behaviors genetic or learned?" is a common question from addicts who are looking for an explanation for why they would continue in the insanity of their destructive, addictive behaviors. Quite simply, the answer is that we are born with a sinful nature so our genes are "fallen." Since the sins of Adam and Eve at the Fall, everyone is born with "genetic defects" of some type and everyone is destined to physically die.

Romans 5:12 states it best: **"Therefore, just as sin came into the world through one man, and death through sin, and so death spread to all men because all sinned."** The one man through whom sin entered into this world was Adam in Genesis 3. Adam was the representative of all mankind. Some say that this is not fair: "Adam sinned, but if I were there to choose, then I would have made a right choice." The Bible disagrees and tells us that "**all have sinned and fallen short of the glory of God.**"[83] Do not be self-righteous and think you could have chosen better than Adam.

God's Explanation

God is not silent about our genetic predisposition toward particular sins. God's Word in Hebrews 12:1 views you as having a **"sin which clings so closely"** to you. In other words, you know that every human being is inclined to sin in general because of a sin nature; however, each individual person differs in the *specific type*

---

[83] Romans 3:23.

of sin in which he indulges. Therefore, those persons who do not struggle with a chemical addiction do not understand how someone could struggle with it. You can be certain that those who do not struggle with a chemical addiction do struggle with some type of sin in an "addictive" manner such as the love of work or the love of control.

Each person has a "sin of preference" that "clings so closely." These could be such sins as lying, coveting, drinking to excess, sexual immorality, murdering, gossiping, and the like.[84] The King James Version of the Bible in Hebrews 12:1 states that this sin "so easily besets" a person. Everyone has a particular type of sin with which they struggle more than other sins. The sin "besets" you by entrapping you and knocking you off of the path in your walk with Christ. Your relationship with God is hindered as a result. What is your particular "besetting" sin? Do you have more than one? What sin "clings closely" to you that you could even be labeled and described as that type of sinner (such as a drunkard, liar, adulterer, man-pleaser, or glutton, to name a few)?

As mentioned previously, if you are prone to sin by drinking or doing anything pleasurable to excess, the Bible labels you as a "drunkard" or "idolater." You may have a "besetting sin" for alcohol, drugs, and mood-altering substances. If so, then you must take responsibility for your sin of preference and build in boundaries and safeguards to protect you from committing such sins in the future. Later chapters of this book will help you to do just that.

The "Go Button"

The following illustration is a helpful metaphor of how one has a sin of preference. In this illustration, all people have both types of buttons: the "go button" and the "stop button." (The wiring of each button is connected to the sinful, human heart.) The majority of people who choose to drink alcohol today do so because they enjoy the initial "buzz" feeling that comes with it. What happens next is where we see two very different responses. One response is to stop drinking because the person despises the out of control feeling. The other response is to continue drinking (go) because the person desires to have that out of control feeling.

A person who chooses to use his or her "stop button" drinks one

---

[84] Galatians 5:19-21.

or two alcoholic beverages and starts to get a "buzz." The same "stop button" person then drinks one or two more alcoholic beverages and begins to feel as if he is really losing control. He thinks, "I don't like this out of control feeling. I need to stop drinking right now," and he stops drinking. This person chooses to use the "stop button."

On the other hand, a person who chooses to use his or her "go button" drinks one or two alcoholic beverages and starts to get a "buzz." The "go button" person drinks one or two more alcoholic beverages and begins to feel as if he or she is really losing control. However, loving this out of control feeling, the "go button" person thinks, "I like this feeling. I want to keep drinking more," and keeps drinking and drinking and drinking...you get the picture. This person chooses to push the "go button" when drinking alcohol or using drugs and wants to keep going. The sin that "clings so closely" to this person is drunkenness. He might also easily fit the category of 'lover of pleasure.'

Neither group understands the other group. People who choose to hit the "stop button" do not understand the people who choose to hit the "go button" and vice versa. The out of control feeling is drunkenness and ironically feels the same for both the "stop button" and "go button" persons; however, this same feeling produces a very different reaction! "Go button" pushers do not understand why "stop button" pushers would ever want to stop drinking. The stop button person realizes he doesn't like being out of control and can't understand the "go button" person. He says, "I hate this." One group's choice to either stop or go is perplexing to the opposite group.[85]

"Stop Button" Chemistry?

There is a theory being tested in the realm of physiology and neurology called the "kindling effect."[86] The central idea in this theory is that there are natural enzymes and chemicals in the body

---

[85] This analogy can apply to drugs and other pleasures as well as to alcohol. I have even found it to be true for responses to anesthesia used for surgery. "Stop button" pushers hate the out of control feeling that anesthesia gives while "go button" pushers love that same feeling. It is a very interesting observation.

[86] From notes taken in a course taught by Dr. Merrill Norton, Univ. of Georgia, at an ASADS (Alabama School of Alcohol and Drug Studies) conference in 2005.

that act as a buffer to counteract the effects of toxic drugs like cocaine, alcohol, nicotine, and marijuana.[87] When a "stop button" pusher ingests one of these drugs, the person may not experience the intoxicating power of the drug because of the buffering effect of the counteracting enzymes (chemicals) in the body. The theorists believe that some people have this first line of defense built into their bodies to protect them from physical addiction. Perhaps, before the Fall of mankind in the garden recorded in Genesis, we all had these perfectly working buffering enzymes.

"Stop button" persons must be warned that repeated use of a substance will often lead to a breakdown in this physical line of defense. When that breakdown occurs, physical addiction may result for anyone. Repeated use wears down your own body's God-given defense and may result in a "stop button" person becoming addicted.

The "kindling effect," also known as the "buffering effect," is still only a theory. It is being tested but is not proven fact at this time. Whether it is proven or not, every person has the potential to become physically addicted to drugs and alcohol. Prevention is the best medicine; it is better to never use addictive substances rather than to experiment with them.

"Go Button" Chemistry?

In contrast, "go button" pushers cannot curse God if the "kindling" theory is proven to be true and they do not have a buffering enzyme! The reason they cannot curse God is because they are responsible for their sin nature and could refuse to take that first drug or alcoholic drink. Substance abusers cannot play the role of a victim because it is one's sin choice to have the desire for drunkenness which is idolatry.

Typically, what happens to the "go button" pusher is that the first time he experiments by using his drug of choice to excess (remember that alcohol is a drug!), he says to himself, "Wow, this is the best thing since sliced bread. I've never felt this good before. Why haven't

---

[87] Neurologists think that there is nothing in the body that can act as a buffer for crystal meth (methamphetamine) resulting in its highly addictive properties and huge potential for dependency. This drug is ruining lives like no other illegal drug ever has so I urge you to never try it. It's also known as crank, ice, and meth. Many who study it think that users of this drug become physically addicted after the first use.

I done this sooner?" The "go button" pusher's eyes are now opened to the sin and there is no going back. It is similar to what happened to Adam and Eve in the Garden of Eden right after they ate of the forbidden fruit. In Genesis 3:7 it states: **"Then the eyes of both were opened, and they knew that they were naked."**

Just like Adam and Eve in Genesis 3:7, the "go button" pusher's eyes are opened to the experience of the sin after he partakes of the desired drug. He now knows what the drug feels like and what it can do for him. There is no going back to the day when the addict had never experienced what the drug feels like just as Adam and Eve could not go back into the Garden of Eden after just one sin. Genesis 3:23-24 states:

> **Therefore the Lord God sent him out from the garden of Eden to work the ground from which he was taken. He drove out the man, and at the east of the garden of Eden he placed the cherubim and a flaming sword that turned every way to guard the way to the tree of life.**

Don't you think Adam and Eve regretted their decision to sin and wanted to return to the days when they knew no sin? Do you wish you had never tasted or tried the substance so you would not know what it feels like for you? Now you love the feeling of the drug, how it relieves your misery and pain, and what it does for you temporarily. It takes you out of reality and into a "perfect" world. However, there is no turning back now, and you cannot return to the paradise of the Garden of Eden of not knowing what feelings the drug produces. But there is hope for

- better feelings
- better experiences
- more peace beyond your capacity to understand
- freedom from the bondage of sin
- rich fellowship with your Savior
- mercy and healing of relationships
- forgiveness from God and potential for forgiveness from others

You cannot conceive of things that God has prepared for you if you love Him. **"But, as it is written, 'What no eye has seen, nor ear**

heard, nor the heart of man imagined, what God has prepared for those who love him.'"[88]

If you are influenced by the world's theory of addiction as a disease, you may be thinking, "Well, if God made me with the potential to push the "go button," then I'm not responsible for my actions." Wrong! You chose to continue pushing your "go button." Many have attempted to blame God by using the excuse of 'God made me this way' in order to keep sinning by excessively using drugs or alcohol. If, indeed, you recognize that you tend to push the "go button," then you actually have a *greater* responsibility to not drink or drug excessively. It has been argued that "go button" pushers may not process alcohol and other drugs in their bodies as well as "stop button" pushers, but whether there is a physical, genetic reason or not, you are still responsible for your choices and how you respond to the heart of the problem.

"Why did God do this to me? Why did he create me with the potential 'hardwiring' of a drunkard?" are questions often asked but with a wrong motive. Is it God's fault that you like this feeling so much? God created all things including you; therefore, He knows you better than you know yourself. He created you *to worship Him,* and He wants you to be "addicted" to worshiping Him alone. The crucial matter is that an "addiction" to anything other than God is a focus upon pleasing yourself, or idolatry. The reality is that you need to focus upon pleasing God and others.

21st Century Idolatry

Theoretically, anyone can become physically addicted to alcohol or drugs. "Go button" pushers excessively satisfy their natural appetites of thirst, hunger, sex, work, and sleep, so they must guard their hearts when doing anything pleasurable. Essentially, this love of pleasure is idolatry–worshiping the creation rather than the Creator.

What or who is the thing (idol) that is being worshiped? At the core, it is the worship of self (not the worship of any one particular substance or pleasure) because the idol is desired for selfish reasons. For this reason, you must recognize addiction as a spiritual problem of the heart. Idolatry is a foreign concept to our modern minds, but idolatry is alive and well today in the hearts of people. In Bible times,

---

[88] I Corinthians 2:9.

men and women worshiped idols of various forms, often in the likeness of animals or humans. The idol became an object the person could see and touch when praying. No faith was required to worship because one could see and touch the idol.

People worshiped different idols because they wanted different things. For example, if a Hebrew wanted a financial blessing, he might worship the idol for the god named Molech. The worship of the idol always came down to a selfish, self-centered view of what the person *desired to receive* from the idol. The idol was a "god" designed to serve the idolater who was really acting in the place of god. In Christianity, biblical churches teach that worship is God-centered and consists of what a person *desires to give to God*. Acts 20:35 states:

In all things I have shown you that by working hard in this way we must help the weak and remember the words of the Lord Jesus, how he himself said, 'It is more blessed to give than to receive.'

So What Do I Do With the "Go Button"?

Every person likely pushes the "go button" for some type of temporary pleasure or pursuit. "Go button" pushing is just another label for "idolatry." So are you now required to abstain from every appetite known to man? No, of course not, but you are to be moderate in the fulfillment of all appetites. Will you ever be able to drink, eat, work, partake in marital sex, or sleep again? Find out what God's protective parameters are for experiencing each appetite. Find out what pleases Him first.

Do you find yourself engaging <u>excessively</u> in various pleasurable activities? If you are, you may be an "all or nothing" type of person who takes things to an extreme measure. *The only extreme that I can recommend is the "radical amputation" and abstinence from strong drink and intoxicating substances.* Do not drink or take the first pleasure because your appetites coupled with your impaired judgment from the substance will lead to excess. It is almost a guarantee, so do not deceive yourself by thinking, "Maybe I can drink like other people. Maybe this time will be different. Maybe I can just drink one or two and stop." Addicts often wish they could drink and take drugs like "normal" people, but they cannot. Rather than listen to yourself at moments of temptation and deception, you must talk to yourself with biblical truth and act upon it.

In time, the Lord will make you more moderate in satisfying your appetites. For now, however, *you need to admit your tendency to go to the extreme in this one area of addiction*, that you are a "go button" pusher. You can begin to channel this way of thinking and acting toward bringing glory to your wonderful Creator. Praise the Lord that He will begin teaching you to be moderate in all things and pray that you will learn to produce the fruit of the Spirit of self-control.[89] If you are married to someone who pushes the "stop button" with regard to alcohol and drugs, you can learn how to be moderate from your spouse.

After consulting with your primary physician, I recommend that "go button" pushers willingly abstain from alcohol and other narcotic drugs for a period of at least six months if at all possible. The biblical principle of abstinence is called the "expediency principle"[90] and it is mentioned in two places in the Bible. First, I Corinthians 6:12 states: **"'All things are lawful for me,' but not all things are helpful. 'All things are lawful for me,' but I will not be enslaved by anything."** Second, I Corinthians 10:23 states: **"'All things are lawful," but not all things are helpful. 'All things are lawful,' but not all things build up."** I urge you abstain temporarily until you can learn to be more self-controlled. *Talk to your medical doctor first and submit to his or her medical advice before proceeding in this.*

In the secular world, the term "harm reduction" refers to controlled drinking and drugging. I do not encourage this. You are beginning the new process of transforming your addiction to drugs into an addiction for serving Christ. Christian addicts should abstain from alcohol and drugs for a long period of time before ever using those substances again. In reality, most Christian "go button" pushers recognize that they can never drink and take drugs without going to excess so they avoid drinking entirely as they operate under the biblical "expediency principle." Not all things that are lawful "build" the addict up, and not all of those same things are advantageous and expedient to the Christian "go button" pusher. Often, the "go button" Christian must "radically amputate"[91] alcohol and drugs out of his life for an extended period of time.

---

[89] Galatians 5:21.
[90] Adams, Jay, The Christian Counselor's New Testament, Hackettstown, NJ: Timeless Texts, p. 518.
[91] Matthew 5:27-30.

God Owns You

Some ask "Why, Lord, did you create me this way?" as if being "hardwired" to worship God is a bad thing. God wants you to worship and serve Him in an extreme manner. Those who followed Jesus thought he was extreme at times during His ministry because He radically obeyed the Father's will. Being a follower of Christ is an extreme, radical way to live and is what Christians should desire. You can never pay God back for salvation, nor can you pay *up* to God in advance in order to earn salvation. However, if you are a Christian who has been shown much love by receiving the precious gift of salvation, then you will want to please God by paying *out* good works unto Him.[92] You cannot earn salvation from God. You are not working for God as you would work for a paycheck from an employer. My hope is that you will see how good God is and because He is so good, you will desire to do good works for His glory.

As your Creator, God made you as He wanted you to be, and to bring Him glory. Mankind is now a strange combination of being made in His image yet being marred by the fallen genetics of sin. In Romans 9:20-21, Paul writes to the church at Rome:

> **But who are you, O man, to answer back to God? Will what is molded say to its molder, "Why have you made me like this?" Has the potter no right over the clay, to make out of the same lump one vessel for honored use and another for dishonorable use?**

God is the Creator and "Molder" while you are the clay that is being "molded" by God. The Lord does whatever He pleases. He is your Creator. He is Sovereign. He glorifies Himself through us because we are created in His image. Look at how much glory He gets when He uses fallible, fallen man to do His will!

Use the "Go Button" for the Lord

It has been my experience that persons who have been born again by the Holy Spirit and who have used the "go button" for drugs and alcohol make excellent transformed Christians because they have

---

[92] Reeder, Harry, "Transformed by Truth: Traveling the Bible Highway 66," sermon series preached at Briarwood Presbyterian Church, Birmingham, AL, on December 5, 2004.

been forgiven much; therefore, they love much. In Luke 7:47, Jesus taught His disciples about the sinning woman who blessed Jesus with the alabaster flask of oil: **"Therefore I tell you, her sins, which are many, are forgiven—for she loved much. But he who is forgiven little, loves little."**

"Go button" pushers *ought to go to the extreme* as this woman did, in serving God because God is changing them from their selfish nature into new creations in Christ. What a radical transformation! Our Heavenly Father uses these people in unique and providentially ordained ways.[93]

For this reason, you are not to be ashamed of using the "go button" for worship of God. You are to be ashamed if you continue to use the "go button" by squandering it upon pleasing yourself with continued substance abuse (or any other selfish desire). Take responsibility now for your actions by repenting and being used by Him and for His glory. Repent from your selfish heart desires and shameful deeds of the past by seeking to please God and love others first. God is forgiving of repentant Christians. If you are using your "go button" for God, then get ready to live an exciting life full of the blessings of God Almighty!

Nurturing

At the beginning of this chapter, the question was asked, "Are my addictive behaviors genetic or learned?" So now we turn to the role of nurture, or learning, in this issue. To answer this question in a nutshell, learning is most often accomplished through modeling. If you have children, you know this is true because all children model their parents' words and behaviors. If you do not have children, you know how much you have turned out to be like the persons who raised you, and you might not like it in some ways! The Bible warns you in Proverbs 22:24-25: **"Make no friendship with a man given to anger, nor go with a wrathful man, lest you learn his ways and entangle yourself in a snare."** The Bible also warns you in I Corinthians 15:33: **"Do not be misled: Bad company ruins good morals."**

---

[93] Asceticism is not what is intended here. God is not pleased with ascetics who think that their extreme deprivation is what pleases Him. Rather, you are to pursue a relationship with God and an attitude of serving Him faithfully.

The persons with whom you choose to spend the most time are going to be the biggest influences in your life. You will become like them because you will mimic their words and behaviors. Whether you realize it or not, you will be changed by their influence as you observe, model, practice, and learn many of their ways. You are designed by God to be a creature that is influenced by others. Because of this truth, you must replace your old friends with godly new friends.

To the Christian in particular, God warns you in Proverbs 23:20-21: **"Be not among drunkards or among gluttonous eaters of meat, for the drunkard and the glutton will come to poverty, and slumber will clothe them with rags."** If you tend to be a "go button" pusher, you must take extra precautions not to associate with persons who continually give themselves over to drinking to excess because you will be influenced by their way of thinking, and you will end up in physical and spiritual poverty. Only associate with another "go button" pusher if they have turned their "go buttons" "on" toward serving our Lord Jesus Christ. Find a same-sex, more mature Christian to model in your transformation process.

There are many great Christians who have turned the misuse and abuse of the "go button" into a blessing from God. Some of the best preachers have been "go button" pushers who are now "on fire" and passionate about their Savior and Redeemer, the Lord Jesus Christ. Like these men of God, you also must learn to use the "go button" for the higher calling–for the ultimate benefit of the kingdom of the Lord.

Prayer of Heart Change and Application

Dear Heavenly Father, you have a good purpose for making me and because of my sin nature, I am a "go button" person. I look forward to serving you with my "go button." I want to turn my "go button" "on" for you, Lord, rather than to fulfill my temporary desires and passions. Father, transform me from being selfish into becoming more focused upon pleasing you and serving others. Amen.

Chapter 11
The Perishing Mentality

Proverbs 31 is a passage of Scripture familiar to Christians because it is often used to teach the character of a godly wife. What many Christians do not realize is that verses 4 through 7 of that Proverb teach some powerful truths about the purpose and power of alcohol and drugs. Let's look at this text and see what dwells in the heart of someone who is addicted.

Proverbs 31:4-5 states: **"It is not for kings, O Lemuel, it is not for kings to drink wine, or for rulers to take strong drink, lest they drink and forget what has been decreed and pervert the rights of all the afflicted."** These two verses are straightforward warnings to those in leadership positions, such as rulers and kings, to abstain from taking even the first drink of strong, intoxicating substances. The reason is clearly stated that drinking alcohol makes one "forget" to do what is right. Does the law change? No. What changes? The leader changes as he becomes someone who is *not* thinking of others but is primarily concerned with pleasing himself. The leader's judgment becomes cloudy and he is not concerned with doing what is right in the sight of God as evidenced by the statement that he "perverts the rights of all the afflicted." He ceases to be a loving servant of God and of the people he oversees.

Now, apply this biblical principle of abstaining from alcohol and drugs to your situation: When you drink alcohol, do you make decisions that are righteous or self-righteous? When you drink alcohol, do you think of those you have been given the responsibility to oversee? For example, the husband who goes to the bar after work on Friday nights has been given the responsibility to love his wife in a sacrificial and giving way. If she is waiting for him at home, wondering where he is, and worried about whether or not he is safe, is he being a responsible, loving husband? No, this husband is being unloving, self-centered, and neglectful of his responsibility to love his wife. He has conveniently "forgotten," as the proverb says, what is right and is doing what he wants to do with no regard for his wife.

Drinking excessively and drugging are selfish behaviors regardless of how they are explained, rationalized, or justified. People drink together at parties, houses, and bars but they are not having self-less fellowship. They may be laughing, talking, and dancing but everyone at that function is primarily consumed with pleasing him or herself. After a few hours of prolonged drinking, people at the party "forget" what is right and "forget" to consider the needs of others. This passage of Scripture is talking to rulers and kings, but as you can see it can be applied to any leadership position – husbands, fathers, mothers, employers, elders, deacons, presidents, and pastors.

Perishing Mentality of Despair and Hopelessness

God plainly states the medicinal and primary purpose of alcohol and drugs in Proverbs 31:6-7: **"Give strong drink to the one who is perishing, and wine to those in bitter distress; let them drink and forget their poverty and remember their misery no more."** God is referring to both alcohol and mood-altering drugs by using the phrase, "strong drink." The person referred to in this proverb is "perishing." In other words, he or she is failing in health so badly and experiencing the "bitter distress" of suffering since death seems imminent.

In this circumstance, the Bible says it is appropriate for this person to ingest "strong drink." Why? *To forget his poverty and to remember his misery no more* is the biblical reason. The intoxicating substance can be a beneficial medicine to the physically "perishing" person by providing much needed pain relief. Drugs and alcohol are designed by God for this purpose alone – to be a blessing to those truly perishing in their physical bodies!

Proverbs 31:6-7 teaches that a central heart problem for the substance abuser is that he often has a "perishing" mentality. The common worldly label for this mentality is "stinking thinking." Although he may not be physically dying, the addict who continues to be enslaved to his abuse of a substance believes the lie that he is "perishing." He tells himself such things as the following:

- My life is a waste.
- No one loves me.
- Life has been unfair to me.
- God has been unfair to me.
- My family would be better off if I were dead.
- I would be better off dead.

These are grave and serious lies as they demonstrate the suicidal and despairing thoughts the addict believes in his heart. In reality, he *is* perishing – mentally and spiritually.

The addict believes his life is a waste and he has been 'dealt a bad hand' in the card game of life.[94] He is discontent. He is pessimistic because he chooses to focus upon the problems that have occurred in his life rather than the blessings. He sees the glass as half-empty rather than half-full; therefore, out of his pessimism, he is "perishing" in the thoughts of his mind. His mentality is like that of a non-Christian who has no eternal hope and is resting on his deathbed. His bitterness and emotional pain is very real, but it is rooted in this "perishing" mentality that must be put-off and eliminated from his life. He continues to live for himself but is never completely satisfied so he despairs.

The substance abuser is suffering in the sheer agony of the circumstances of his life. He wants pain relief from his terminal "cancer of the soul," and he knows that alcohol and drugs temporarily relieve the emotional pain just as they do for a true cancer patient. However, the emotional pain may go away for awhile, but the circumstances remain the same and often worsen. Just as the cancer is not cured by the pain medications given to the cancer patient, the serious, spiritual (or heart) problem of the substance abuser is not cured by the drug of his or her choice.

Self-Pity = Pride

Self-pity is at the root of this "perishing" mentality for the substance abuser. Self-pity is the energy force that fuels the engine of this defeatist mentality. Many people do not understand that self-pity is really a manifestation of pride. It is not the typical form that pride takes. You may think of a prideful person as someone who is bold, loud, confident, arrogant, and cocky. However, self-pity is the prideful idea that "I am not getting what I deserve; I deserve better."

Pride drives a person full of self-pity because the person is overly focused upon self and has unrealistic expectations of how life *should be* treating him. The person full of self-pity thinks he knows better than God what he needs. He thinks God is not giving him what he deserves so he is discontent. He is overly absorbed with himself.

Who is truly sovereign in a mindset like this? The sovereignty of God means that no person or thing is bigger and more powerful than God. God is at the top of the list. The Christian substance abuser's "perishing" mentality fueled by prideful, self-righteous, and self-pitying thoughts leads to destruction. The addict begins to act, think,

---

[94] This is the reason I speculate that the theory of addiction as a "disease" is so popular today.

and talk as if he is God. The addict who thinks like this is his own god. This is the definition and epitome of idolatry!

The Connection of Thoughts, Emotions, and Actions

There is a strong, cyclical relationship between thoughts, emotions, and actions. Thoughts produce emotions which produce actions which produce more thoughts and emotions. It is not the other way around. You are not designed to feel emotions *apart* from your thinking! God created you to think first, and then to feel emotions.

The system of beliefs in this country is so feelings-oriented that we tend to focus on feelings before focusing upon thoughts. This is backwards. Feelings are important, but they are not primary. Thoughts are primary since they produce feelings and emotions! Both your thoughts and emotions are internal processes in your spiritual heart.

From your thinking and emotion, you act. If you act rightly, then your thoughts and emotions will be positive. For example, if you help someone by raking leaves for them, then your righteous actions will produce in you the right thoughts and emotions of joy and happiness. On the other hand, if you hurt someone by driving drunk and causing an accident, then your unrighteous actions will produce in you the unrighteous thoughts and emotions of guilt and sorrow. The cyclical process again is: the thoughts and emotions of your heart lead to your actions, which produce more thoughts and emotions.

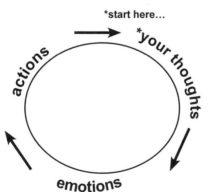

You can see how critical your mind is to the battle of addiction. Your mind is where it all begins, and that is why it is crucial that your mind be transformed by God's truth. You must begin to think like God - meaning you must live your life under the principles found in the Holy Scriptures. Then you will experience godly feelings and exhibit godly actions, all as a result of thinking biblically.[95]

The Christian addict's objective is to put-off his perishing thinking and to replace it with God's joyful thinking. God's way of thinking is found in biblical principles. When you begin with God's way of thinking, it leads you to have godly emotions and actions. Therefore, the following diagram is the biblical one that is desired by all Christians:

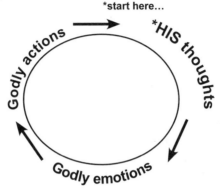

God Examines the Heart

God determines what is sinful and communicates it to us in His Word. He has always levied judgments based upon heart motives, and we can see this in the extensive detailed laws given to Moses. Just look at the different consequences for murders described under various circumstances in the book of Numbers (footnote 95). Jesus, however, dramatically illustrates the *holiness of heart* that God requires in Matthew 5:

> You have heard that it was said to those of old, 'You shall not murder; and whoever murders will be liable to judgment.' But I say to you that everyone who is angry with his brother will be liable to judgment; whoever insults his brother will be liable to the council; and whoever says, 'You fool!' will be liable to the hell of fire.

In this passage of Scripture, Jesus is teaching that sinful anger may manifest in a variety of ways but he names four of them as:

• Murder

• Anger in one's heart toward his brother

---

[95] Diagram adapted from a class taught by Lou Priolo called "Introduction to Biblical Counseling."

- Insulting words
- Speaking an angry curse like, 'You fool!'

Each of these manifestations of sinful anger has different consequences. From God's perspective, all of these manifestations of sin are equally wrong. Sin is sin is sin. Jesus tells us, however, that different sins have different earthly consequences. Obviously, murder is an extreme example and there are extreme consequences such as receiving the death penalty for murder. However, no one on earth may ever know that you committed murder in your heart when you wished that someone who hurt you would die. But God knows.

The point is that God examines the motives of mankind. The descriptions of what is sinful and what is not sinful are only found in the pages of the Bible. Hebrews 4:12 states:

> **Indeed, the word of God is living and active, sharper than any two-edged sword, piercing until it divides soul from spirit, joints from marrow; it is able to judge the thoughts and intentions of the heart.**

You may have heard the phrase: "You only have one thing to change: everything." Well, the Bible says that two things must change: your thoughts and your behaviors.[96] You first need to change your thoughts because your behaviors will follow your thoughts. For this reason, you must begin to think like God and as a result, act in an obedient way that pleases Him.

Suppose it is time for the annual Christmas party at your job and you know that alcohol is always consumed. If you wisely decide not to attend the party this year because it is too great a temptation for you, God will be pleased with you although your co-workers may view you as a "party-pooper" or "Grinch." If your heart's desire is to avoid the temptation, it should not matter what people think of you. You are trying to please God first and foremost. As you grow in Christ, you may be able to attend the party in a few years, but that is not a decision you have to make right now.

Escape: "Emotional Pain Relief"

Avoiding pain at all costs is called the "escape" of "emotional pain relief." Escaping to a pleasurable activity comes in many

---

[96] Some biblical counselors consider thoughts to be behaviors. I make a distinction but I can see their point.

forms: alcohol, drugs, food, sex, sleep, work, vacations, shopping, television, video games, books, magazines, internet chat rooms, and sports, just to name a few! Are these things bad? No, of course, all of these things are not intrinsically bad. Again, you must analyze your heart's motivation for *why* you *want* to escape. Do you desire to escape from perishing thoughts and feelings of despair about your life's circumstances rather than facing them biblically? What else is motivating your strong desire for escape?

The United States of America encourages a culture of escape. Because of large amounts of wealth Americans can afford to enjoy many different forms of escape and entertainment. Often, I hear Christians tell me, "You *need* a vacation," meaning that I *need* an escape from the rigors of everyday life. The only *needs* people have are food, water, clothing, and shelter. A vacation is not a need but a desire. What people are saying is that it is permissible to escape from the problems of life because as this thinking goes, 'everyone deserves a break from reality'.

An "escape" to a pleasurable activity is not a new concept as you can read in Genesis 9 (Noah), and 19 (Lot). The desire to "escape" from this sinful, fallen world has existed for thousands of years. In biblical days, the author of Psalm 55 desired an "escape," too. Psalm 55:6-7 states: **"And I say, 'Oh, that I had wings like a dove! I would fly away and be at rest; yes, I would wander far away; I would lodge in the wilderness.'"** The substance abuser uses drugs and alcohol to "escape" far away from the pressures and realities of this fallen world and to "escape" to a temporary pleasure.

What Did Jesus Do?

Jesus escaped from this fallen world at times, too, but we know that Jesus was without sin so He did it righteously. Christians should model Jesus when they desire to "escape." Jesus did "escape" from the pressures of the multitudes that followed Him and from His disciples who followed Him as well.[97] The purpose of Jesus' "escape" from people is given in Scripture, namely that Jesus wanted to be with His Heavenly Father. Jesus turned to no other "escape" than spending time with His Father in heaven! Jesus did not have things that Americans value such as video games, televisions, or favorite clothing stores to turn to for an "escape." Do you really think Jesus would have done these things for hours and hours just to "escape" from the trials of His life on earth? No. Jesus' "escape" is the

---

[97] Luke 6:12 and Luke 22:41 are two examples when Jesus withdrew for the purpose of escape from people to be with His Heavenly Father.

only acceptable one to God, and that is spending time in intimate fellowship with God. You can turn to God, too, because you want to cultivate your relationship with Him and because He can solve your problems according to His Will.

Again, it is a matter of your heart. It is not a sin to go shopping. However, it may be a sin if your shopping is motivated by feelings of hurt, anger, or bitterness in an attempt to feel better by "escaping" from the hurt. Instead, you must put off all means of "escape" and make them secondary to the "putting on" of spending time with your Sovereign Creator. Pray and talk to the Lord. Then read the Bible so you can learn and hear what God has to say to you. You will find that God's Word offers encouragement, proper perspective, hope, and joy for the Christian.

We live in a fallen world where everyone sins by being selfish. Everyone has to deal with wanting to escape from painful circumstances or emotions caused by the hurt and rejection of a loved one. The pain of life is no different for the Christian, but what is different is the severity of your emotional pain. Perhaps you feel the hurt of rejection very deeply because of your tremendous sensitivity and tender-heart towards people. If you feel emotions at an extreme measure from a perceived rejection, it is essential that you learn to overcome these emotions by making cognitive choices that please God. In other words, you cannot be ruled by your emotions; rather, you must learn to rule your emotions.

During the active physical addiction, you habitually learned to respond to pain by doing things that are pleasurable and give you a short period of escape from the painful rigors of life. What you did not expect is that these pleasurable things would eventually rule you and you would cease to have control over your drug of choice. I Corinthians 6:12 puts it this way: **"All things are lawful for me," but not all things are helpful. "All things are lawful for me," but I will not be enslaved by anything."** Physical addiction enslaves the addict as he becomes ruled by his desire for the drug of choice due to the physiological cravings along with the habituated patterns of thinking and acting.

Escape to the Word of God!

Here is an illustration about the power of "putting off" and "putting on" in terms of thinking and acting.

A man who smoked cigarettes for thirty years wanted to quit. Every time he tried to quit, he failed. He asked his counselor how he could ever overcome his addiction to cigarettes. Instead of recommending that he begin chewing nicotine gum or wear a nicotine patch, the counselor asked him, "Where do you keep your pack of cigarettes?" Puzzled, he responded, "In my front shirt pocket on the left-hand side." The counselor handed him a pocket-sized Bible and said, "Replace your cigarettes with this small Bible since they are about the same size." He agreed and went to work the next day. At break time, he walked outside to smoke, reached into his front shirt pocket, and to his surprise (temporarily) pulled out the pocket-sized Bible. He began reading, got immersed in a passage of Scripture, forgot about his craving, did not smoke a cigarette, and went back inside when the whistle blew. He did this for the next forty days (and even longer) and quit smoking. Not only did he quit smoking, but more significantly he began a new habit of reading his Bible.

This man read the Bible to "escape" from the rigors and pain of everyday frustrations and problems. He avoided the pain just as he had always done before with a cigarette, but now he was addicted to the Bible which had become pleasurable for him! The heart of his addictive problem was to experience some temporary pleasure to momentarily escape from the emotional agonies of life. Now, instead of having to deal with the terrible side effects from smoking cigarettes, he was addicted to doing something that had benefit both in his present life and also in the eternal life to come. I Timothy 4:7-8 states it in this manner:

> **Have nothing to do with irreverent, silly myths. Rather train yourself for godliness; for while bodily training is of some value, godliness is of value in every way, as it holds promise for the present life and also for the life to come.**

Genesis 25:29-34 records an interesting exchange between Jacob and Esau that can be applied to addiction:

> **Once when Jacob was cooking stew, Esau came in from the field, and he was exhausted. And Esau said to Jacob, "Let me eat some of that red stew, for I am exhausted!" (Therefore his name was called Edom.) Jacob said, "Sell me your birthright now." Esau said, "I am about to die; of what use is a birthright to me?" Jacob said, "Swear to me now." So he swore to him and sold his birthright to Jacob. Then Jacob gave Esau bread and lentil stew, and he ate and drank and rose and went his way. Thus Esau despised his birthright.**

There is much to learn from this passage of Scripture, but what is significant for now is that Esau sold his birthright, or his future blessing to which he was entitled, for a temporary pleasure to satisfy a temporary, natural appetite. Does this sound like substance abuse? Yes, it is the fulfillment of a "right now" desire rather than the denial of that pleasure in obedience to God and the promise of future blessing.

Do not deceive yourself; living to please self is short-sighted, temporarily pleasurable, and empty. Living selfishly lacks purpose and fulfillment because God has designed everyone to be dependent upon Him and others. Who wants to live for a selfish sinner, even if it is yourself? You will continually hunger for more because God created us with appetites that can never be completely satisfied on earth. The addict needs to satisfy himself by continually living for the Lord Jesus Christ. The "perishing" mentality must be replaced by a proper attitude of a "joyful" mentality that is described in more detail later in the book.

Prayer of Heart Change and Application

Dear Heavenly Father, I have been guilty of having a perishing mentality at times in my life. Help me take my pain to your throne and not attempt to escape it. I want you to replace that attitude with a "joyful" mentality. I want to have a joyful spirit that rejoices in the fact that I have eternal life and fellowship with you, regardless of my current circumstances. Though this life is full of trials and problems, I want to maintain a joyful attitude because you are not going to leave or forsake me regardless of my sin. Remind me of your good promises to me and to my family, Lord, and help me to keep your commandments in my everyday walk. Amen.

Chapter 12
Heart Problems

Christians who struggle with the idolatry of addiction have several heart problems: bitterness, guilt leading to the avoidance of emotional pain, discontentment with a desire for a "quick fix," loneliness, depression and despair, people-pleasing, and the fear of man. We will look at each of these problems that are ruled by our emotions.

Ruled by Emotions

Substance abusers tend to make feelings-oriented decisions rather than principle-oriented decisions.[98] They feel emotions to the extreme, and these can be powerful influences that affect their behavior; sometimes leading them astray. The transforming addict must learn to be ruled by the commands of God rather than by personal emotions.

Substance abusers primarily communicate and think out of emotion. Often, their first response to stimuli is emotional rather than logical. For example, someone asks an addict in active addiction: "What are your thoughts about that movie you watched this weekend?" The addict likely would answer by exuding emotion rather than thoughts. Typically, they would respond like this: "What a romantic movie! I cried. It is a tremendous love story with an exciting ending. I was so moved. I loved it." Lots of emotional words and inflections are used by this person. They use superlatives like always, never, worst, and best, because these words communicate extreme emotion. They like to emote and when they do experience an emotion, they prefer it to feel good! Obviously, they seek pleasure and avoid pain. Drugs and alcohol are effective for them because they enhance the already powerful emotions in an addict. They want to experience an emotion to its fullest extent.

Bitterness

Proverbs 31:6 says that the "perishing" person is in "bitter distress." The New King James version of the Bible describes the

---

[98] "Feelings-oriented" and "principle-oriented" are descriptions taken from my notes on a presentation by Jay Adams at the National Association of Nouthetic Counselors (NANC) conference in 2002.

person as "bitter of heart." [99] Bitterness is a major heart problem for the substance abuser. Addicts tend to be very tender-hearted toward strangers and social causes (like feeding the poor), yet they act selfishly around their loved ones when in active addiction. They tend to be the loyal type of friend who will do anything for anyone else. When an addict asks for help from a fellow addict, he usually gets some assistance; money, more drugs, or whatever the need may be. In fact, addicts who are seeking help to change their behavior tend to sympathize with other addicts and are more accepting of those who are unlovely according to society's standards primarily because they are, or have been, in the "same shoes."

In contrast, substance abusers tend to be overly critical of themselves when soberly reflecting upon their own behaviors. They also tend to be very critical of those who hurt and reject them whether it is a perceived or real hurt. This is where bitterness begins to creep into their hearts. In his book, *The Heart of Anger*, Lou Priolo writes that the first step in the process of becoming rebellious occurs when someone experiences a hurt.[100] Proverbs 18:14 says: **"a crushed spirit who can bear?"** and this crushed spirit is the feeling of hurt and rejection that is produced when one is emotionally harmed. It feels unbearable.

Furthermore, because the person "plays the tape" of the hurt over and over in his mind, he is reminding himself of that hurt so much that it keeps the wound fresh. It is similar to having a cut on your arm that begins to heal and grows a scab over the wound. If you were to pull that scab off of your arm, you would "re-feel" the hurt and pain of that wound again. Resentment is the same "re-feeling" only with emotional pain rather than physical pain. When you remind yourself, the offender, or third parties about the emotional hurt you experienced, you are re-opening that wound and experiencing the pain for a second time. How will the wound ever heal if it is not left alone?

As this "seed" of hurt is continually brought to one's remembrance, the hurt turns into bitterness. Bitterness, or what the world refers to as "resentment," is cultivated and rooted in one's heart if not handled biblically. Hebrews 12:15 says: **"See to it that no one fails to obtain the grace of God; that no 'root of bitterness' springs up and causes trouble, and by it many become defiled."** When the addict is so critical of himself and overly sensitive to the

[99] *The New King James Version.* 1996, c1982 . Thomas Nelson: Nashville
[100] Priolo, Lou. *The Heart of Anger*, Calvary Press, pp. 21-22.

criticism of others, he tends to be driven to drink to excess to avoid the hurts and emotional pains of everyday life. Addicts are often their own best critics and they are overly sensitive when others criticize them, or when they perceive that others are being too critical and harsh. Because the addict has a big, tender heart, he can be hurt easily by others. He must become a little more thick-skinned; he must not allow others to hurt him so intensely. Sometimes this is a pride issue in that the addict *thinks* too highly of himself ("How could they do that to me?"), and as a result, he gets hurt easily.[101]

The church must help people learn how to forgive each other for hurts, real and perceived. We need to be the forerunners in leading people away from bitterness and resentment, fear of rejection and the like. *Most Christian substance abusers and addicts want to receive forgiveness for their addictive behaviors, but truly repentant ones must learn how to grant forgiveness to those that have hurt, rejected, and offended them.* We in the church would be well served to practice biblical forgiveness more regularly.

Forgiveness: The Antidote to Bitterness

The Bible has much to say about forgiveness, as it is an essential teaching for fallible Christians. In the Lord's Prayer in Matthew 6:12, Jesus states: **"and forgive us our debts, as we also have forgiven our debtors."** Debts that we owe to God are a direct result of our many sins. We are asking Him to replace our sin record with the perfect record of Christ. In turn, God asks us to replace the sin records of others with the perfect record of Christ when they sin against us, repent, and ask us to forgive them.

Forgiveness is not easily understood in the natural man's mind. People sinfully want others to feel the same pain and hurt that they felt when offended. The true Christian must understand the real forgiveness of God the Father through the sacrifice of His Son. Knowing the kind of suffering and emotional pain Jesus experienced on the cross, how can the true Christian not forgive others of their small offenses when he has been forgiven by God of many great offenses? Jesus taught His disciples about forgiving others in Luke 17:3-4:

---

[101]The world has learned that the substance abuser is "bitter of heart," too, because secular programs often deal with resentments in secular substance abuse counseling.

Pay attention to yourselves! If your brother sins, rebuke him, and if he repents, forgive him, and if he sins against you seven times in the day, and turns to you seven times, saying, 'I repent,' you must forgive him.

Forgiveness is commanded by God and is not optional for Christians. It may surprise you how the process of forgiveness starts. According to Luke 17:3, the Christian who was sinned against, offended, and hurt must go to his brother in Christ and rebuke him for the offense. In other words, the wounded person must confront the offender. Many substance abusers want to *avoid conflict* at all costs in order to keep the peace, but this is not the biblical model. God calls Christians to be peacemakers who are not afraid of resolving a conflict in a biblically appropriate manner. Out of a righteous motive of holding a sinning brother accountable for his God-given responsibilities, a hurt Christian must lovingly and appropriately confront his sinning brother, and this is not optional!

Next, Luke 17:3 says that if the confronted brother or sister repents by asking for forgiveness, then the hurt, offended Christian must forgive him. Forgiveness is a promise. It is a promise not to bring it up again to yourself, the person who hurt you, or a third party (which would be gossip). Forgiveness is an act of your will. It is a choice you make. God says He remembers your sins no more. God does not forget your sins because He is God and knows all things. Instead, God actively chooses not to remember them by replacing His thoughts of your sin with the sacrifice His Son Jesus made upon the cross. God chooses not to remember your sin and not to remind Himself of it. In the same manner, you must choose not to remember the sin of those who have hurt you.[102]

Forgiveness is an active choice rather than a passive one. You may have to *continually remind yourself* not to hold a grudge against someone who has asked for your forgiveness. You have to *make the effort to change* your thoughts about that person's actions and how it hurt you. You may not *feel* like forgiving them, and you may not necessarily *feel better* as a result of having forgiven this person who has hurt you. However, you must actively *choose to not remember* it anymore by not reminding yourself of the offense.

---

[102] Adams, Jay, <u>From Forgiven to Forgiving</u>, Amityville, NY: Calvary Press, p. 12.

You must choose to not remember it because when you remember how this person hurt you, it stirs up all of the emotions associated with the hurt. You then recall the hurt, disappointment, anger, confusion, and any other emotion that you experienced from the offense against you. It is critical that you do not bring the matter back to your remembrance by talking about it again to a third party, the offender, or yourself. If you do remind yourself of the person's hurtful actions against you after having forgiven them, you must then repent because forgiveness is not optional; it is a command of God.

It may be difficult for you to forget the hurts you experienced by this person because you are sensitive to the criticism of others. You must put these principles in place in order to forgive first and then forget. Forgetting may never happen, but it definitely will not happen until you first forgive. If you still struggle with forgiving the person (as evidenced by whenever you see them you are reminded of how the person hurt you in the past), then make a written list of all of the good things that have resulted from your relationship with this person.

- How have you grown closer to the Lord as a result of this hurtful and painful experience?

- Write down a "gratitude list" specifically about the instance and the person who hurt you.

- Replace your negative, "perishing" thoughts with positive, uplifting thoughts about the person.

- Write a list of specific Bible verses associated with thankfulness to memorize to replace your negative thoughts about the person and the act.

- Use Appendix H to help you. God can and will use this experience to draw you closer to Him.

Guilt - Leading to the Avoidance of Emotional Pain

It has already been mentioned that the addict is seeking pleasure while avoiding emotional pain at all costs by staying active in the addiction. What does this emotional pain consist of? Often, the problem is rooted in the guilt experienced from a conflict and the emotional pain that was never biblically resolved. As a result, the guilt never disappears. For example, a son or a spouse has allowed himself to become addicted to a substance and has betrayed the trust and confidence of family members by using family resources to support his addiction. Now, when the repentant addict comes out of the active using phase of the intoxicant, the pain is still there. The pain may even be worse resulting in the desire to continue using the drug to excess. It is a vicious cycle, continuing until the guilt and pain are addressed in a biblical manner that is pleasing to God.

What is the biblical manner in which to address the pain? Proverbs 28:13 states: **"Whoever conceals his transgressions will not prosper, but he who confesses and forsakes them will obtain mercy."** The first step of the healing process for the pain is to confess your sin. Admit your problem. Do not hide it by attempting to "conceal" it from the Lord, who is already aware of it. If you are feeling guilty about something, confess it to a counselor, close Christian friend, or a pastor. Pray with them and ask God to forgive you.

The second step is to make restitution which is "forsaking" your sin. Find a way to right the wrong you committed. There are a variety of ways to do this and a variety of situations that require this type of restitution so we are not able to address every circumstance specifically. If you cannot find a way to repay the wrong you committed, ask the trusted Christian person to whom you confessed your sin what he suggests you do for restitution. You can also ask the person whom you offended how you can make appropriate restitution for your wrongdoing.

Discontentment with a Desire for the "Quick Fix"

A major heart problem for the addict is discontentment, which feeds the "perishing" mentality. Rather than being content with where God has stationed him in life, he thinks God has "dealt him a poor hand". The world calls this discontentment "pessimism" and it reigns supreme in the mind of an active abuser. In fact, the continued usage of intoxicants to excess becomes a self-fulfilling prophecy to the active user who continues to become discontent. "God must really hate me because of all of the problems in my life," thinks the discontent one. Discontentment is a dangerous mindset for the clean and sober person because it can lead to active addiction rather quickly.

The addicted person's best idea to eliminate discontentment is by applying a "quick fix," or temporary solution. To illustrate, a mechanic who puts freon in a leaky air conditioner of a motor vehicle is not fixing the problem; he is only providing quick, temporary relief from the heat of summer. When the freon leaks out again, the same problem will reappear. In order to truly fix the problem the mechanic replaces the air conditioner's leaky hose with one that does not leak and then adds the freon. The "quick fix" mechanic does not want to put forth the extra effort required to truly fix the heart of the problem.

Substance abusers think they have the "quick fix" answer— seeking pleasure while avoiding their emotional pain. It temporarily works until the high wears off, and then all of the problems reappear. The "quick fix" is a desire for magic dust or a magic pill to change the way I think and feel. The "quick fix" mentality believes the lie that one does not have to do any work to fix the problem. It is akin to the idea of buying a one dollar lottery ticket with the unrealistic dream of winning three million dollars when the odds are astronomically against winning.

What's not good in Genesis? Loneliness

When the addict feels lonely, he feels it in an extreme measure. Remember that the substance abuser tends to feel all emotions to extremes. When he is down, he really gets down and out. When he is up, he really feels great! Loneliness is common for both men and women. God created the desire in us to marry someone of the opposite sex for companionship. Eve was formed by God and given in marriage to Adam explicitly for companionship. Eve filled a void that Adam experienced right after being created and living with the animals.[103] Before The Fall and sin of mankind, God said that **"it was not good that the man should be alone"** in Genesis 2:18. Until that point in Genesis, God said that everything he made was good. The first time God said anything in His creation was "not good" was in reference to it not being a good situation for man to be alone in Genesis 2:18.

Loneliness is a normal experience in life. Even though it overwhelms the addict, God intends for him or her to use the feeling of being lonely like a thermometer. It can be illustrated this way: the thermometer measures how lonely the Christian has become so that he can adjust his thermostat (his relationship to the Lord). The feelings of great loneliness indicate to him how far away he currently is from God and how much he needs to adjust his "thermostat." God

---

[103]Genesis 2:18-25.

has not gone anywhere, but the substance abuser has drifted away from the Lord and is therefore experiencing a degree of loneliness. The lonely Christian can adjust his thermostat by drawing close to God in a number of ways, including church attendance, prayer, Bible study, singing praise to God, and fellowship with believers. Often, meaningful fellowship with a like-minded believer in Christ is the best remedy.

Depression and Despair

Normal sadness can lead to depression and despair for the addict who experiences emotions to extreme. But the "perishing" mentality feeds depression and despair, too, as the substance abusing Christian centers his thinking upon how bad things are rather than upon the blessings he has received from the Lord. Addicts tend to experience deep lows stemming from:

- Guilt
- Perceived and/or real hurts
- An elevated, incorrect view of self as most important

The "perishing mentality," or "stinking thinking" as the world calls it, contributes greatly to depression because one's thoughts create one's emotions.

We've already addressed how to biblically handle guilt, how to respond to hurts, and how to battle the "perishing mentality." Some of those same methods apply to depression. Depression and despair are very real to the substance abuser, but he must not give in to these feelings to the point of not meeting his responsibilities. Christians who are depressed and in despair have no hope and have given up on finding help. They have been overwhelmed by the cares and responsibilities of this world. The faith they have in a loving, caring, and Sovereign God has been engulfed by their feelings of hopelessness in this "perishing" mindset.

While very real, the "perishing mentality" is foolishness at its core because the Christian has chosen to believe the lie that God is not lovingly concerned about his or her circumstances. He or she has not realized that God has chosen to allow these circumstances to be present to help the addict grow and draw nearer to Him. Romans 8:28 states: **"And we know that for those who love God all things work together for good, for those who are called according to his purpose."** If the Christian addict loves God, then this specific verse of the Bible states that God uses everything that the Christian experiences in his life for his benefit and good. The verse does not promise that everything will be good. The promise is that God will turn the bad and the good circumstances into a blessing for the Christian who loves God.

The depressed Christian must choose to do the right thing by fulfilling his responsibilities in life. Again, he must not be only a hearer of God's word, but he must also be a doer of it. He can experience the feeling of sadness but he cannot stay sad or depressed to the point of neglecting his God-given responsibilities. He must be an "overcomer" of his feelings and actively complete his obligations unto God. This may not be the solution the addict wants to hear because many Christians want a magic pill and a quick fix to their problems; however, God holds us responsible and accountable to Him for our actions. Therefore, if you are a Christian, you have certain responsibilities and commands to follow that have been instituted by God in the Bible. You do not have the option of remaining in a state of despair and depression to the neglect of your responsibilities before the Lord.

Quite often, depression is caused by the anger and guilt of having done something that was sinful. For example, a drug addict who is stealing pain medication from his father (who takes it to ease the pain of his terminal cancer) will most likely experience large amounts of guilt and shame for his selfish actions. Without true repentance, these actions cause the guilt to mount and may lead to severe depression. The solution for the addict is to confess and forsake his sin by asking for forgiveness and paying restitution to his father. Once he does so, the sorrow and depression caused by his sinful actions turn to rejoicing and a clear conscience before God and man. Again, does this sound too easy? Then, take this challenge: try it and see whether it is easy or not. You will learn that it takes real courage and humility to confess sin rather than hide it. As a result of being obedient, you will also see the wonderful blessings of doing things God's way.

People-pleasing, Fear of Man, and Love of Approval

Some Christians avoid conflict and confronting another person because they are concerned about what people are going to think. The Bible calls this type of person a "people-pleaser."[104] This person

---

[104]Ephesians 6:6 and Colossians 3:22.

is more interested in *looking like* a good person rather than *being* a good person by obeying the Lord. It is the fear of man rather than the fear of God. Christians are often riddled with fear: afraid to share the Gospel with strangers, afraid to take a stand on current moral issues, and afraid to look as though they are not perfect to unbelievers and believers. Christians must quit trying to appear as though they are perfect people. At the root, this is a pride issue that involves the love of approval and keeping up an appearance of how they want to be perceived rather than being who they truly are.

Often, a "people-pleaser" is someone who portrays what he *thinks* someone else wants him to be. Many of these ideas and thoughts of how he "should" appear to the people he wants to impress are self-imposed. In other words, these ideas and thoughts are generated by the people-pleasing substance abuser based upon his perceptions of these other people. The Christian ends up being a fake rather than himself. He may "wear a different mask" around some people in an effort to have people like him. The Christian addict considers himself a "people person."

It can become embarrassing if he occasionally forgets to wear the right "mask" around someone he wants to impress. If this happens, he has to tell more lies to "save face" and avoid embarrassment. What can be really devastating is when two different people with whom he wears two totally different "masks" meet in an unexpected situation. Then the people-pleaser faces a huge problem by having to be two different people at the same time. Unfortunately, most addicts are adequately skilled at keeping this charade without being exposed for who they truly are.

Some persons in active addiction are people-pleasing to avoid conflict because they feel ashamed and guilty for their sinful actions. A truly repentant drunkard becomes more and more transparent as he grows in Christ. By "transparent," it is meant that the formerly addicted person lives his life in an open manner since he no longer has anything to hide. He is no longer ashamed of his behavior and it is reflected in how he openly lives his life. His transformation allows him to become transparent to those who care the most about him. The transformed Christian addict is not consumed with what others think because he now has a clear conscience before the Lord, a new identity in Christ Jesus, and he is living in obedience to the Word of God.

Work, Work, and More Work

Some addicts have a "quick fix" mentality when it comes to prayer. Have you ever said, "I pray everyday to you, Lord, but what else do I need to do to overcome this addiction?" Prayer is essential for a Christian addict, but some believe in the secular idea that they are supposed to "let go and let God" without doing any of the hard work. The real solution is work. There is no "quick fix." Work, work, and more work! In order for the person who uses the "go button" in a positive manner to overcome the addiction, hard work is required. Often the Christian who grows in Christ is like a runner in a marathon who must pace himself rather than a sprinter of a short distance.

Do you remember Adam's consequence for his sin against God when he ate the forbidden fruit in the Garden of Eden? Genesis 3:23 tells us: **"therefore the Lord God sent him out from the garden of Eden to _work_ the ground from which he was taken."** In addition, this work that Adam had to do was *hard work.* Genesis 3:17b-19: **cursed is the ground because of you; in pain you shall eat of it all the days of your life; thorns and thistles it shall bring forth for you; and you shall eat the plants of the field. By the sweat of your face you shall eat bread, till you return to the ground** (Emphasis mine). Do not be deceived: to overcome your addiction you must work hard! Your sin has the same consequence in your life that Adam's sin did for him.

Contentment is Learned

How does one overcome this "perishing" mentality fed by discontentment? The hard work begins by replacing these harmful thoughts with grateful thoughts. Contentment is learned according to the Apostle Paul in Philippians 4:11: **"Not that I am speaking of being in need, for I have learned in whatever situation I am to be content."** Contentment begins by understanding that a Sovereign and loving God knows what is best for the addict. God has allowed the addict to be right where He wants him to be. Contentment is best learned by looking for the blessings and choosing to think on the circumstances as blessings rather than thinking of them as a curse.

Does a loving, Heavenly Father curse an obedient child? God does not curse His children but He does discipline them. Hebrews 12:6 tells you: **"For the Lord disciplines the one he loves, and chastises every son whom he receives."** Is God disciplining you right now? If you are a believer in Christ Jesus, then be content that God loves you as His son, and He wants you to change your behavior. If you are an unbeliever, then you will forever remain discontent in your substance abuse until you place your trust in the Lord Jesus Christ. Christians must learn contentment by focusing their thoughts on the things listed in Philippians 4:8: **"Finally, brothers, whatever is true, whatever is honorable, whatever is just, whatever is pure, whatever is lovely, whatever is commendable, if there is any excellence, if there is anything worthy of praise, think about these things."**

Identity in Christ

The repentant Christian no longer has to hide, lie, or attempt to appear perfect to other people (wear a mask) because his identity is in Christ.[105] Others do not (or, rather, should not) expect you to be perfect in this life so you do not have to portray a false image of being faultless. You have faults, problems, and struggles in this life but Christ is able to strengthen you to overcome those weaknesses. Quit trying to wear masks to hide your flaws from people. You have flaws. By acting as if you are perfect, you are lying to yourself, others, and God. Perfectionism is offensive to God because it is rooted in pride: only One Person, the Lord Jesus Christ, is perfect. At heart, the thinking of a perfectionist says, "I am capable of being like God (who really is perfect). I can work hard to achieve perfection. I will make people think I am perfect. God would want me to appear to be perfect." Those are all lies of Satan and underestimate the power of sin and our sin nature. Be authentic. Be someone who struggles but by God's grace continues to persevere in a fallen world full of challenges in this life.

Most addicts and many Christians struggle with an "identity crisis." They do not know who they are and who they are supposed to become. You are to *become more like Christ Jesus* every day that you live, but you are an imperfect creature dealing with the consequences of sin in a sin-cursed world. You will become more like Jesus by the power of the Holy Spirit working in conjunction with the Word of God. Because of God's grace, you are a "new creation."[106]

Remember however, that you will not be perfect until you die and are given a new, glorified body in the afterlife. For now, your

---

[105] II Corinthians 5:17.
[106] II Corinthians 5:17.

identity is not about you. Your identity is who you are in Christ alone. When God looks at a Christian, He sees the righteousness of Christ and not the sinner. Christians are thankful that God sees them in their new identity rather than in their old one that was destined for an eternity in hell.

A wonderful passage of Scripture that comforts many repentant Christians is this one in I Corinthians 6:9-11:

> **Do you not know that the unrighteous will not inherit the kingdom of God? Do not be deceived: neither the sexually immoral, nor idolaters, nor adulterers, nor men who practice homosexuality, nor thieves, nor the greedy, nor drunkards, nor revilers, nor swindlers will inherit the kingdom of God. And such were some of you. But you were washed, you were sanctified, you were justified in the name of the Lord Jesus Christ and by the Spirit of our God.**

Prayer of Heart Change and Application

Dear Heavenly Father, in this fallen world, I struggle with these heart problems of bitterness, guilt, discontentment, loneliness, depression, despair, people-pleasing, a desire for a "quick fix," pride, self-pity, and selfishness. I know that you have a good purpose even when I experience these bad heart problems: You want me to draw closer to you. Father, please remind me to draw close to you when I feel this way. Enable me to overcome my emotions by remaining obedient to you regardless of the problems I experience and hurts I feel. I want my emotions to work for me rather than against me, Lord, and for your glory. Make me more Christ-like each day. Remind me that I have a new identity and I can be authentic to everyone I meet because it is you alone whom I must please. Amen.

Section 2

Reproof

Chapter 13
How Many Enemies Do You Have?

A "reproof" is defined as a "criticism for a fault."[107] It is also called a "rebuke" by some versions of the Bible. Sinful persons often need a reproof from the Lord. Sometimes a "reproof" is necessary because the Lord wants to turn you from walking down the wrong path of serving yourself to serving Him. Sometimes, a "reproof" hurts. Hebrews 12:11 states: **"For the moment all discipline seems painful rather than pleasant, but later it yields the peaceful fruit of righteousness to those who have been trained by it."** Quite likely, you have already been reproved several times in this book. The focus of this section is to become a little more specific in pinpointing the heart of your problem which is you. We are all in need of a Savior. We all need transformation to grow in Christ and become more like Christ.

Three Enemies

The battle with substance abuse and addiction is not easy because you have three enemies: Satan, the world, and your own flesh. Even if you had just one of these enemies, it would be difficult to have victory over addiction. Having three enemies makes it three times as challenging because you do not always recognize which enemy you are facing at any given time. However, it is not your job to try to differentiate, label, and separate your enemies into the appropriate category. Your job is to respond to the spiritual warfare in a manner that pleases God. James 4:7 tells us: **"Submit yourselves therefore to God. Resist the devil, and he will flee from you."** I will describe these enemies for you.

Two External Enemies

Your first enemy is Satan. Satan does not have any spiritual authority over the Christian. Sometimes Christians allow themselves to be deceived into thinking that Satan exercises power over them. James 4:7 commands the Christian to do two things. First, the Christian must submit to God's will. Christian addicts often ask

---

[107]Merriam-Webster, I. (1996, c1993). Merriam-Webster's collegiate dictionary. Includes index. (10th ed.). Springfield, Mass., U.S.A.: Merriam-Webster.

God, "I pray everyday to you, Lord, but what else do I need to do to overcome this addiction?" A Christian who asks this question is only doing the first part of this command in James 4:7: submitting to God. It is an essential part of James 4:7 but it is only half of the command.

The second half of the command is to "resist the devil." Most defeated Christians stop prior to resisting the devil thinking that submitting and praying to God is all that is required in order to have the devil "flee" from them. To resist the devil, the Christian has to *do* something. The Christian has to act. Too many defeated Christians are passively praying for God to do something while they *do* very little themselves. Praying is important but one cannot stop there. Actions must follow prayer and James 4:7 tells the Christian to "resist the devil."

How do you resist the devil? It is not necessary to verbally "rebuke the devil" as some Christian circles recommend, but you do have to resist the devil's temptations for you to sin. *You are in spiritual warfare with the devil, and the battle is in your mind.* The actions you must begin to take are actions of *replacing* your thoughts. You cannot be passive and allow your mind to think Satan's thoughts. You must recognize the enemy's lie, renounce it as a lie, and replace the lie with a biblical truth. Then, you meditate[108] upon God's Scriptural truths and your thinking is now actively resisting the devil. Your actions and even your emotions will follow your thoughts.

You cannot fight Satan in your own strength or you will lose every time. *Renewing your mind with biblical truths is essential.* Jesus Himself first submitted to God and then resisted the devil by speaking God's Word to Satan. The devil fled from Him![109] Why do Christians think it will be any different for them? If Jesus used Scripture to defeat Satan, Christian addicts also must renew their minds with Scripture and attack the trial in God's way rather than in their own thinking, strength, or plan. When you submit to God's will and actively resist the devil in your thought life and actions, the devil will flee from you according to James 4:7. The devil cannot stand against the power of God's Word. Once Satan flees, you still have to do battle with two more enemies.

---

[108]By meditate, I mean "allow your thinking to dwell upon" God's truth all day long if necessary. Fill your mind with God's Word. Let God's Word renew your mind.

[109]Read Matthew 4:1-11.

Your second external enemy is the world. By the term "world" I do not mean all the people in the world; I am referring to the world system, the world's way of thinking, and the world's view on life – that *this is all there is.* On television, the ***commercialism*** of the world perpetuates the following lies of Satan:

- Alcohol use and even abuse is fun (beer commercials on television).
- Alcohol use doesn't hurt anyone as long as you don't drive drunk.
- It's a private choice.
- It's ok to relax and drink.
- Alcohol is a great way to deal with the horrible things you've experienced.
- Alcohol enables you to be the most fun for other people.
- You deserve a break, a nice little escape.
- You have been good this week (or this year, or this quarter, or today).
- Celebrate your achievements better with alcohol.

As you meet unsaved people, you will be bombarded with their worldview that substance abuse and addiction are justifiable. Some examples of the common lies of the world that are perpetuated in ***secular treatment centers*** are as follows:

- Addiction is something you have power over *without* the help of Jesus.
- God exists for your happiness and to serve you.
- You are a helpless victim of addiction with no hope for change apart from your own efforts.
- God's Word is insufficient and ignorant on the subject of addiction.
- You have to be a stumbling, bumbling, everyday drinker or drug user in order to be an addict who is out of fellowship with God.

This second enemy operates just like Satan in that the world challenges your thinking first. Your enemies understand that if they can conquer your thinking, they can conquer you. God teaches the Christian substance abuser and addict in Proverbs 23:7a: **"Eat thou not the bread of him that hath an evil eye, neither desire thou**

119

his dainty meats: For as he thinketh in his heart, so is he: Eat and drink, saith he to thee; but his heart is not with thee" (KJV). God designed humans in such a way that their minds are connected to their hearts.

It is natural for you to think about what your heart desires. Your heart desires the things it is allowed to "see." For example, you see a commercial on television with a hot, sizzling steak and you begin to think about it. You might not be aware of your thoughts about the steak but your heart is aware of it. God created mankind with minds that can think, meditate, and process information obtained from the five senses: seeing, hearing, tasting, smelling, and touching. This simple concept is absolutely essential to understand because you cannot allow yourself to be passive in your thinking. Television advertisers understand this powerful concept better than most Christians. This is why they spend billions of dollars each year on marketing their products to viewers.

Here are some helpful, practical ideas to implement when you are tempted by the world's lies:

- If you see an image on television that promotes sin and lies, then change the channel or turn off the television.
- Do not entertain worldly thoughts in your mind. Replace them with biblical truths.
- Be active and resist the lies of this world whose father is Satan, the father of lies.
- You can resist the lies of this world by not going to certain places like bars, some restaurants, parties, and neighborhoods where you once purchased drugs.
- Avoid certain people and things that trigger a desire to use drugs or alcohol.

One Internal Enemy

Both Satan and the world are powerful enemies that operate *outside* of you yet try to influence your thinking. They try to infiltrate your mind so that you perceive them as internal enemies, but they only get inside of your thought life if you allow it. Your third enemy may be the most powerful because it is lurking within your very being; it is *your "flesh."* When the Bible speaks of your "flesh," it refers to all of your thinking, speaking, and actions. These are all born in your sin nature. Your habitual practice of sin is contained in your "flesh." *Did you know that prior to being born again, you were a slave to sin and that you practiced sinning just as someone practices the piano or practices his golf swing?* These sinful practices are habitual, and you bring them into your new walk with Christ in the Holy Spirit. The solution is learning to replace your sinful practices with godly practices. How does this happen?

The Struggle

Be honest. Have you ever tried to quit using drugs and alcohol but failed? Have you ever asked, "Lord, will you just take away my desire for this addictive behavior so that I will have victory?" Some have pleaded with God by asking, "Lord, will you please remove this addictive substance from the entire earth so that I will be able to walk closer to you?" Does God have a plan and purpose for your struggles with addiction? The answer for the Christian is 'yes.'

One way God humbles His people who are pridefully doing things their own way is by allowing them to fall. Proverbs 16:18 states: **"Pride goes before destruction, and a haughty spirit before a fall."** Through your struggling, God is reminding you that you are a created, finite being who is dependent upon Him for everything. God is the only Being who is perfect and perfectly good. God is teaching you the virtue of humility and total dependence upon Him alone.

Condemnation vs. Conviction

The apostle Paul was one man who knew about humility. How did he know about humility? Read this portion of Scripture written by Paul from Romans 7:15-25:

> **I do not understand my own actions. For I do not do what I want, but I do the very thing I hate. Now if I do what I do not want, I agree with the law, that it is good. So now it is no longer I who do it, but sin that dwells within me. For I know that nothing good dwells in me, that is, in my flesh. For I have the desire to do what is right, but not the ability to carry it out. For I do not do the good I want, but the evil I do not want is what I keep on doing. Now if I do what I do not want, it is no longer I who do it,**

> but sin that dwells within me. So I find it to be a law that when I want to do right, evil lies close at hand. For I delight in the law of God, in my inner being, but I see in my members another law waging war against the law of my mind and making me captive to the law of sin that dwells in my members. Wretched man that I am! Who will deliver me from this body of death? Thanks be to God through Jesus Christ our Lord! So then, I myself serve the law of God with my mind, but with my flesh I serve the law of sin.

Does this sound like a person who is struggling with some type of addiction? Yes, Paul knew very well how weak he was in his flesh. *His understanding of his weakness helped him to comprehend his dependence upon the Lord for strength.*

The good news is that the very next chapter: Romans 8:1: *"There is therefore now no condemnation to them which are in Christ Jesus, who walk not after the flesh, but after the Spirit."* (KJV) The saved Christian who is repentant and being led by the Holy Spirit (rather than by his own fleshly desires and appetites) is not under the *condemnation* of the Holy Spirit. When he sins, he is under the *conviction* of the Holy Spirit, but he is not condemned by the Spirit to spend eternity in hell.

There is a big difference between the conviction of the Holy Spirit and the condemnation of the Holy Spirit. Christian addicts and substance abusers should be grateful for God's conviction of their sin because it is intended to help them change their destructive behaviors. Condemnation is a reality for unwilling, unrepentant, unbelievers who fail to trust in Christ for salvation.

God Gets the Glory

Your flesh, Satan, and the world are your three enemies and all must be confronted in order to overcome your addiction. The good news is that God has given you three major weapons (and other minor weapons) with which you can confront your three enemies:

- Jesus Christ, to battle Satan (who is already His defeated foe)

- The indwelling of the Holy Spirit
- The Word of God – the Bible

Paul only boasted in the Lord as II Corinthians 10:17-18 states: **"'Let the one who boasts, boast in the Lord.' For it is not the one who commends himself who is approved, but the one whom the Lord commends."** What joy it will be for you when you have victory over your addiction and you can give praise and honor to the Lord who deserves all the credit! What awesome weapons to possess: your Savior, your Sustainer, and your Sword; the Word of God!

Prayer of Heart Change and Application

Dear Heavenly Father, my three enemies are more than I can overcome in my own strength. I need you to win this fight and I thank you for providing me with three awesome weapons with which I can do battle. Father, give me discernment during the battle so that I might choose the right weapon and be victorious. However, even when I fail and lose the battle, Lord, I know that you are humbling me and teaching me to better rely upon you so I am thankful even for the defeats. Amen.

Chapter 14
The Spiritual Consequences of Addiction

Do you remember that part of the definition for "addiction" mentioned earlier is that the addict is harmed in some way as a direct result of the behavior? Typically, the harm comes from neglecting one's God-given responsibilities. Examples of such neglects are:

- failure to pay the bills
- failure to fulfill the duties of a husband, wife, or parent
- neglecting or forsaking participation at church
- failing to be a productive employee
- failing to abide by the laws of society

These failures are easy to identify and are very common "symptoms" of what the world calls addiction. They are really physical or earthly consequences of selfish choices to use drugs and alcohol to escape from God-given responsibilities and the trials of this world. When you fail in your God-given responsibilities, you hurt yourself and your loved ones. Has your addiction caused you to fail God, others, and yourself because you are not being dominated or controlled by the Holy Spirit, instead, are you being led by your own will for drugs and alcohol?

Substance abuse, drunkenness, and addiction have been called "life-dominating sins" because of the profound impact of the sin into every area of life.[110] While I agree that this sin is life-dominating, it is important to note *that every sin has the potential to be life-dominating as sin often takes people farther than they had originally intended to go.* In other words, some think to themselves, "I'll just do it this one time and then stop," but they find themselves committing the sin over and over. Regardless of what type of sin it is, it tends to become life-dominating in one's thoughts, words, or actions.

Substance abuse and addiction are sins of idolatry that are *"life-devastating"* because of the severe physical and spiritual consequences that result.[111] Addiction tends to bring devastating

---

[110]Mack, Wayne, Homework Manual, Vol. 1, United States of America: P& R Publishing, pgs.105-106

[111]Ephesians 5:18-21.

consequences to a believer's life in a relatively short amount of time. Different sins have different physical consequences. For example, the sin of committing murder leads to prison and possibly the death penalty, whereas the sin of stealing a pack of gum may lead to a lesser consequence such as a monetary fine. In God's eyes, both of these sins are equally wrong and have equal spiritual consequences though the physical consequences imposed upon these sins in society adequately fit the crime. To read about many of the various consequences of addiction as evidenced in the Bible, turn to Appendix D.

Substance abuse, drunkenness, and addiction can lead to the following types of temporal, physical, and earthly consequences: divorce, loss of parental rights, imprisonment, and death. However, your most severe consequence of substance abuse is the inability to enjoy a close relationship with your Creator and Heavenly Father. This is a spiritual consequence. You must not allow yourself to become an "idolater" who worships a pleasure created by God rather than worshiping God Himself. You will find yourself traveling down your own path and you will get lost. The children of Israel in many Old Testament passages of Scripture were guilty of idolatry and they were lost for forty years in the wilderness!

To determine the extent of your current addiction problem, turn to Appendix E. Answer those questions honestly and assess how much damage you have already done to your life in the areas listed. While there are many devastating physical consequences for substance abuse and addiction, a Christian who continues to indulge faces two extremely severe spiritual consequences that most people do not think about: *the quenching of the Spirit and the searing of the conscience.*

Spiritual Consequence #1: Quenching of the Spirit

In I Thessalonians 5:19, you are commanded: **"Do not quench the Spirit."** What this means is that the ability of the Holy Spirit to teach, illuminate God's Word, and convict you is hindered, or handcuffed, by your acts of disobedience. "It is the effective working of the Holy Spirit that Paul warned against hindering. His *fire* can be diminished or even snuffed *out* if He is resisted. The Holy Spirit's working can be opposed by believers."[112]

---

[112]Walvoord, J. F., Zuck, R. B., & Dallas Theological Seminary. 1983-c1985. *The Bible Knowledge Commentary : An Exposition of the Scriptures.* Victor Books: Wheaton, IL

Can God really be hindered? God is certainly not hindered by anything that man does, but man stunts his own spiritual growth by continuing to sin. The Bible teaches mankind to **"work out your own salvation with fear and trembling"** (Philippians 2:12). This work that man does is in conjunction with the Holy Spirit and the Word of God as the Bible says, **"for it is God who works in you, both to will and to work for his good pleasure"** (Philippians 2:13). These two truths—that man is responsible, and that God is Sovereign—work simultaneously and are beyond mankind's comprehension, or ability to understand.

Here is an illustration to help you understand how man can stunt his own spiritual growth. It has been said that smoking cigarettes can stunt your growth. For a growing teenager, this statement can be true because nicotine suppresses your appetite. If you do not eat properly as a teenager, you will not receive the proper nutrients and you will not grow and develop in a healthy manner.[113]

Spiritually speaking, you are a child of God whose spiritual appetite is suppressed by your continual sin; therefore, you are not receiving all of the spiritual nutrients you need to grow. The Bible is the spiritual food you should be eating and the Holy Spirit dwelling in you helps you to digest and understand what God is saying.[114] Your disobedience is the nicotine, or poison, that stunts your spiritual growth and suppresses your spiritual appetite so that you do not *want* to feast on the Word of God even though you are a Christian. You are feeding your flesh and not your inner, spiritual person. It is a walk down that spiral staircase of not feeling close to God and not wanting to read the Bible or pray to God. Needless to say, it is a dark, lonely, and dangerous place to be when you are in direct disobedience to God.

Spiritual Solution for Quenching the Holy Spirit: Brokenness

Genuine brokenness in your heart leads to humility and practical repentance for your sin and acts of disobedience. Brokenness is first required to begin spiraling upward and out of this black hole

---

[113]The same is also said to be true for Ritalin™ because one of its side effects suppresses the appetite. You may want to consider this side effect before giving it to a young, growing child. Research the side effects of any medication before you allow your children to be placed on it. Talk to your medical doctor soon.

[114]John 14:26.

in which you find yourself. Are you truly broken about your sin of excessive drinking or using drugs? What does brokenness look like? Psalm 107:4-22 gives you a picture of being broken about your sin:

> Some wandered in desert wastes, finding no way to a city to dwell in; hungry and thirsty, their soul fainted within them. Then they cried to the Lord in their trouble, and he delivered them from their distress. He led them by a straight way till they reached a city to dwell in. Let them thank the Lord for his steadfast love, for his wondrous works to the children of men! For he satisfies the longing soul, and the hungry soul he fills with good things. Some sat in darkness and in the shadow of death, prisoners in affliction and in irons, for they had rebelled against the words of God, and spurned the counsel of the Most High. So he bowed their hearts down with hard labor; they fell down, with none to help. Then they cried to the Lord in their trouble, and he delivered them from their distress. He brought them out of darkness and the shadow of death, and burst their bonds apart. Let them thank the Lord for his steadfast love, for his wondrous works to the children of men! For he shatters the doors of bronze and cuts in two the bars of iron. Some were fools through their sinful ways, and because of their iniquities suffered affliction; they loathed any kind of food, and they drew near to the gates of death. Then they cried to the Lord in their trouble, and he delivered them from their distress. He sent out his word and healed them, and delivered them from their destruction. Let them thank the Lord for his steadfast love, for his wondrous works to the children of men! And let them offer sacrifices of thanksgiving, and tell of his deeds in songs of joy!

Are you like the people described in the above psalm? *Are you broken about your sin to the point that you are crying out to the Lord to save you from the trouble that your addiction has caused you?* You must be broken about your sin and see it as offensive to your loving Heavenly Father. Call out to the Lord to send His Word to forgive, heal, and deliver you from your destruction. During His healing process, as He delivers you from the bondage of addiction, your desire to thank Him, praise Him, and tell others about Him will increase because He is worthy of all praise.

Spiritual Consequence #2: Searing of the Conscience

The sinning Christian who is quenching the Holy Spirit soon experiences the second life-devastating consequence which is to be grouped with the "**liars whose consciences are seared**"[115] as with a hot iron. If you have ever cooked a piece of meat and turned up the fire really high to sear it, then you know what this means. Searing a piece of meat seals in the juices and the flavor of the meat on the inside because there is a hard exterior. In a similar manner, when your conscience gets *seared by continual sin,* a hard exterior forms around the outside of your spiritual heart and conscience so that you become hard-hearted, or hardened, to God's Word. In this hardened state

- You become less sensitive to the leading of the Holy Spirit.
- You read the Bible but it does not make sense, is painful, and lacks any relevance to you.
- It becomes difficult to see anything good in the Bible because of the sinful condition of your life.
- Your mind becomes warped and you do not see God's love clearly. You may think people are against you when they really love you and desire to help you.
- You do not follow the Holy Spirit's loving leadership designed to help and protect you.
- Ironically, you (the addict) are often the *last* person to realize that you are a slave to your addiction! Family, friends, and co-workers see it before you do!

Lying and Deception

An additional sin that commonly accompanies substance abuse, drunkenness, and addiction is deception. Substance abusers and addicts may deceive in a number of the following ways:

- outright lies
- concealment

---

[115]I Timothy 4:2.

- denial
- "I don't know"
- hidden agenda
- insinuation
- truth plus a lie
- fabrication
- blameshifting
- false accusations
- diversion
- partial truth
- exaggeration
- covering up past sins
- joking
- slandering
- body language lies
- incongruence
- claiming to be close to God but continuing to sin
- making commitments with no intention of keeping them
- giving the appearance of one emotion to cover up the existence of another emotion
- planting evidence
- "acting."[116]

Lying contributes to a seared conscience because one lie leads to another and then to another and so forth. As you tell more and more lies, you deceive others, but you may deceive yourself by forgetting what is actually true. You rationalize your sin to yourself and begin to believe your own lies. Minimizing the truth is also a form of lying that downplays the seriousness of the sinful choices you are making.

This horrible combination of the sins of lying and addiction stop you from growing spiritually, cause you to be "hard-hearted" toward God and others, and make you feel as though God is very far away. Your relationship with Him is temporarily hindered in such a way that you think God is not concerned about you. The truth is that God

[116]Priolo, Lou, "The Lou Priolo Audio Library: *Biblical Guidelines for Deception*, CD #60," Chesterton, IN: Sound Word Associates.

is right where He says He would be and He will never forsake or leave you.[117] Your continual sin has caused you to separate from your close relationship with God just as the prodigal son separated when he left his father in the parable that Jesus told in Luke 15:11-32.

Who causes this separation? Is it God or is it you due to your sin of drunkenness? The answers to these questions come in Isaiah 59:1-3:

> **"Behold, the Lord's hand is not shortened, that it cannot save, or his ear dull, that it cannot hear; but your iniquities have made a separation between you and your God, and your sins have hidden his face from you so that he does not hear. For your hands are defiled with blood and your fingers with iniquity; your lips have spoken lies; your tongue mutters wickedness."**

Does the addict in active addiction speak lies? Immersed in an active addiction, does the addict's tongue speak about wicked things? Unfortunately, you know that 'yes' is the answer to both of these questions. Therefore, *you are responsible* for your separation from God. Your relationship is hindered because you turned from Him not because He turned from you! Sin separates us from God just as it did Adam and Eve in the Garden of Eden in Genesis 3.

Spiritual Solution for a "Seared Conscience" and Hard Heart: Repentance

After your spirit is broken,[118] repentance must follow as it did for the prodigal son.[119] After he squandered all of his possessions and a severe famine arose in the land, the prodigal son began to be in need in Luke 15:14. Are you in need yet? Or do you have an "enabler," someone who continues to give you money, food, shelter, or some other type of assistance so that you can choose to spend your money on alcohol or drugs?

Do not miss the significance of the "severe famine" in Luke 15:14-16 because in today's language it simply means that all of the addict's "enablers" and resources have dried up because no one in

[117]Hebrews 13:5.
[118]Matthew 5:3-4.
[119]Luke 15:11-32.

the land had anything to spare to give to this prodigal son. Until he became "in need" and realized the futility of his lifestyle of slavery to sin, the prodigal son did not come to his senses (Luke 15:17). Have you run out of money, lost your home, lost your family, and lost your true friends as a result of your substance abuse? If not, you may not be at the place where you come to your senses and see your need for repentance. If you do realize the condition you are in, then ask for God's forgiveness with a broken and contrite heart today.[120]

For the Christian, repentance follows brokenness and is essential to restoring your relationship with God. Repentance is not an immediate, "quick fix" deliverance by God. Repentance is a repeated process of decisions that you make. It is a two-fold, continuing process of

1. Making decisions daily that deny your selfish, sinful desires

2. Accepting God's commands for actions that please Him.

It does not take years for you to become repentant and obedient to God. Repentance is immediate and decisive. **"Repent, for the kingdom of heaven is at hand."**[121] You can live the peaceful, forgiven, and abundant life of the kingdom of God right now because it is at your fingertips.

What does repentance look like? Jesus was teaching in the temple, when the chief priests and elders began questioning Him, and He told this parable of the two sons, which is a powerful yet simple illustration of repentance in Matthew 21:28-32:

> **What do you think? A man had two sons. And he went to the first and said, 'Son, go and work in the vineyard today.' And he answered, 'I will not,' but afterward he changed his mind and went. And he went to the other son and said the same. And he answered, 'I go, sir,' but did not go. Which of the two did the will of his father?" They said, "The first." Jesus said to them, "Truly, I say to you, the tax collectors and the prostitutes go into the kingdom of God before you. For John came to you in the way of righteousness, and you did not believe him, but the tax collectors and the prostitutes believed him. And even when you saw it, you did not afterward change your minds and believe him.**

[120]Matthew 5:3-5.
[121]Matthew 3:2.

Is it too late for you to repent? No, because Jesus says that even the people society views as the most corrupt, evil, and hopeless in the world (prostitutes and tax collectors in verse 31 above) are capable of being saved by God as they believe and trust in Him. Believing and trusting result in true actions of repentance and obedience.

One final biblical example concerning repentance is recorded in King Solomon's prayer to dedicate the temple in II Chronicles 6:36-40:

> **If they sin against you—for there is no one who does not sin—and you are angry with them and give them to an enemy, so that they are carried away captive to a land far or near, yet if they turn their heart in the land to which they have been carried captive, and _repent_ and _plead_ with you in the land of their captivity, saying, 'We have sinned and have acted perversely and wickedly,' _if they repent with all their mind and with all their heart_ in the land of their captivity to which they were carried captive, and pray toward their land, which you gave to their fathers, the city that you have chosen and the house that I have built for your name, then hear from heaven your dwelling place their prayer and their pleas, and maintain their cause and forgive your people who have sinned against you. Now, O my God, let your eyes be open and your ears attentive to the prayer of this place** (Emphasis mine).

Although this passage is not specifically about addiction, Solomon is asking the Lord to hear the repentant prayers of the people when they turn away from their sin and turn toward Him. *He pleads with God to be merciful by not giving them what they deserve!* The prayer of the repentant addict ought to be modeled by this prayer of Solomon.

A final way to demonstrate repentance is by being a "truth teller." Be someone who is an open book. In other words, be someone who has no secrets to hide and is authentic. People are drawn to genuine, authentic persons because they can be trusted. The repentant addict who no longer has anything to hide and has no lies to remember is now free to be authentic. There is no mask to wear! Allow the truth to set you free.[122]

---

[122] John 8:32.

If you are currently addicted to anything, surely by now, you are waking up from your disobedience like the prodigal son who realized he was literally eating with pigs. Do you see that your addiction is leading you down the same path as the prodigal son – into the pig trough? Are you ready to come back to the Heavenly Father just as the prodigal son did in Luke 15:17-21? This solution may seem too easy to be true for you right now. Believe in the Lord Jesus Christ to complete this good work of sanctification in you and you will experience the "transforming" freedom in Christ, contentment, peace, and joy. Philippians 1:6 states: **"And I am sure of this, that he who began a good work in you will bring it to completion at the day of Jesus Christ."**

Prayer of Heart Change and Application

Dear Heavenly Father, I do not want to continue to have my life devastated by the consequences of quenching the power of the Holy Spirit in my life and by searing my conscience so that I am unable to hear from you. Father, those are devastating places to be. I need to allow you to work in and through me as well as allow you to speak to me by the Holy Spirit through the Holy Scriptures. I ask you to reverse these consequences and bring me back to a right relationship with you where I can receive and hear clearly from you. Amen.

Chapter 15
Manifestations of Pride

Someone asked me, "What are the top three problems an addict must face?" My answer was, "Pride, pride, and pride." In reality, pride manifests in three common ways for the addict: boasting, self-pity, and selfishness.

The "boasting" type of pride is what you commonly see at football games after a touchdown (or any ordinary achievement). Self-pity is a type of pride in reverse. As mentioned earlier, self-pity is the idea that I deserve better than what I am receiving in life and from God. The third type of pride—selfishness—is a type of pride that centers one's attention upon pleasing self above all. Selfishness is self-gratification to the extent that the person has no regard for how his actions may affect anyone else.

There is no exception to this rule. Selfishness drives a drunkard, addict, or substance abuser. Is the female drug addict really concerned about her parents and children when she goes to the crack house to smoke crack cocaine? Who else is the drunkard thinking of when he picks up a six-pack? The behaviors are selfish, and they do not hurt just the addict; they hurt his relationship with the Lord, his spouse, his children, and those who care most for him. The Christian must begin to lovingly think and act for the well-being of others rather than thinking and acting only for self. Though a Christian is saved, now he must begin to change into the image of Christ in a process called "sanctification." The same power that saves a lost soul is the same power that sanctifies him.

Temptations to Sin: Lust of the Flesh, Lust of the Eyes, and Pride of Life

> **Do not love the world or the things in the world. If anyone loves the world, the love of the Father is not in him. For all that is in the world—the desires of the flesh and the desires of the eyes and pride in possessions—is not from the Father but is from the world. And the world is passing away along with its desires, but whoever does the will of God abides forever (I John 2:15-17).**

The substance abuser is tempted to sin just as Adam, Eve, and even Jesus were tempted to sin in three ways:

- Lust of the flesh
- Lust of the eyes
- The pride of life.[123]

Essentially, pride in the heart of a Christian leads one to think he is wiser than God, and this is often the root cause for falling into each of these three temptations. When we think we are better than we are, we believe we can triumph over our flesh. When we dabble in addictive substances, we are demonstrating pride before the Lord, as if we can cope without His grace. Our heavenly father, who disciplines in love, then allows us to see our arrogance and prove our weakness as we experience the fruit of our actions: disgrace, loss of family and friends, poverty, or some other affliction. Overwhelmed by all of this, the addict must turn in humility to the One who created him to give him the strength to repent and change direction. If the temptation can be avoided, the best advice is to flee from it rather than trying to face it within one's own strength. Christians must turn to the Holy Spirit for guidance and God's Word for empowerment to defeat the enemy.

<u>Lust of the Flesh:</u> Satan used the natural appetites of the body to tempt Eve to sin in Genesis 3:6a: **"So when the woman saw that the tree was good for food."** This temptation drew her away from the will of God. Satan tempted her to question God's Word by saying, "Did God actually say, 'You shall not eat of any tree in the garden'?" Satan was trying to cast doubt about God's Word when it comes to fulfilling one's natural appetites. In other words, Satan was suggesting to Adam and Eve, "If you are truly hungry, does it really matter whether you eat from this tree or not? Does it really matter that God forbids it? You are hungry. Eat. God wants you to be happy, right? Does God love you?" Satan was tempting them to act upon their feelings and natural desire to eat food without considering the parameters God had placed around them.

How did Jesus respond to this same temptation in Matthew 4:1-4?

> **Then Jesus was led up by the Spirit into the wilderness to be tempted by the devil. And after fasting forty days and forty nights, he was hungry.**

---

[123]Genesis 3 and Matthew 4.

> And the tempter came and said to him, If you are
> the Son of God, command these stones to become
> loaves of bread. But he answered, It is written, 'Man
> shall not live by bread alone, but by every word that
> comes from the mouth of God.'

For forty days, Jesus had not eaten and he was experiencing the natural appetite of hunger. Did He give in to his feelings of hunger? Did He to do what He wanted to do which was to fulfill a natural desire? No, instead, Jesus accurately quoted the Holy Scriptures when He said that one is to live according to obedience to the Word of God rather than by one's natural appetites. Repentant addicts must learn to live according to the commands of God found in the Bible rather than their feelings, desires, and appetites. Christian addicts must depend upon God to satisfy these desires rather than turning to temporary pleasures.

Lust of the Eyes: Satan tempted Eve in Genesis 3:6b: **"that it was a delight to the eyes,"** meaning the fruit would meet her selfish and covetous desires. The fruit delighted her eyes because her desire was for temporary satisfaction. She was coveting the fruit. In other words, her desire to eat the fruit was akin to the adage: "The grass is greener on the other side." She mistakenly believed the lie that this delightful and appealing fruit would make her happy. Addicts often believe that they cannot be happy unless they partake in this intoxicating substance that appears to be so satisfying. Once again, it is rooted in being discontent, and the "perishing" mentality feeds it. How did Jesus handle this temptation? In Matthew 4:8-11, it states:

> Again, the devil took him to a very high mountain
> and showed him all the kingdoms of the world and
> their glory. And he said to him, 'All these I will give
> you, if you will fall down and worship me.' Then
> Jesus said to him, 'Be gone, Satan! For it is written,
> 'You shall worship the Lord your God and him only
> shall you serve.' Then the devil left him, and behold,
> angels came and were ministering to him.

Satan quoted the Word of God correctly but twisted the true meaning of the Scriptures. Satan wants to cast doubt upon the Word of God and cause you to fail to place your confidence in God and His Word. Jesus rightly quotes and applies Scripture stating that God is not to be tested as God does not lie. His promises will be kept, and He promises to be all you need to lead a fulfilling life.

Pride of Life: Satan tempts Adam and Eve by stating in Genesis 3:6c: **"that the tree was to be desired to make one wise"** meaning that they would become **"like God."**[124] Unfortunately, everyone is tempted to want to be like God and many people try to act as if they are God. The pride in this type of thinking is idolatry as one desires to exalt himself to the same status as God. This temptation leads one into the disobedience of worshiping himself rather than the Creator. Pride and the idolatrous desire of worshiping and pleasing oneself are at the heart of addiction. How did Jesus respond to this same temptation? In Matthew 4:5-7, it states:

> **Then the devil took him to the holy city and set him on the pinnacle of the temple and said to him, "If you are the Son of God, throw yourself down, for it is written, 'He will command his angels concerning you,' and 'On their hands they will bear you up, lest you strike your foot against a stone.'" Jesus said to him, "Again it is written, 'You shall not put the Lord your God to the test.'**

Jesus told Satan that He would only worship and serve God. Jesus was not interested in the selfish, temporary pleasures of the world that feed one's pride. Jesus submitted His will to the Father and humbled Himself. Again, Jesus rightly quoted and applied God's Word to His circumstance. God's Word is powerful and you may not be able to utilize it often right now because you are not reading, studying, and memorizing Bible verses diligently. The Bible is a very powerful weapon for the addict. The booklet, *Understanding Temptation: The War Within Your Heart*, will enhance your understanding of these three temptations.

Humility is the antidote for pride. Humility is focusing upon God and others rather than self. Stuart Scott defines humility as: "The mindset of Christ (a servant's mindset): a focus on God and others, a pursuit of the recognition and the exaltation of God, and a desire to glorify and please God in all things and by all things He has given."[125] When a Christian addict begins to exhibit behaviors that reflect this type of humble attitude, those closest to him will be convinced that his heart has been radically changed by the Lord.

---

[124]Genesis 3:5.
[125]Scott, Stuart, *From Pride to Humility: A Biblical Perspective*, United States of America: Focus Publishing, p 17-18.

An addict will bend or break a rule if it is perceived as "unjust" or "unnecessary" in his eyes, reflecting a selfish, prideful heart. Pride is very much involved in a "go button's" heart when he wants to help everyone else but rejects the help offered by others. Some addicts refuse the help of others out of a desire to avoid accountability. Other addicts want help but only on their terms. They are unwilling to submit to someone else's rules and suggestions. Heart attitudes produce all types of selfish, manipulative, controlling, and dishonest words, actions, and thoughts.

At times, the addict struggles with the love of control since he rebelliously desires to do things his own way. The Bible warns in Proverbs 14:12: **"There is a way that seems right to a man, but its end is the way to death."** Wanting to control things is proudly attempting to act like God rather than submitting to His will. The Christian who wants to control his life needs to relinquish that control to God who is a Sovereign, loving, and caring master.

Everyone is a slave to something. In Romans 6:16-19, the Bible clearly teaches that you will be a slave to sin or a slave to righteousness. As you will read, there is no "in between" for any person:

> **Do you not know that if you present yourselves to anyone as obedient slaves, you are slaves of the one whom you obey, either of sin, which leads to death, or of obedience, which leads to righteousness? But thanks be to God, that you who were once slaves of sin have become obedient from the heart to the standard of teaching to which you were committed, and, having been set free from sin, have become slaves of righteousness. I am speaking in human terms, because of your natural limitations. For just as you once presented your members as slaves to impurity and to lawlessness leading to more lawlessness, so now present your members as slaves to righteousness leading to sanctification.**

Prayer of Heart Change and Application

Lord God, Give me the mindset of Christ so that I may lower myself and exalt you, my Loving Creator and Heavenly Father. Enable me to experience the power of the Bible to defeat Satan's lies just as Jesus did. Teach me to love Your Word, Lord, and give me wisdom and understanding when I study your Word. I am not sure how to change but I ask you to help me to put-off the pride in my heart and help me to put on a humble, teachable attitude. I confess my boasting, self-pity, and selfishness and ask you to forgive me. Not only do I seek your forgiveness, but I seek change in this area. Amen.

Chapter 16
What to do First: Put–Off

There are many practical things you can and must do immediately to overcome your addiction problem. Regardless of the severity of your substance abuse, the first thing to do is to confess your sin problem of addiction to God in prayer and to a close, trusted Christian friend. If you are married, it is best that this person be your spouse. If you are not married, confess to a leader in your church. Spoken confession is important for three reasons. First, your confession acknowledges the extent of this life-devastating problem to yourself. Second, your confession acknowledges your need for the help of others to confront this life-devastating problem. You cannot adequately defeat an addiction without the help of God and others. Third, confession acknowledges your responsibility for your addiction-related actions.

Denial and Self-deception

Self-deception, which the secular world often calls "denial," is a huge problem for the addict. Jeremiah 17:9-10 states: **"The heart is deceitful above all things, and desperately sick; who can understand it? I the Lord search the heart and test the mind, to give every man according to his ways, according to the fruit of his deeds."** When Scripture states that **"the heart is deceitful above all things,"** it implies that an unbeliever cannot fully know what's in his own heart because it is so wicked and "sick." Only the Lord knows fully what's in the heart according to Jeremiah 17:10 and only the Lord has the power to "give to every man according to his ways" and the "fruit of his deeds." When someone is in "denial," he is not confessing how powerfully gripping this sinful addiction and substance abuse problem is to his life. In reality, he is not *willing* or *honest* to work on his addiction; therefore, he denies that his addiction is a problem:

- "I can handle it."
- "It's not that bad."
- "I won't ever do it again. I've learned my lesson this time."

These are common phrases often heard from someone who is *unwilling*. Some counselors refer to this as "self-deception" and "being in denial" but there is no real deception here. In reality, there is a lack of *willingness*! Willingness is the essential ingredient in overcoming addiction.

- Are you willing to do anything and everything to overcome this problem?
- Do you want to overcome it or do you merely want to co-exist with the problem?

Confession is a first step but confession alone is not enough. Many people confess their addiction but *do* very little about the problem. It is possible for you to become a transformed addict. Proverbs 28:13 states: **"Whoever conceals his transgressions will not prosper, but he who confesses *and forsakes* them will obtain mercy."** Are you "concealing" your addiction from yourself and from those who love you? If so, then you must honestly confess your addiction problem to a trusted, Christian friend.

Honesty is related to willingness and is another essential ingredient in overcoming addiction. Lying and deception go hand in hand with addiction because you are trying to hide your sin. You know that what you are doing is wrong so you hide it. Trust with loved ones is destroyed once your problem and related deceptions come to light. In reality, not much of a relationship exists between you and your friends and family because you may have been seeing people as *objects* to be used and manipulated for your own purposes and self-gratification. Now you must openly and willingly confess the truth to those persons closest to you and ask them to stand with you as you overcome your addiction.

A failure to accept full responsibility for addiction is an *insurmountable wall* that cannot be overcome. Addiction counselors know this is true and that is why they "confront the denial" of the addict who continues to shift the blame, minimize, lie, and fail to take responsibility for his addiction. Unless you can honestly confess that the "buck stops here" and "I am responsible for this mess of my life," you are unable to proceed much further along the path of transformation. You are standing at the insurmountable wall. You are stuck and there is no pulling you out of your addiction until you recognize the truth that you are completely to blame for this addiction. You alone are responsible. You cannot go over or around this wall because it must be torn down. The tearing down of this insurmountable wall begins when you accept responsibility for your substance abuse, addiction, and sin.

Do not blame Satan either. Did Satan go into the package store and buy your alcohol? Did Satan go to your drug dealer and buy your drugs? No, you did. Did Satan light your crack cocaine pipe? No, you did. Do not play the "blame game" because you will ultimately lose. You are responsible. You cannot blame the alcohol, drugs, parents, spouse, children, job, society, a "disease," unfair laws, or finances for your addiction. It is solely your fault because you responded to pressures in an unbiblical way of escape called substance abuse. If you are an addict and you fail to see your responsibility for your addiction, then you are not ready to deal with it biblically. If you continue to blame everyone and everything except yourself, there is no help for you.

Forsaking Your Sin

If you are willing to take the step of honest confession, the next step is the forsaking of—or renouncing by turning away from—your sinful addictive behaviors and actions. You are abandoning your old way of life as you would abandon an old, beat up car after a car accident. This part of the transformation process is extremely important. It is called the "put off" stage of the process of being transformed into the image of Christ. Confession is merely words spoken, but forsaking sin consists of both thoughts and actions. That means you must be willing to do everything in your power to avoid temptations. This is crucial in the early stages of the process of overcoming your sin problem. Temptations can consist of people, places, and things that trigger your desire to use a drug or to drink.

Restrictions

Willingness to forsake your sinful temptations means that you are going to have to restrict yourself or have someone else levy restrictions upon you. Restriction is one of those terms that we don't like to see applied to our lives.

Everyone wants God's grace and mercy but few want discipline implemented in their own lives. Christians often perpetuate the thinking that they have "liberty in Christ" so they can do anything, go anywhere, and talk to anybody. Christian liberty is truly a biblical principle, and it can be experienced by a faithful, responsible, and Christian transformed addict or abuser, but only when the person has first disciplined his life according to biblical standards.

God gives you boundaries and restrictions because He loves you—not because He is punishing you. God is not a cosmic killjoy who loves to tease, punish, and ruin people by killing their fun. One aspect of God's character as revealed in the Word of God is love and sometimes that is why God restricts people whose lives would otherwise be out of control without it. The Christian substance abuser and addict who is trying to overcome his addiction requires boundaries—and lots of them!

For this reason, it is imperative that the Christian addict *willingly* allow a loved one or leader in the church to impose restrictions, or boundaries, upon them in an attempt to help. The Christian addict needs structure. Be honest with the person who is helping you and use Appendix F to help you to create a "contract" to which you must adhere immediately so that you may learn to become disciplined in your life. Do not look at this contract as a list of restrictions. Rather, look at it as a loving, helpful tool that will ultimately make you a better person and draw you closer to God.

Prayer of Heart Change and Application

Dear Heavenly Father, I confess that I have often lived out of control. I have not been disciplined and I need others who are godly people to provide me with structure so that I will not fulfill my temporary cravings, appetites, and desires. I recognize that you have provided me with loved ones and church leaders to help me. Lord, I need your help to make me willing to submit to these people who love me. Let the Holy Spirit dominate me so that I can willingly abide by their rules rather than my own rules. Help me to do this until I can begin operating in a disciplined, self-controlled way on my own. Amen.

Section 3

Correction

Chapter 17

What to Do Second:
Renewing Your Mind

In this section called "correction," the focus is upon "setting one right" which is what the Greek word in II Timothy 3:16 means. In the first section, you received "teaching" so you would not be "unknowing." In the second section, you received "reproof" so you would not continue making repeated errors. Now, in this third section, you will receive "correction" so you will be "set right" upon the path which is the Lord's path. You will learn what to do in order to overcome your struggles with idolatry and drunkenness.

A Teachable Spirit

Many Christians underestimate the power of the world's messages upon their thinking. The lessons that Jesus taught were radically opposed to the world's system. For example, Paul said in Acts 20:35 that Jesus taught "it is more blessed to give than to receive." What a radically different message from the world that promotes the selfish ideas of "you deserve the best" and "you have to look after number one." The gospel tells us that we deserve an eternity in hell yet God gives us the free gift of eternal life in Heaven with Him.

In this chapter, you will examine how important it is to think like God. You cannot think like God unless you listen to what God says in His Word. The Bible is so important for you to read and study, so that you will change your ideas to match biblical ideas. Remember that we are all born with a sinful nature that is anti-God until we are "born again" and given a new nature: the indwelling of the Holy Spirit that enables us to rightly interpret the Bible.

In this chapter, you will again be challenged to think about addiction as a sin issue rather than as a "disease concept." It is crucial that you think of this issue in a like manner with God. Mind renewal is hard work. It requires a teachable spirit on your part, a learner's heart to strive to understand what the Lord says about addiction, and a practitioner's commitment to implement these hard truths into your daily thinking and actions.

An essential element for effective communication between two persons is that they speak the same language. Have you ever tried to speak to someone who only spoke French or Spanish when you speak only English? It is frustrating, fruitless, and without non-verbal communication such as hand gestures, both of you are ready to call it quits very soon. These same feelings of frustration may happen when you try to ask God about your substance abuse or addiction. There is a fundamental communication problem between you and God that leads to many misunderstandings about what God says about addiction. These misunderstandings are not God's fault. Any misunderstandings stem from within us – our sinful nature – because we approach the problem from a man-centered view rather than from a God-centered view. Are you willing to put your ideas aside and be open-minded to what God's Word says? Are you teachable?

Again, let me contrast the world's approach to addiction with the biblical approach. The world's thoughts are: *"We need to categorize this problem by giving it a label; therefore, we will name all of these observable behaviors and situations: addiction, alcoholism, drug abuse, chemical dependency, co-dependency, disease, etc."* It is a good idea to categorize a problem and to give it a label since it helps others to identify the same problem when it manifests in various persons and places so that the common problem can be effectively treated. In fact, the idea of labeling stems from the need for good communication.

God Himself has already categorized and labeled this problem as sin. It is the sin of "idolatry" in general and God even gives it the specific name of "drunkenness." God says that a person who gives himself or herself over to this type of sin repetitively is a "drunkard." The only problem with the word "drunkard" is that modern society has painted the incorrect image of a drunkard as someone who is never capable of being sober and stays drunken one hundred percent of the time.

If you have ever seen the Andy Griffith Show, then you may remember Otis, the "town drunk," who staggered, slurred, stumbled, and bumbled his way around town nearly every time he appeared in the show. The picture is that of a person who is never capable of having a moment of sobriety. The show dramatized only one aspect of the drunkard and substance abuser: the outward behaviors while intoxicated.

A true depiction of the drunkard as a whole person portrays someone who willfully chooses to occasionally disobey God in his thoughts, words, and behaviors; however, those occasional choices increase with more regularity and habitual strength. Eventually, the drunkard becomes so enslaved to the thoughts of drinking and drugging that he has a new identity of a sinner, idolater, or drunkard.

The truth is that many drunkards function well on the job never missing a single day of work. The reality is that drunkards and drug addicts are not *always* intoxicated. Even the phrase "getting drunk" implies someone who is sober at first and then goes into a state of drunkenness. Once in this state of drunkenness, he cannot stand upright, cannot walk a straight line without falling down, and cannot put together a meaningful, coherent sentence. Society has taken a narrow view of the word "drunk" and even suggests that you are "shamed" by the use of that word. Some secular group therapists will not allow their counselees to use "junkie," "drunk," or "drunkard" to describe their behavior because it is "demeaning and cruel" in the worldly counselors' darkened opinion.

Is the word "drunkard" too harsh and mean-spirited to describe someone who continually gives themselves over to the sin of drunkenness? The Lord Jesus Himself uses it to describe this person.[126] It is a true description and name for the problem and it gives the Christian hope. How? *God calls sin "sin" and by doing so, God gives real hope to the drunkard because Jesus Christ died upon the cross for sin.* The Lord Jesus Christ gave His life for sin. Your only hope is to call it "sin" just as God does. You must take full responsibility for your sin so that you can experience God's forgiveness fully. Victims of a "disease" who sincerely believe it is not their fault fail to accept responsibility for their actions and do not get to fully experience the wonderful blessing of the gift of God's forgiveness. They are stuck in front of the "Insurmountable Wall" mentioned in the chapter entitled: "What to Do First: Put – Off".

Anything short of calling drunkenness a sin minimizes the very sacrifice of Christ and is a sin itself because you are acting rebelliously and foolishly as if you know better than God. Proverbs 16:25 says, **"There is a way that seems right to a man, but its end is**

---

[126]The Gospels give us three verses when Jesus used the term: Matthew 11:19, Matthew 24:49, and Luke7:34. Twice Jesus defended Himself against the false accusation that He was a sinner. Had His accusers lived in this day, they would have called Him an "alcoholic with a disease of addiction." Note that Jesus Himself utilized the term, "drunkard." You can, too.

the way to death." You must change your thoughts about addiction to match God's thoughts so that you will become more like God in your thinking and in your behaviors.

A Learner's Heart

Is it really a sin to drink alcohol or use drugs? Have you ever asked anyone this question and not gotten a straight answer from them? One reason people avoid answering this question directly is that it is a sweeping question about the behavior of drinking alcohol in general, rather than a specific question about a certain person in a particular circumstance. If the answer to the question is 'yes,' then the follow-up questions are: "How do you explain all of the Christians who drink or take prescription medications? Are these Christians all in sin? Can they all be wrong?" Some ask: "If drinking alcohol is not a sin, then are you giving an "alcoholic" or "drug addict" a license to continue to sin?"

As you can see, this general question about drinking as a sin may lead to confusion and controversy. Therefore, a better way to frame the question is to be specific by asking yourself the following: "Is it really a sin for *me* to drink alcohol or use this drug?" This revised question deals with the motives in *your heart*. Although God's Word gives you principles dealing with behavior in general, biblical principles are most beneficial when applied to your specific circumstances in a practical manner. This technique of specific, pinpointed discipleship is often accomplished in a biblical counseling session.

A Practitioner's Commitment

Addicts and substance abusers drink alcohol and use drugs for the wrong heart motive: to please self. It is a selfish desire and often leads to excessive behavior because alcohol and drugs do not satisfy the real desire of the heart: to know God intimately and personally. Living a life for God's glory knowing that you are created for His purposes is the best way to live. A life lived only to please self will lead to an unfulfilled, unproductive, and unsatisfying life. A life lived ensnared to sin is certainly not God's best for the addict and is one reason why the Lord hates sin. Sin is rebellion against God. It is a heart set on having its own way.

The Bible plainly teaches that drinking to excess, called "drunkenness," is a sin. Ephesians 5:18 says, **"And do not get drunk**

with wine, for that is debauchery, but be filled with the Spirit." Notice that these are not options, but they are commands of God. First,

- *God commands the Christian not to be under the domination of wine because it is sin.* The command to not get drunk with wine is called a "put off." Sometimes the Bible refers to it as "denying oneself." It is not easy but it is necessary.

- Second, in this particular verse, *God commands the Christian to be dominated by, or filled with, the Holy Spirit.* This is what the Bible says that you need to "put on".

Putting off and putting on are biblical concepts essential to the transformation process from addict to servant of God. However, if an addict merely changes what he is addicted to without any real heart change, little has been accomplished. Unfortunately, this is what happens in many secular treatment centers.

Real heart change occurs when motives, thoughts, and desires in the transforming addict change. These areas of the mind of the addict must change, or be renewed, and this is the middle step between the "put off" and "put on" dynamic for biblical change. The *renewing of the mind step is found* in verse 23 of this passage of Scripture:[127]

> **...to put off your old self, which belongs to your former manner of life and is corrupt through deceitful desires, and to be renewed in the spirit of your minds, and to put on the new self, created after the likeness of God in true righteousness nd holiness (Ephesians 4:22-24).**

Do not make the common yet sinful mistake of "exchanging one temporary pleasure for another temporary pleasure." Temporarily, this approach works effectively because it takes time before you become addicted to the newer pleasure (develop your new habits). During this time of creating and strengthening new habits for the new pleasure, your family members, friends, and loved ones mistakenly think that you have truly been "transformed." What is the truth, however, about your outward actions compared to your heart?

---

[127]The concept of "renewing the mind" was strengthened in me thanks to the teaching of Dr. Howard A. Eyrich during a D.Min. course I took in biblical counseling in the Fall of 2006 at Birmingham Theological Seminary.

If this is what has happened to you in your past failures at overcoming addiction, it will become very clear to you what God commands. It is quite similar to exchanging one pleasure for another. God wants you to replace one sinful addiction with a righteous addiction that pleases Him. God knows how He made you. You may think you have an "addictive personality." Even if that were true, you are responsible for directing it to God. God wants you to channel your passion for your addictive object to Him because He is the only healthy "object" to be focused upon.

Being Renewed in Your Mind is Essential

God has taught us that the middle step of "renewing your mind" is essential for the new, righteous "addiction" to be healthy, beneficial to you, and glorifying to God. *To be renewed in your mind means that you must hate what you once loved.* In other words, you must see alcohol and drug usage as your enemy. Your thinking about drugs and alcohol must change from "friend" to "foe." They are not helpful to you. Pray that the Holy Spirit would not only help you change your thoughts but would also change your desires for alcohol and drugs. If you will do your part to change your thinking, I believe God will change your desire for alcohol and drugs.

Ephesians 4:23 says that you are **"to be renewed in the spirit of your minds."** The battlefield is your mind. For illustration purposes, imagine we are doing a brain transplant on you. As your surgeon, I will cut open the top of your cranium and remove your brain. By disconnecting your brain and taking it out, every thought of yours that does not agree with God's Word is removed. Next, I will replace your brain with a Bible. With this new and improved "Bible-brain," you will now think new thoughts that agree with God's thoughts because it is His Word, after all. With this new "Bible-brain," you will not only think like God but you will speak to people in a godly manner and you will act in a godly manner.

Now, the above illustration is a transplant and quick fix solution that as we all know really cannot happen. What God wants to happen is a process that He calls "renewal." *Renewing your mind is hard work, and there is no substitute for Bible reading, study, meditation, and memorization.* When you became a Christian, you did not get a brand new mind. Your old mind still has some really wrong patterns of thinking. The old mind must be renewed, or made like new by being rejuvenated. The word "renew" implies that the mind had become faded like an old couch needing restoration. When the upholstery is replaced and the inner parts and stuffing in the couch replenished, the old couch now looks like a new couch. In reality, it is the same old couch with some renewed parts.

Your mind is the same old mind but it needs some new thoughts. Those new thoughts must be derived from the Holy Scriptures and then applied as a practical "put on." Mind renewal is actually an act of the will as you choose to think differently about drugs and alcohol. The Bible says in Romans 12:2: **"Do not be conformed to this world, but be transformed by the renewal of your mind, that by testing you may discern what is the will of God, what is good and acceptable and perfect."** The renewal of the mind must occur for the addict to become less self-centered, more giving, and more pleasing to God. The renewal of the mind must occur or you will become addicted and enslaved to another temporary pleasure such as food, television, gambling, and the like for an escape. The world calls this an "addictive personality" and it is a half-truth, but regardless of who you are, you must become "addicted to Jesus" by worshiping God every day of your life.

The Holy Spirit works in conjunction with the truth of the Word of God. Did you make the connection between the Holy Spirit and the Bible? Some Christians do not fully comprehend the connection between the Holy Spirit and the Bible. God teaches that we will become powerful by learning and applying biblical truths. The power will come from the Holy Spirit as the Holy Spirit utilizes the Word of God that is within your mind. In John 4:23-24, Jesus said: **"But the hour is coming, and is now here, when the true worshipers will worship the Father _in spirit and truth,_ for the Father is seeking such people to worship him. God is spirit, and those who worship him must worship _in spirit and truth"_** (Emphasis mine). Do not miss the significance of this teaching or you will limit the power of God in your own life. Utilize Appendix G to help you begin the process of renewing your mind.

You need two things to have a renewed mind: the Holy Spirit and God's Word. You must do your part to faithfully read, study, and memorize God's Word. There is no substitute. The Holy Spirit will enable you to understand His Word and to rightly apply it in your life. The Lord will renew your mind if you have a teachable spirit, a learner's heart, and a practitioner's commitment to implement His truths into your life by the power of the Holy Spirit.

Prayer of Heart Change and Application

Dear Heavenly Father, I need you to renew my mind. Help me to hate what I once loved and thought was good. Renew my mind, Lord. Enable me to see that I was only serving myself and not you when I was in active addiction. Give me a teachable spirit, a learner's heart, and a practitioner's commitment to implement your truths into my life. Amen.

Chapter 18
The Battle in the Mind

The Truth about Alcohol and Drugs

God does not say anywhere in His Word that the drinking of wine is a sin. If God had said so, you could decisively conclude that it is a sin to drink alcohol or use a drug any time anywhere. Then you could simply obey God by never drinking again, and live a pleasing life unto Him. However, God did not say that it is a sin to drink. No one must add to or subtract from the Word of God. John warns us regarding his prophecy in the book of Revelation 22:18-19:

> **I warn everyone who hears the words of the prophecy of this book: if anyone adds to them, God will add to him the plagues described in this book, and if anyone takes away from the words of the book of this prophecy, God will take away his share in the tree of life and in the holy city, which are described in this book.**

Therefore, no one should ever add to God's Word by completely forbidding someone to ever drink wine or use prescription medications. God has a purpose for strong wine, alcohol, and drugs as you have discovered.

God does say it is a sin to be drunk with wine to excess.[128] The world calls this "substance abuse." As with any sin, if you drink to excess, you must confess it as sin, ask for God's forgiveness, ask for forgiveness from any others you may have offended, and repent by radically changing your behavior. You must consider "radical amputation," or abstaining from any volitional (willful) alcohol and drug use (unless prescribed by a medical doctor). You "radically amputate" and eliminate the occasional use of drugs and alcohol because it has often led you to excessive use and sin (more on this topic in the chapter called "Taking a Nazirite Vow Under the Care of a Physician").

God commands you to turn away from the sin of drunkenness because it will enslave and dominate you, bringing you to utter

---

[128] Ephesians 5:18

155

ruin. Drunkenness is a powerful and cruel master as we studied in Proverbs 23:29-35. Repentance from the sin of drunkenness is not always easy because it affects you in so many ways. *Are you ready for change? Do you want what God wants for your life though it may be the most difficult thing you have ever had to do?*

Theoretically, there is no excuse for a Christian to continue to quench the Holy Spirit by allowing sin to dominate him and to reign supreme in his own flesh and bones. Romans 6:12 commands you: **"Let not sin therefore reign in your mortal bodies, to make you obey their passions."** This means you are not to allow yourself to yield to sinful, selfish, and temporary pleasurable appetites that your flesh desires. This also means that as a Christian you are not to become enslaved to "physical" addiction and substance abuse. Because you are a Christian, the indwelling power of the Holy Spirit to choose what is right and the powerful Word of God are major weapons to tear down the strongholds of sin. Finding a biblical church is another wonderful resource for a Christian who truly wants to be free from addiction.

Although some have argued that there is not enough help out there for addicted persons, the problem is neither a lack of help nor a lack of programs. There is certainly not a lack of revealed truth. The real problem is that people suppress the truth[129] and deny God's solutions to their problems because they *want* to do things "their way."[130] Substance abusers must ask God to change their "want to" into what His "want to" is for them. In other words, the substance abuser must put off his desires, renew his mind by the truth of the Word of God, and put on God's desires in a meaningful and practical way.

Do you continue to drink or use drugs because you want to do things your own way? If so, you must submit to God's Word for guidance with this problem of addiction. God wants you to be *willing*. He wants your heart to desire His will. Matthew 26:39 describes Jesus in the Garden of Gethsemane: **"And going a little farther he fell on his face and prayed, saying, "My Father, if it be possible, let this cup pass from me; nevertheless, not as I will, but as you will."** Do you wrongly pray for God to change His will into what your will already is? Or do you rightly pray as Jesus did in the above verse: that God's will be done regardless of your feelings? God wants your

---

[129]Romans 1:18-23
[130]Proverbs 16:25

heart to be willing to do His will in His way even if that way seems difficult. God wants your mind to be *transformed by His truth*! Are you ready?

Attention, Christian addict! God Your Creator:

- has given you the truth about addiction in His Word
- has arranged a path of forgiveness through Christ Jesus His Son
- has equipped you with the power to change through His Holy Spirit

Hallelujah! What a Savior!

How to Fight Cravings

In the physical component of addiction your flesh has a stronghold on the battlefield of cravings. If at all possible, you need to avoid the temptation to use your drug of choice. You have five senses: sight, taste, smell, hearing, and touching. When you see, taste, smell, hear, or touch something that reminds your brain of how you have sinfully fulfilled an appetite in the past, you may begin to experience a real, physiological craving in your body like sweating or salivating. Your body is anticipating the fulfillment of its natural appetite with what it remembers to be very pleasing and effective. The drug felt good and your body remembers it. Even if you begin to experience a craving of some kind, you are *not* defeated so do not give up at this stage of the battle!

In the process of your transformation, the concept of renewing your mind must be practically applied to fight cravings. Your body has been defeated as evidenced by the craving, but you still have power in your mind to overcome this craving. Too many Christian addicts give up once they start to experience a physical craving in their body. They sweat, salivate, and excitedly anticipate the use of the drug they desire more than anything. Their body is the first line of defense against the addiction and it has been beaten, but you still have a greater battlefield—your mind—**if *you have it trained correctly.***

Taking Thoughts Captive

II Corinthians 10:5 states: **"We destroy arguments and every lofty opinion raised against the knowledge of God, and take every**

thought captive to obey Christ." When your body has become your "enemy" due to the temporary craving you are experiencing, your thoughts must do battle *against* your body. To speak in military terms, your mind must make your body "retreat" to get you out of that situation. You must remind yourself that this drug of choice is *not* a friend and will ultimately destroy you by greatly hindering your fellowship with God and leading to terrible consequences. Immediately, you must **"take any thoughts captive"**[131] – thoughts that are the lies that encourage you to "give in," to indulge your cravings.

By taking thoughts captive, the Bible means that these thoughts cannot be allowed to run freely through your mind. The mind must capture the thoughts and place them in chains in a prison cell of the brain.

How do you take your thoughts captive? You recognize them as lies from Satan and meditate instead on Scripture. *You renounce and put-off the thought that is a lie from Satan and you replace it by announcing the truth of Scripture*. You put on the truth of the Bible in place of the lie you had believed. You cannot be passive about this because you are in constant spiritual warfare (Ephesians 6:12). Knowing the truth of God's Word helps you to identify the lies of Satan that you believe to be true but lead to death.

Again, new thoughts reminding you that your drug of choice is not a friend must immediately replace any old thoughts promoting surrender to the craving. The Bible says in Romans 12:2: **"Do not be conformed to this world, but be transformed by the renewal of your mind, that by testing you may discern what is the will of God, what is good and acceptable and perfect."** Is your mind renewed to the point that you can now discern what the righteous will of God is for your life? If not, then you need to memorize this verse of Scripture and others relating to the renewing of your mind so that you can be victorious over your powerful, physiological cravings. *Renewing your thoughts by memorizing verses of Scripture is the most powerful weapon against cravings.* Jesus quoted the Word of God to Satan to defeat His enemy and Christians must do the same.

Seven Practical Examples of Resisting the Devil and Temptation

Diligent studying of the Word of God at this point in your transformation process will teach you how to obtain deliverance

---

[131] II Corinthians 10:5b

from sin: **"Thy word have I hid in my heart that I might not sin against thee" (Psalm 119:11, KJV).** Here are seven practical ways to resist the devil and the lies of the world:

1. *Prepare a Philippians 4:8 "Think List"* ahead of time in anticipation of the temptation that you will face in addiction.[132] Philippians 4:8 states: **"Finally, brothers, whatever is true, whatever is honorable, whatever is just, whatever is pure, whatever is lovely, whatever is commendable, if there is any excellence, if there is anything worthy of praise, think about these things."** This list must be composed of things that you can "think on" that are "true, honorable, just, pure, lovely, commendable, excellent, and worthy of praise." Keep a copy of this list in your purse, wallet, car, house, office, and anywhere else where you can have quick access to it. Focus your thoughts and attention on these things in your life that are blessings. Such items may include your relationships with loved ones, vacations you are planning, funny occurrences that have happened to you or your family, and certainly God's Word.

2. *Change a thought about someone from a negative to a positive.* Do not assume the worst about them but believe the best about them according to I Corinthians 13:7: **"Love bears all things, believes all things, hopes all things, endures all things."** Search for a positive truth about them on which to focus and think on that aspect in a variety of ways. It is better to err on the side of love.

3. *Change the subject of conversations when talk begins to become ungodly* (e.g. break-time on the job). Have a gratitude list of things, personal stories, or subjects that you can readily talk about to avoid gossip and foolish talk. Ephesians 5:4 states: **"Let there be no filthiness nor foolish talk nor crude joking, which are out of place, but instead let there be thanksgiving."** Do not miss the significance of replacing negative, perishing thoughts with positive, grateful thoughts.

4. *Abstain (or stay away) from the resemblance or appearance of evil* (for example, going a different route home from work to avoid passing by the bar or usual hang-out). I Thessalonians 5:22 states: **"Abstain from every form of evil."** Restrictions like these are freeing. Ask any transformed addict. If you are going to a loved one's holiday party and you know that alcohol will be served there, plan to be drinking an alternative beverage and get it in your

---

[132] Adams, Jay, <u>The Christian Counselor's New Testament</u>, Hackettstown, NJ: Timeless Texts, p. 613.

hand as soon as you walk in the door before an alcoholic drink is offered to you. It would be better to skip the party altogether, but that is not always possible. Proverbs 14:16 says: **"One who is wise is cautious and turns away from evil, but a fool is reckless and careless."** Actually attending this party would not even be wise until there has been much evidence (sometimes many years' worth) to suggest that transformation is occurring (such as, faithful adherence to restrictions has been demonstrated). Attendance at this party in particular is not advisable for one who has just recently come over the "Insurmountable Wall".

5. *Have an answer ready for those who will say,* "Ah, come on, don't be a party-pooper. Just have one drink." The best answer is one that glorifies God but, "No, thank you," and a smile works just as well. Prepare your answer well in advance and practice saying it. Here are some possibilities:

A. I'm in the process of transformation from pleasure dominating me to God dominating me.

B. God is not pleased with how I act when I drink or when I am drunk.

C. I am not pleased with how I act when I drink or when I am drunk.

D. I'm finding out the truth about addiction.

These answers need to be short and then the conversation moved on to something else. These answers need to *be **not arrogant*** suggesting that you have all the answers for the world's problems, *but honest* that you are growing and changing your desires. This takes a big supply of humility and *meekness from the Holy Spirit*. Again, do not attempt to attend parties without a trusted Christian friend early in the process of transformation.

6. *Mute the television or radio* and/or leave the room when commercials are aired that promote discontentment, pleasure with no consequences, and other evil desires of the flesh. Learn to recognize these lies.

7. *Avoid channel surfing* by using a programming guide. Plan what you will watch and watch it only. Be active not passive.

A note of warning: you might be able to do all of the suggestions in the list above, but, without *a **true change of heart*** by the Holy Spirit, you will not experience lasting change. Furthermore, without the Holy Spirit changing your heart, *your motives* for following the list are self-serving rather than God-pleasing. In other words, remember that your primary goal must be to please and serve God. Your secondary goal is to create godly habits that produce blessings of lasting change for you personally.

What Does Being Godly Look Like?

One way to measure godliness is to use the fruit of the Spirit in Galatians 5:22-23 as a "measuring stick:" **"love, joy, peace, patience, kindness, goodness, faithfulness, gentleness, (and) self-control."** Use a scale from one to ten for each fruit to rate how much fruit you are displaying to the world. Ask a spouse or close Christian friend to rate you, also. When the Christian addict begins to worship his Creator rather than some temporary pleasure that can never fully satisfy, then he will begin to exhibit some of this fruit of the Spirit in his life on a consistent basis. In addition, he will be preparing himself for the eternal "life to come" as mentioned previously in I Timothy 4:8.

Do you know someone you consider to be "godly"? This godly person did not instantly become godly by swallowing a "pink godly pill." There is no such thing! The idea of instant godliness is just as silly. Godliness takes practice and godly people have been practicing at it for a long time. They still fail occasionally but even when they fail, they often handle their failure in a godly manner. Begin practicing your godliness today by becoming more obedient in your thought-life, spoken words, and actions. Renew your mind with God's Word so you can think, speak, and act like the Lord Jesus Christ who is your ultimate model for godliness.

Prayer of Heart Change and Application

Dear Heavenly Father, I am without excuse. I am to blame. Please forgive me for living life independently of you. Renew my mind, Lord. Help me to take my thoughts captive and to replace them with thoughts that are true and pleasing to you. Give me new thoughts so that I can win the battle of addiction that begins in my mind. I need to see addiction as you see it so I can be transformed into someone who acts, speaks, and thinks more like You, Lord. Mold me, shape me, and conform me into the image of Your Son, Jesus, everyday. Thank you, Father. Amen.

Section 4

Training in Righteousness

Chapter 19
What to Do Third: Put-On

In this final section, you will be instructed how to put what you are learning into practice. It takes training *and* practice to learn how to play a sport like baseball with excellence. If you only read this book and the biblical principles presented and do not put them into practice, this book will be limited in its effectiveness. It is up to you to be a "doer of the Word" and not just a hearer (or reader) of the Word of God.[133]

Change of Mind Leads to Change of Actions

As you have already learned, repentance is action. Since actions speak much louder than words, as a "transforming" addict, you must not only change your thinking but you must begin changing your actions, too. A heart willing to obey God precedes one's actions. This step of the process of transformation is called "putting on." Even if you think your heart has not been changed yet by God, you need to "put on" obedience to Him regardless of your thoughts and feelings.

Here is an illustration. In the Bible, God gives us parameters for how a Christian is to live life. Think of these parameters as a giant circle. Inside the circle is obedient living according to God's commands and outside the circle is disobedient living according to your own way. If you are involved in active addiction, you are living outside the circle. Whether you want to or not, you must place yourself inside the circle and live life on God's terms. Even if your heart has not changed, you will reap the benefits of living inside the circle because God's way helps you improve your interpersonal well-being: relationships with friends, family, and children, finances, legal problems, and the struggles of daily living. Changing your thoughts and gaining knowledge without putting it into action is not sufficient to become truly "transformed." Step three of the process is "putting on" righteous living.

Wisdom Contains Both Knowledge (Information) and Obedience (Action)

You might think that wisdom is how much information, or knowledge, you put into your brain, but Jesus taught that an

---

[133]James 1:22.

important piece of wisdom is actual obedience, or action. To conclude the teachings Jesus gave to His followers in the Sermon on the Mount, Jesus compares the wise man and the foolish man in Matthew 7:24-27:

> **Everyone then who hears these words of mine and does them will be like a wise man who built his house on the rock. And the rain fell, and the floods came, and the winds blew and beat on that house, but it did not fall, because it had been founded on the rock. And everyone who hears these words of mine and does not do them will be like a foolish man who built his house on the sand. And the rain fell, and the floods came, and the winds blew and beat against that house, and it fell, and great was the fall of it.**

Both men are similar in that they:

- Both built houses
- Both *heard* the Word of God (so they possessed the same knowledge)
- Both experienced the storms of life

To relate it to modern times, the wise man and the fool are sitting together in the pew, receiving the same teaching, hearing the same sermons, struggling with the same substance abuse problem, and reading from the same Bible containing God's Word. The fool, however, chooses *not* to put these teachings into action. The fool does not apply the principles he heard and learned from God's Word to his own life. In contrast, the wise man chooses to apply these principles to his life and therefore, his house is built upon a solid foundation of rock.

When the problem of substance abuse storms houses (rain, wind, and flood), the wise man's house stands, but the fool's house falls because the house did not have a solid foundation. It was built upon the sand of disobedient actions. Great is the destruction of the fool's house because he lived disobediently to God's Word.

Wisdom comes from not only hearing the Word of God, but from putting the Word into practice in our life. Just as you learn to ride a bike, play the piano, or play a sport, you must practice the wise spiritual principles found in God's Word. The world thinks a fool is just a stupid and ignorant person. Biblically, a fool is not ignorant of the truth since he knows what is right as Proverbs 10:23 says, **"Doing wrong is like a joke to a fool, but wisdom is pleasure to a man of understanding."** Many times, a fool is rebellious in that he knows what is right to do, but chooses not to do things in God's way. The fool chooses to do what seems right in his own mind.[134]

Wisdom is both hearing and doing what is right in a way that pleases God first. Once the Holy Spirit enables you to obtain knowledge by understanding the Word of God, He also enables you to *do* the Word by putting these principles into practice. Philippians 2:13 states: **"for it is God who works in you, both to will and to work for his good pleasure."**

Be wise by doing. If you fail to do what you know is right, you quench the fire of the Holy Spirit inside of you. You then hinder two of your abilities:

First, you hinder your ability to understand God and you become warped in your thinking about Him. You start thinking wrong thoughts about God's character such as: "God doesn't care *about me.* God doesn't want the best for me. God is punishing me."

Second, you hinder your ability to act in a God-pleasing manner. God made you His ambassador, or representative, so you don't want to hinder your glorifying of Christ's name by failing to act obediently.

Consequences Can Produce Humility

The addict is enslaved to the desire to escape from life. He is pursuing the selfish fulfillment of his appetites to the neglect of his responsibilities. When you neglect responsibilities, negative consequences usually result such as the electrical power is turned off, the car is repossessed by the bank, or you are evicted from your apartment for failing to pay rent.

These consequences are not completely bad, however, since they provide an excellent opportunity for God to give you what you really need: humility.[135]

Humility is required for repentance to take place. It is humbling to lose your car or lose your place to live, but one of the purposes of the

---

[134]Proverbs 12:15.
[135]Luke 15:11-32. Read about the prodigal son for an example of consequences leading to humility.

consequence is that God is reminding you of your dependence upon Him. If you have lost your home, you must humbly ask someone for help. Unfortunately, many addicts will lie about how they lost their home or try to portray themselves as a victim of circumstance rather than taking responsibility. When that happens, you have missed an opportunity to humbly repent.

The prodigal son in Luke 15 did not miss his opportunity to repent. Luke 15:14 states: **"And when he had spent everything, a severe famine arose in that country, and he began to be in need."** Interestingly, the prodigal son spent all that he had and then the famine that arose in the country meant that no one else had anything to spare to help him. In other words, his resources dried up. His "enablers" were no longer "enabling him" as the world says. What happened to the prodigal son when he spent all he had? What happened when he had no one else to turn to? He "began to be in need." Did he repent right then at the beginning of his "need"? No! Amazingly, his situation had to get worse before he "came to his senses" the Bible says in Luke 15:17. The prodigal son made himself a slave to someone (sounds like the slavery of addiction!) and was so destitute that he "longed to be fed" with the food the pigs ate. Finally, through his consequences, the Lord opened his eyes and he put on an attitude of humility and repentance to return to his father who represents our Father in Heaven.

Repentance: Part of the Daily Walk

Repentance is the action part of wisdom. Repentance restores one's relationship with God. Repentance restores one's communication with God. Communication is not just talking, or praying to God, but it is *listening* to God. How do you listen to God? You read His Word and meditate upon it day and night.[136] To oversimplify matters, prayer is talking to the Lord and reading the Bible is listening to God talk; thus, the Bible is called "God's Word" because He is speaking. The Holy Spirit opens the "ears" of one's understanding of God's Word. For the Christian, repentance is as essential as believing in Christ in order to walk in fellowship with the Lord. Repentance is often taught as a "one time" action. While repentance is an essential component of salvation, it is not limited to being a "one time" event. *Christians must repent and believe, or trust, in God every day of their lives for the forgiveness of sin.*

---

[136]Psalm 1:2.

Secular Groups Have One Idea Right – Sanctification is a Gradual Process

After being saved by grace, Christians still are not perfect and need forgiveness. Many persons are inaccurate in their thinking that the Christian is supposed to *never again struggle* with sin – or even never again struggle with *certain kinds* of sin they wrongly deem to be the "worst sins." The church is filled with many people who hold this view and put on a false appearance of having their lives altogether perfect and orderly with no problems at all and certainly no struggles with sin. The pride rooted in this way of thinking is dangerous because it makes it more difficult *to humble yourself and ask for help in the very place that the most help can be offered: the Bible-teaching church of the Lord Jesus Christ.*

The result is that Christian addicts and substance abusers go to treatment programs and then reject the church because it is full of "hypocrites" according to the way they see things. These same Christians are drawn away to the secular organizations that promote spiritual growth as a *gradual process*. In this sense, secular modalities have the correct perspective on the truth when compared to these churches that promote the demonstration of "perfection at all costs."

It is no wonder that many Christians are more attracted to the secular modalities of "spirituality" that promote the biblical truth of growing in Christ as a gradual, lifelong process for Christians. When churches promote the unbiblical idea of reaching a point in life where a Christian can become perfect, or sinless, they are driving addicts—and all those that struggle with sin for that matter—away from the church and to secular modalities. Churches that promote "perfection" in this life are not biblically grounded in this doctrine of sanctification.

You, however, are responsible for finding a Bible teaching church that has a correct understanding of repentance in the process of growth in Christ. The leaders of the church are responsible for shepherding and ministering to hurting souls while teaching biblical truths, such as growing in Christ, accurately. Resolve to begin *doing* the work of obedient Christian living today, fully relying upon the sanctification of the Holy Spirit and the promise of forgiveness when you stumble and repent and forsake your sin.

Prayer of Heart Change and Application

Dear Heavenly Father, You are so good to me and I thank you for loving me enough to allow me to experience consequences that bring me to my knees with a humble spirit. I do see purpose in the problems that have resulted from my selfish, addicted ways and I truly am grateful to you for allowing me to experience those consequences so that you and I might become closer. I need You, Father, to guide me. I repent of my sin and ask you to help me to back up these words with repentant actions. I want to demonstrate my love for you and the wisdom you have given me in a real, practical, and honoring way. Therefore, Father, guide me in your truth and direct my steps so that you may receive glory. Amen.

Chapter 20

Responsibility, Gratitude and Submission: More to Put-On

Godly Sorrow vs. Worldly Sorrow

Family members of an addict have a difficult time trying to determine whether their loved one is truly repentant from their addictive behaviors and sin. They wonder if the addict is truly sorry about the sin or if he is only sorry about the consequence he is experiencing as a result of the sin. Family members want to help someone who is putting forth the maximum effort to overcome their addiction. The dilemma is often stated in these questions: "She seems to be clean and sober now, but how can I be sure that she is not going to go back to drugs and alcohol? How do I know? What do I look for?" True repentance manifests in identifiable ways. Here are some questions:

- Are your words matching your actions? Others can *observe* your actions if you are repentant.

- Are you sorry about your sinful and selfish actions?

- Are you "grieving" your past actions?

- Will you now put forth your best effort to drastically change your behavior?

In fact, the Bible identifies two types of sorrow in II Corinthians 7:10: **"For godly grief produces a repentance that leads to salvation without regret, whereas worldly grief produces death."** Anyone who has experienced the death of a loved one has experienced the emotion of grief and the subsequent actions of weeping over their loss. If you are truly convicted of your sin by the Holy Spirit, you will be grieved by your past actions to the point of doing everything you can to fight addiction. II Corinthians 7:10 says that you will be **"without regret"** meaning you will not be resentful to the newly imposed restrictions in your life.

If you are experiencing the type of "worldly grief" mentioned in this verse, then you will only be:

- sorry you got caught

- sorry you have caused problems for some of the people in your life

- sorry for the consequences you may be suffering
- sorry for things that are "worldly," or only temporal

"Worldly grief" is not concerned with providing restitution to "fix" the problems your addiction has caused other people. In this type of grieving and sorrow, you are primarily focused upon thoughts such as: "I screwed up again, and now everyone knows it."

The type of sorrow and grief that your loved ones are really eager to see is the type of "godly grief" produced by the conviction of the Holy Spirit. With godly grief, you are sorry and grieved that you have offended a holy God who is your Creator and who loves you. Only then will you be able to embrace (not resent) the restrictions imposed on you by yourself or others to help you continue on the path of transformation.

You have proven by your past actions that you cannot be trusted with regard to substances that alter your mood. If you have not been faithful, honest, and truthful, you must *willingly* place yourself under certain restrictions in order to avoid the temptations for drinking and drugging. Willingness is the essential ingredient for success in overcoming a substance abuse problem and any life-devastating sin problem. When willingness is in your heart, any and all restrictions upon your freedoms are welcomed because you are willing to do anything to "transform" from drugs and alcohol. In biblical words, you are repentant and your actions now match your words of repentance. You have fruit!

If you are truly being transformed, you will want to demonstrate your willingness to those who care the most for you. You want your loved ones to see that you care for them and are becoming more responsible. In contrast, if you are in active addiction, you are going to exhibit words and actions of self-centeredness and irresponsibility. The bottom line is that you will not be thinking of others or show concern for them. With true repentance, there are at least three pieces of evidence to look for in your life:

1. Responsibility
2. Gratitude
3. A submissive spirit

Responsibility

Why is responsibility such a big issue in the process of transformation? Responsibility is a big deal to God, your Creator.

Recall that in Genesis 3:12-13, Adam blamed God and Eve for his sinful decision, and Eve blamed the serpent:

> **The man said, "The woman whom you gave to be with me, she gave me fruit of the tree, and I ate." Then the Lord God said to the woman, "What is this that you have done?" The woman said, "The serpent deceived me, and I ate."**

You can exhibit responsibility for your actions by coming in before curfew, coming straight home rather than going to bars, and calling home if there is a delay of any kind. This demonstrates concern for your loved ones. Responsibility is critical to successful transformation. It really is a fruit that demonstrates that a genuine change of heart has occurred. Responsibility for one's actions shows that one is beginning to become more honest and transparent in his behavior. The deceptive behaviors of your past begin to disappear as you demonstrate that you are not afraid to accept responsibility for your failures and actions.

Did Adam and Eve take ownership of their sinful choices according to the above two verses? No, both were guilty of shifting the blame to someone or something else. Adam's blame-shifting is particularly despicable because he essentially blamed his Creator for his sin by referring to Eve as **"the woman whom _You_ gave to be with me"**. Adam indirectly implies blame on the Lord!

Take responsibility for your sin. Take responsibility for how prone you are to over-indulge your appetites. Taking responsibility means

1. Recognizing a potential temptation
2. Taking precautionary measures, or restrictions, *prior* to allowing the temptation to occur

In other words, do not walk into a situation that is dangerously tempting and say, "Well, the Bible tells me to resist temptation. I know there are some temptations inside this beer joint, so I'm just going to go inside and resist those temptations." No, in order for you to be responsible, you must avoid temptation and any appearance of evil. Place restrictions upon yourself and follow those restrictions as though you would be put to death for breaking one of them! It is a serious matter, and you must become responsible in this far-reaching manner.

Confession vs. Admission

Let's take it a step further. The secular world tells addicts to "admit" their problem of addiction. Admission occurs *after* one has been confronted. There can be admission of guilt without any grieving at all. For example, a person is confronted by a loved one who is trying to convince the addict that he has a problem with drugs after his fourth arrest for driving while intoxicated (D.W.I. also known as D.U.I., or driving under the influence). After the loved one confronts him, he shrugs it off and says, "Yeah, I did it but everyone is human. Plus, I have a disease. I can't help myself." Admission of guilt occurred after the confrontation but there was a failure by the addict to accept responsibility for his actions. *Admission alone is inadequate if the addict fails to acknowledge his responsibility for the behavior.*

Another example is a mother who says to her son, "Johnny, did you steal that candy bar?" The son *admits* his guilt by stating, "Yes, mother, I stole it." There is a confrontation and an admission of guilt. This scenario is better than the first but the Word of God encourages the addict to go one step further than the little boy in this example. The Bible tells Christians to "confess" their sin problem of addiction. Confession occurs *before* an addict has to be confronted! In the example above, the Bible encourages the son to *confess* to his mother, "Mother, there is something I must tell you. I stole that candy bar." The son is giving his mother information that was unknown to her prior to the confession. Plus, the mother did not have to drag the information out of him.

The worldly approach encourages admission because it does not acknowledge the biblical standards for sin that God sets. Confession involves calling the problem what the Lord calls it. If God calls it sin, you must agree to call it sin and confess your thoughts, words, and actions as sinful. When you do so, you will find mercy in the love of Christ and the atoning work that He did on Calvary. Most often, transformed addicts will want to proactively *confess* their sins, faults, and mistakes rather than reactively *admitting* them after being confronted by a loved one.

The major problem with *admission* is the deception involved in wanting to conceal the sin rather than openly *confessing* it. I John 1:9-10 states: **"If we confess our sins, he is faithful and just to forgive us our sins and to cleanse us from all unrighteousness. If we say we have not sinned, we make him a liar, and his word is not in us."** The Bible does not say in verse 9 above, "If we *admit* our sins, then he is faithful…" The heart of this issue is that in the case of admission of guilt one is simply "getting caught" after trying to hide the sin. *True confession and repentance reflects a heart that desires accountability; a heart that wants someone to speak into their lives and help them grow in this area of struggle – a heart that longs to be pleasing to God.*

The Bible encourages Christians to confess their sins because responsibility goes hand in hand with confession. Do you remember studying Proverbs 28:13? **"Whoever conceals his transgressions will not prosper, but he who confesses and forsakes them will obtain mercy."** The important action that follows a confession is to forsake, or renounce by turning away from, your transgressions that are violations of God's laws. Responsibility is a key element for both the confession part and the forsaking part of repentance.

- When you are responsible, you take preventative measures to insure that you do not get tempted to partake in drugs and alcohol.

- When you are responsible, you forsake alcohol and drugs by avoiding parties, bars, and places where you know that alcohol will be served.

- When you are responsible, you avoid and forsake persons with whom you used to drink alcohol and deal drugs.

- When you are responsible, you plan ahead to avoid any places, persons, and items that could tempt you to be irresponsible by giving into your addiction.

- When you are responsible, you confess your sin, ask for forgiveness, and have repentant actions that match your confession of guilt.

When someone is willing and making strong efforts and practical actions to overcome an addiction, the person grows in the area of responsibility.

Gratitude

After you have learned to put-off and put-on, verse 19 reveals that you, the former drunkard, begin to exhibit a thankful heart as you are "addressing" others with singing. This person must put-on a "joyful" mentality to replace his "perishing" mentality. Gratitude is the second evident fruit of repentance. Let's look again at Ephesians 5:18-21:

> **And do not get drunk with wine, for that is debauchery, but be filled with the Spirit, addressing one another in psalms and hymns and spiritual songs, singing and making melody to the Lord with all your heart, giving thanks always and for everything to God the Father in the name of our Lord Jesus Christ, submitting to one another out of reverence for Christ.**

Deliverance from the bondage of addiction produces singing unto the Lord from the bottom of one's heart. Have you ever heard a testimony from someone who has been set free from addiction? If you have, then you know that the person is enthusiastic and passionate about what the Lord has done for them. The filling of the Holy Spirit produces the fruit of **"love, joy, peace, patience, kindness, goodness, faithfulness, gentleness, self-control"** and it becomes clearly evident to other people! Because of being filled with the Holy Spirit, the Christian will exhibit two changes evident to everyone who loves that person.

1. *Eternally Focused, Heavenly Minded*

The first change is that the filling of the Spirit leads to loving God more. The repentant person seeks to learn more about God and His ways. Also, the repentant person seeks to glorify God in his actions. The filling of the Spirit leads to having an eternal focus rather than a temporal, pleasure-driven focus. The repentant person becomes "heavenly-minded."

2. *Others Focused, Loving Others*

The second change produced by the filling of the Holy Spirit leads to loving others more. The repentant person begins to love others first and to put the needs of others before his own selfish desires. Typically, addicts have tender hearts toward the needs of the homeless, strangers, widows, orphans, and other groups of people, and yet they struggle sometimes in seeing the needs or meeting the needs of those who live in the same house. A dramatic change produced by the Spirit will be evident to those around you when you put others ahead of yourself.

Others will note the change in you because Luke 6:45 states: **"The good person out of the good treasure of his heart produces good, and the evil person out of his evil treasure produces evil, for out of the abundance of the heart his mouth speaks."** In Ephesians

5:19, the Spirit-filled person is **"singing and making melody to the Lord with all your heart"** The grateful Christian addict is overjoyed at the goodness of God causing his words to pour out grace to other people. What others begin to hear out of the mouth of the Christian addict are words that are so beautiful that it sounds like singing!

Remember that Proverbs 31:6-7 says, **"Give strong drink to the one who is perishing, and wine to those in bitter distress; let them drink and forget their poverty and remember their misery no more."** The old mentality of the addicted person still enslaved to substance abuse and addiction is a "perishing" mentality of being depressed and in "bitter distress." (Review chapters on Idolatry and the Perishing Mentality) The new mentality of the addicted person set free from substance abuse and addiction is one of thankfulness as Ephesians 5:20 describes that he is **"giving thanks always and for everything to God the Father in the name of our Lord Jesus Christ."** Do not miss the significance of this verse! The repentant person is thankful for *everything*, including the good and the bad that happens to him.

Just What Is "My Good" Anyway?

God does not promise that all things will be good from this point forward for the reformed addict. In Romans 8:28, God says: **"And we know that for those who love God all things work together for good, for those who are called according to _His_ purpose"** *(emphasis mine)*. All things will eventually work out for the benefit of *those who love God* and are called according to His purpose. What is the "good" in Romans 8:28 that will benefit the transformed addict? The "good" means that God will use all things in your life to draw you closer to Him because He loves you and is working in your life for your sanctification. Your relationship with God will become more intimate than ever before.

Most people are deceived by thinking that the "good" in Romans 8:28 is *their* idea of what good should be. In other words, they think "good" should mean that they will hit the lottery; be rich; have an attractive, flawless spouse; own a new home with a white, picket fence; have perfect children; be honored in their community for their generosity; and so forth. But all these things have a temporal focus. God has an eternal focus and a purpose for your life since He is the potter and you are the clay. Your new life in Christ belongs to Him alone and you are now His servant to be used however He pleases.

The best news of all is that God is love and He is good. He only wants what is best for you and He will sustain you. One of His "best" goals for you is to make you mature in your faith, thinking, feelings, and acting. For this reason, the Spirit-filled person has reason to be joyful as he begins to enjoy the kingdom of God **"for the kingdom of God is not a matter of eating and drinking but of righteousness and peace and joy in the Holy Spirit"**[137] while living here on the earth! This change in living is very dramatic.

Submission

The third evidence of repentance and change in a Christian substance abuser's life is an attitude of being submissive. Submission is an extremely difficult area for any person (even more so for an addict) to address because of the natural rebellion that rules the sinner's heart. You are probably saying, "I agreed with most of what you said in this book until you used that awful word: submission." Americans often view authority as oppressive and generally have a negative view of authority primarily because the culture fosters the idea that "you are the final authority in anything that pertains to you."

Satan also propagates the lie that God's authority is not good and loving authority. Satan has been promoting this lie since Adam and Eve in Genesis 3:1-5. Do not believe the lie that the authority you have given yourself is as good as God's authority you have given yourself is as good as God's authority over you. Do you think you can trust yourself more than the Lord of heaven and earth? Where is God's authority in your life? Is He your Creator and do you belong to Him?

In active physical addiction, a person primarily does what he wants to do. Even if not using alcohol or drugs, the person in this "perishing" mentality is self-centered and primarily does what will best relieve his misery and pain. The world describes this condition as being a "dry drunk" because there is no heart change, even though the one, specific behavior of drunkenness is changed. The person continues to be selfish and primarily exhibits his self-interests to those who care most about him.

Interestingly, a very recent article published in Newsweek[138]

---

[137]Romans 14:17.
[138]From an article entitled: "What Addicts Need" published in Newsweek March 3, 2008 issue.

reported that there is now a drug named, "Vivitrol®, a monthly injection that prevents patients from drinking alcohol by obliterating its ability to intoxicate." People all over the world can be given a "vaccine" to guard them against intoxication, thus supposedly preventing addiction. So we once again observe the world's answer to addiction: prevent the outward behavior, with no regard for the *heart of addiction*. The person who receives this vaccine is still capable of having a heart of addiction, one that wants to use the "go button" for anything pleasurable.

On the other hand, the transformed person who has experienced a genuine change of heart, does not exhibit the selfishness, stubbornness, and rebellion of the "dry drunk." Ephesians 5:21 tells you that the transformed addict is now submitting to another person *"out of reverence for Christ."* The transformed addict is now teachable and willing as evidenced by a submissive spirit. The aspect of a submissive lifestyle is a radical transformation of the reformed addict. This is true evidence of the power of God because substance abusers are not submissive by nature. Substance abusers are the opposite of submissive. They are called idolatrous, rebellious, and foolish according to the Bible.

To Whom Must I Submit?

How does this submission manifest itself practically in your life? You need to find a Bible-teaching church and submit to its leadership. Within the church, find an individual who is more mature in the Christian faith than you to disciple and counsel you. Ideally, a pastor, assistant pastor, elder, or deacon in the church is the best choice since God has ordained the elders of the church to shepherd God's people by being spiritual leaders who look after their souls. In this type of submissive relationship, you would meet regularly with your church leader, read everything that the leader recommends for you to read, and follow the advice of the leader. Substance abuse is spiritual warfare, and you need strong leadership especially since you have always sought to do things "your way." You need to learn God's ways according to Scripture and the best teacher of Scripture is an ordained leader in the church. Shepherding and serving God's people are primary duties of the leadership of the church.[139]

If none of the leaders in the church is available, find a Christian friend who is more spiritually mature in the faith than you are.

---

[139]I Peter 5:2-3.

The world refers to this type of person as a sponsor, a mentor, or a spiritual coach, but these titles lack the necessary spiritual authority of a leader of the church. God gives authority to spiritual leaders in the church. However, because it is so essential for the repentant, addicted person to be brought under the submission of a Christian leader, I recommend getting a trusted friend to shepherd, disciple, and train you if a church leader is not available.

If the submission process takes the form of one friend to another friend for the transformed addict, you want to be sure you know what the Bible means by "submission." Your submission to this friend comes only from your "reverence for Christ" as Ephesians chapter 5 verse 21 mentions. Reverencing Christ means fearing God. Proverbs 9:10 says, **"The fear of the Lord is the beginning of wisdom,"** and it is out of this respect and fear for God that you are willing to submit to a trusted Christian brother. By submitting, you are *willingly* placing your trust in God that He will guide your friend to teach you about the character of your Heavenly Father. As long as your friend's counsel is biblically-derived, follow his instruction to the best of your ability. If your friend or any spiritual leader commands or asks you to sin, you are not obligated to follow that command or request because you are never permitted to sin against God for any reason.

The submission involved in Ephesians 5:21 is a command of God but is a result of a changed and *willing* heart that wants to learn more about God from a godly leader. It is willful submission. The central issue is that the transformed addict is no longer doing things his way and in his own strength but is ultimately trusting in God by trusting in this shepherd-type person. The transforming addict needs to develop an intimate relationship with someone who is going to **speak the truth in love** at all times. The transforming Christian ought to desire the feedback and constructive criticism of someone who knows him or her intimately.

Men ought to submit to men and women ought to submit to women. It is not a good idea to mix the sexes when suggesting friendship, discipleship, and submission for the substance abuser. The only exception is in the area of spouses. Ephesians 5:22 states: **"Wives, submit to your own husbands, as to the Lord."** It is best for wives to submit to their husbands first and to develop a submissive-type relationship with a more spiritually mature woman second.

A relationship with another godly woman can be a great

blessing. The only warning is that sometimes people are deceived by others who appear to be godly but do not know the Word of God. Therefore, use great caution and discernment in selecting a mentor who not only knows but also lives obediently to the Word of God. For wives, it is wise to have the husband be directly involved in the choice of this outside friend. A husband's insight and approval of the establishment of this relationship is important. Often a pastor's recommendation is valuable.

Likewise, a wonderful resource to help change a husband is a godly wife.[140] The husband is encouraged to sit down with his wife to devise a "covenant plan for change" for the mutual benefit of their marriage. Mutually agreed upon parameters can be set at that time. For example, the wife may want the husband home by 5:30 p.m. and the repentant husband would want to honor that request of his wife as unto the Lord. The husband may think that 5:30 is not realistic so the two of them may agree upon 6:00 p.m. as an arrival time.

If both spouses are Christians, then some parameters could be easily established in an effort to help the person stay on the clean and sober path of transformation. If only one of the spouses is a Christian, then outside help in terms of a mediator may be needed. If help is needed, go to a pastor, elder, deacon, biblical counselor, or trusted Christian friend to help mediate this process.

Submission to God by Having a Disciplined Lifestyle

You must willingly submit to God and can do so by developing structure and discipline. Because you have led such an unstructured and undisciplined life, I recommend that you write out a schedule of planned activities for your entire day, week, and month. Again, use Appendix F as a guideline to help you with this assignment. You need to live according to this schedule and not waver from it for any reason. You should get up much earlier than you are accustomed, and become a creature of the day rather than of the night according to I Thessalonians 5:7-8. A disciplined lifestyle will yield much fruit for you.

Additionally, Appendix I is a quick reference to help you recognize the typical changes you should experience while you are in the process of transformation. While not specific, this appendix is very helpful in determining your progress. The Bible says that what

---

[140]Ephesians 5:21.

is in the heart will eventually come out of the mouth. What is in your heart will also become outwardly visible by your actions. Luke 6:45 states: **"The good person out of the good treasure of his heart produces good, and the evil person out of his evil treasure produces evil, for out of the abundance of the heart his mouth speaks."** My prayer for you is that God will reveal to you whether or not you have truly experienced a heart change.

A Few Thoughts about Group Meetings

The Christian substance abuser and addict must be cautious about the types of group activities he chooses to attend. Secular, self-help group meetings are recommended only for *unbelievers – not for Christians.* It is normal for transforming addicts to long to be around other people who "understand" what it is like to be physically addicted. However, sometimes the Christian addict ought to be around others who do *not* think as he does so that he can learn a better way of thinking and acting.

Ideally, Christians should either find or start a small group of three or more, same sex, growing Christians from their local church body. These meetings should consist of prayer, Bible study, discussion, fellowship, and real accountability. Accountability must be open, honest, and deep so that the other members can pray accurately and help appropriately. It is best if a deacon or elder in the church leads these meetings. The length of these meetings is recommended to be at least an hour (longer if time permits) so that each person has adequate time to speak.

A warning is in order here: **"Do not be deceived: Bad company ruins good morals."**[141] It is sometimes easy for a group meeting to get off the track of the transforming truth of God's Word by wallowing in the detailed descriptions of their past sins. Strong Christian leadership is necessary in the beginning stages of these groups.

God's Mighty Resources for You

The Word of God tells us that God has provided many resources for you to begin the lifelong process of change and growth. The main ones are:

- The sacrifice of His Son

---

[141]I Corinthians 15:33.

- The Holy Spirit
- The Bible
- A measure of faith[142]
- Prayer
- The local church body of believers in Christ Jesus
- Elders, deacons, and leaders of the church
- The power to make wise choices and decisions by the Word and the illumination of the Holy Spirit.

These are all excellent resources provided by the Lord for the Christian. They are magnificently sufficient and are far superior to secular treatment programs and worldly wisdom. Responsible Christian substance abusers and addicts must begin to tap into these resources in order for these principles to start working in their life. Then transformation will start taking place.

Prayer of Heart Change and Application

Dear Heavenly Father, Help me to become more responsible, grateful, and submissive to the authorities that you have placed over me. Do not let me blame anyone or anything else for my addictive problems. Place in me a joyful attitude that is grateful for all you have done for me including the gift of eternal life. Cause me to tap into your mighty resources so these changes can take place in my life. Make me willing to submit to others out of my love for you, knowing that I am going to be protected and grow as a result of my willing obedience. Amen.

---

[142]Romans 12:3.

Chapter 21
Seven Things for Which to Pray

Here are seven things that are biblically-mandated for which you should pray:

1. Be Enlightened

You and I need to know what is in our own hearts and what purpose God has called us to fulfill. Pray that the wonderful things in His law will be lit up for you. Psalm 119:18 says, **"Open my eyes, that I may behold wondrous things out of your law."** You and I can prayerfully request the same thing of the Lord when reading the Bible. We must pray that the Holy Spirit will enlighten our eyes as we read His Word in the Holy Scriptures. Paul writes in Ephesians 1:17-18:

> **...that the God of our Lord Jesus Christ, the Father of glory, may give you a spirit of wisdom and of revelation in the knowledge of him, having the eyes of your hearts enlightened, that you may know what is the hope to which he has called you, what are the riches of his glorious inheritance in the saints.**

2. Be Empowered

We must pray that the Holy Spirit will empower us to victory over addiction **"for it is God who works in you, both to will and to work for his good pleasure,"** according to Philippians 2:13. God creates in your heart a change from your desires to fulfill *self-centered and temporary* pleasures to a desire to fulfill *self-less and everlasting* pleasures that please God first and foremost. The primary goal of the biblical counselor is to challenge the Christian addict to desire nothing less than this type of genuine heart change. God must give you power.

The Christian who struggles with excessive drinking has the powerful Person of the Holy Spirit working inside his own heart and mind to bring about changes that are pleasing to God. I Corinthians 6:19 states, **"Or do you not know that your body is a temple of the Holy Spirit within you, whom you have from God?"** We may boldly proclaim the same thing that the Apostle Paul stated in Philippians

185

4:13, **"I can do all things through Him who strengthens me."** The "Him" in this verse is the Person of the Holy Spirit. Jesus said to his followers regarding the promise of the Holy Spirit: **"You know him, for he dwells with you and will be in you."**[143]

3. Be Studious

We must exercise our faith in Jesus Christ and in God's Word. God spoke the world into existence in Genesis 1. Over and over the Bible says "God said" demonstrating the power of His Word to create and to change his creation. Defeated Christians who enter the counseling office have tried to overcome their addiction problem by praying more, going to secular meetings, attending church more frequently, or by asking someone at work for their opinion. However, the defeated person rarely says that he has *vigorously studied the Bible* seeking answers to his addiction problem. **"Do your best to present yourself to God as one approved, a worker who has no need to be ashamed, rightly handling the word of truth."**[144] Another good scriptural command related to being studious is: **"Avoid the irreverent babble and contradictions of what is falsely called "knowledge," for by professing it some have swerved from the faith."**[145]

The Bible is not written like an encyclopedia in which you turn to the "A" section of the book to read about everything that God says about addiction. The Bible is written to provide truthful answers for you, but it is written for the bigger purpose of revealing God's character, thoughts, ways, and life-giving words to you. Join a Bible-teaching church today and seek out those who will join you in your search to learn more about your Creator. Don't you want to know more about the Being who made you?

4. Be Decisive

Revelation says: **"I know your works: you are neither cold nor hot. Would that you were either cold or hot! So, because you are lukewarm, and neither hot nor cold, I will spit you out of my mouth."**[146]

You need to make a decision to obey God regardless of your

---

[143]John 14:17.
[144]II Timothy 2:15.
[145]I Timothy 6:20b.
[146]Revelation 3:15-16.

feelings, thoughts, and ideas. Too many times, people live in the "gray area" of indecision by "staying on the fence." They cannot decide whether to commit to abstaining from drinking alcoholic beverages for an extended period of time or whether they are a social drinker who can drink alcohol responsibly without sin accompanying their actions. Indecision is confusing to the Christian addict. God wants a total commitment from you. After all, His Son gave His life through his sacrificial atoning death. You now belong to God. He has bought you with the price of His only begotten Son. Therefore, commit yourself to living an obedient lifestyle unto God by putting into practice the principles we have studied.

5. Be Diligent

2 Peter 1:10 says, **"Therefore, brothers, be all the more diligent to make your calling and election sure, for if you practice these qualities you will never fall." 2 Peter 3:14** continues **"Therefore, beloved, since you are waiting for these, be diligent to be found by him without spot or blemish, and at peace."** Continually remind yourself that His Word alone is true and sufficient to help you live a godly and pleasing life unto the Lord. Read the book you are now holding in your hands with your copy of God's Word open right beside you. This will result in the Holy Spirit allowing you to **"taste and see that the Lord is good"** as the psalmist writes in Psalm 34:8. God is Sovereign and His counsel will stand forever. Psalm 33:10-11 says, **"The Lord brings the counsel of the nations to nothing; he frustrates the plans of the peoples. The counsel of the Lord stands forever, the plans of his heart to all generations."** God's counsel is far superior to the best wisdom and counsel that mankind has to offer. Don't you want to adopt His wisdom and strategies for attacking this problem of addiction in your life?

God's answers are the only ones you need because they are completely true. This book is intended to teach you what God says about the problem of addiction in His book of Truth called the Bible. What a wonderful blessing it will be to you when you realize that God enables Holy Spirit-filled Christians to understand what He means in His Word, the Bible, and that God empowers Christians to overcome any addiction!

As John 8:31-32 says: **"So Jesus said to the Jews who had believed in him, 'If you abide in my word, you are truly my** disciples, and you will know the truth, and the truth will set you free.'" The Christian can take great comfort in the words Jesus emphatically added when He was confronting the Jews in John 8:36, **"So if the Son sets you free, you will be free indeed."** Hopefully now, you are convinced that God has the resources you need to be free from the bondage of addiction and has given them all to you as a free gift! Abide in the Word diligently and be free!

6. Be Joyful

Recall that the "perishing" mentality must be "put off," and you need a new mentality to "put on" to replace it. The mentality you need to put on is the "joyful" mentality. Remember that being joyful is a state of mind and a way of thinking about your circumstances. Happiness is a fleeting emotion, but biblical joy refers to a purposeful way of thinking.

James 1:2-3 states: **"Count it all joy, my brothers, when you meet trials of various kinds, for you know that the testing of your faith produces steadfastness."** To **"count it all joy"** means to think (or to reckon and determine) that these trials and situational problems that are testing your faith are **good** for you because they will be to your benefit when they end. Joy is focusing upon God's ultimate plan for your life and your growth in Christ. God's perspective of your circumstances is much different than your own perspective because you belong to Him. You are His creation and a new creation in Christ.

You must purpose in your heart to be joyful about your trials and about your station in life. Be content with where the Lord has placed you in His Sovereign plan. A "joyful" mentality is best maintained as one understands God's Sovereign power and God's character. The same God who created all of the billions of stars in the heavens is that same God who loves you. What else do you need to know in order to develop a "joyful" mentality?

God formed you and God has allowed your circumstances to be what they are because He means them to shape you for your good and for His glory. Romans 8:28-29 should remind you:

> And we know that for those who love God all things work together for good, for those who are called according to his purpose. For those whom he foreknew he also predestined to be conformed to the image of his Son, in order that he might be the firstborn among many brothers.

You must now live for God and be addicted to the things of God.

When you keep your eyes on Christ Jesus, you will not sink in the ocean of your problems and circumstances. Matthew 14:28-33 tells the lesson Peter learned about keeping his eyes upon Christ Jesus:

> **And Peter answered him, "Lord, if it is you, command me to come to you on the water." He said, "Come." So Peter got out of the boat and walked on the water and came to Jesus. But when he saw the wind, he was afraid, and beginning to sink he cried out, "Lord, save me." Jesus immediately reached out his hand and took hold of him, saying to him, "O you of little faith, why did you doubt?" And when they got into the boat, the wind ceased. And those in the boat worshiped him, saying, "Truly you are the Son of God."**

Peter became afraid when he looked around at his circumstances, and he began to sink in the water. When Peter changed his focus from Jesus to his circumstances, he began to perish in the water. The grace of God is that he saved Peter despite his fear and lack of faith in Christ Jesus. *Likewise, you have been saved by the grace of God despite your fear and doubt.* You must keep your eyes fixed upon Christ Jesus by truly worshiping God at all times. Worshiping God is putting Him first in every aspect and in every moment of your life. Instead of constantly thinking about drugs, alcohol, and getting "high" due to these "perishing" thoughts, you must continually focus on the blessings of God, His goodness to you, and His purposes for your current set of circumstances. Then (and only then) will you develop a thought-life of being "joyful" despite the trying circumstances of life in a fallen world corrupted by sin. 2 Corinthians 6:2b-10 gives great explanation of this seemingly illogical (to man's finite mind) command to rejoice, or be joyful:

> **Behold, now is the favorable time; behold, now is the day of salvation. We put no obstacle in anyone's way, so that no fault may be found with our ministry, but as servants of God we commend ourselves in every way: by great endurance, in afflictions, hardships, calamities, beatings, imprisonments, riots, labors, sleepless nights, hunger; by purity,**

> knowledge, patience, kindness, the Holy Spirit, genuine love, by truthful speech, and the power of God; with the weapons of righteousness for the right hand and for the left; through honor and dishonor, through slander and praise. We are treated as impostors, and yet are true; as unknown, and yet well known; as dying, and behold, we live; as punished, and yet not killed; as sorrowful, yet always rejoicing; as poor, yet making many rich; as having nothing, yet possessing everything.

Remember that your thoughts are primarily the problem because they lead to emotions and then to actions. Everything begins in your thoughts. Your thoughts must become joyful to the point that you understand God intends your problems to be for your good. *You are not to be a fake by pretending to be externally happy and joyful about life's problems; rather you are to reckon your horrible circumstances as a means to ultimately making you a better person.* In addition, you must realize that life is not "all about you" as you are God's property and He wants to fulfill *His* purpose for your life. As you learn to serve Him, you will be more happy, joyful, and content. As the Holy Spirit works to produce in you more holiness and obedience, then joy will follow. *God is not as interested in your happiness as He is in your holiness.*

7. Be a Standing Stone through Your Life Story

Pray about how to write out your life's story. Use Appendix J to help you do this well. When you reflect back on your life, you can really begin to see God's Sovereign hand of grace and mercy in your life. You will also be reminded of many of the lessons you learned about God throughout your lifetime. You will be surprised at how many of those lessons were taught to you during times of severe emotional suffering, hurt, rejection, and pain. A life story is a wonderful way to erect a "standing stone" to remind you of the testimonies of what God has done in your heart throughout your life.

In the days of Joshua, the Lord commanded His people to erect twelve standing stones so that they would always be reminded of the miracle that God did for them and so they could tell others. Joshua 4:5-7 states:

And Joshua said to them, 'Pass on before the ark of the Lord your God into the midst of the Jordan, and take up each of you a stone upon his shoulder, according to the number of the tribes of the people of Israel, that this may be a sign among you. When your children ask in time to come, 'What do those stones mean to you?' then you shall tell them that the waters of the Jordan were cut off before the ark of the covenant of the Lord. When it passed over the Jordan, the waters of the Jordan were cut off. So these stones shall be to the people of Israel a memorial forever.'

A life story can be kept and shared with your children, grandchildren, and great grandchildren for many years to come. Use your life to glorify the only true God who is worthy of all praise. All who see your story will pause and think, "What happened here? This is not a chance occurrence. These events did not just happen by chance. What did God do here?" Just like the children of Israel you will have an opportunity to share your story.

Prayer of Heart Change and Application

Dear Heavenly Father, Thank you again for the many resources that you have provided for me to overcome drunkenness. I do not have to battle this problem in my own strength because you strengthen me. Help me to be enlightened by your Word, empowered by your Holy Spirit, studious of your Word, decisive about obedience to your Word, diligent to study your Word, joyful in my circumstances, and faithful and not fearful. Take my life story and let it be a standing stone unto Thee. I love you, Lord. Amen.

Chapter 22
Taking a Nazirite Vow Under the Care of a Physician

After having experienced all the awful consequences of drunkenness, the person in Proverbs 23:35 still has not had a heart change because he **"must have another drink."** It is a very tragic picture of the unrepentant, unchanged heart. If a Christian substance abuser is truly repentant and his heart has been changed by the Holy Spirit, then he will want to do everything to demonstrate his willingness to protect himself from recurring temptations and "relapses."[147] This change of heart may manifest itself by the addict's willingness to make a Nazirite vow unto the Lord. Numbers 6:1-8 states what a Nazirite vow entails:

> **And the Lord spoke to Moses, saying, 'Speak to the people of Israel and say to them, when either a man or a woman makes a special vow, the vow of a Nazirite, to separate himself to the Lord, he shall separate himself from wine and strong drink. He shall drink no vinegar made from wine or strong drink and shall not drink any juice of grapes or eat grapes, fresh or dried. All the days of his separation he shall eat nothing that is produced by the grapevine, not even the seeds or the skins. All the days of his vow of separation, no razor shall touch his head. Until the time is completed for which he separates himself to the Lord, he shall be holy. He shall let the locks of hair of his head grow long. All the days that he separates himself to the Lord he shall not go near a dead body. Not even for his father or for his mother, for brother or sister, if they die, shall he make himself unclean, because his separation to God is on his head. All the days of his separation he is holy to the Lord.'**

---

[147]Luke 15:11-32. Specifically, verses 18-21 demonstrate a repentant heart attitude of humility!

There are three parts to swearing a Nazirite vow. First, is to not cut his hair (verse 5). Second, is to not touch a dead body (which is unclean according to the Old Testament law) (verse 6). Third, is to not eat or drink anything from the vine which would include juice, wine, and strong drink (verses 3-4). Obviously, the first two parts of the vow are not the focus of our study, but certainly the third part of the vow pertaining to the drinking of alcohol is relevant.

In verse 8 above, it states that a person who swears a Nazirite vow is holy to the Lord during all of the days he keeps his temporary vow. By being "holy," the Nazirite was dedicating himself to serve the Lord during this period of time and separate himself from the culture around him. He still lived in the world around him and experienced the very real temptations as those around him, but because of his vow to the Lord, he restricted himself from partaking in anything grown from the vine such as strong wine. The extreme manner in which the Nazirite lived his life caused him to constantly be reminded of his lifelong, radical devotion to live for God's glory. It was a sacrifice.

For a Christian substance abuser, at least initially, it is a very good idea to think of yourself as taking a Nazirite vow regarding intoxicating drugs and alcohol. Neither mood-altering drugs nor alcohol are essential to one's life, so you will not die without alcohol. Warning: Withdrawal symptoms are very real and very dangerous at times. You must seek a medical doctor's care before quitting any substance 'cold turkey.'

Scientific studies periodically circulate that a glass of wine or alcoholic beverage is beneficial to one's health. While this may or may not be true, clearly, alcohol results in impaired judgment. Water and food are essential to one's health, but alcohol and drugs are not. They can be harmful, even though they have a purpose and are helpful in the right time and in the right measure.

A Nazirite vow was *willingly* sworn by a Hebrew to indicate that he was going to lead a separate lifestyle from other Hebrews. It was sworn voluntarily and it could be sworn for a temporary period of time.[148] The heart of the Hebrew who swore such a vow demonstrated a dedication to living a holy life pleasing to God without being concerned about what others might think. As mentioned earlier, it is likely that Timothy in the New Testament took a Nazirite vow. Two other persons whose mothers were instructed during pregnancy by

[148]Numbers 6:20.

God's angel to take a Nazirite vow were John the Baptist (Luke 1:15) and Samson. An angel spoke to Samson's mother as Judges 13:3-5 states:

> **And the angel of the Lord appeared to the woman and said to her, 'Behold, you are barren and have not borne children, but you shall conceive and bear a son. Therefore be careful and drink no wine or strong drink, and eat nothing unclean, for behold, you shall conceive and bear a son. No razor shall come upon his head, for the child shall be a Nazirite to God from the womb, and he shall begin to save Israel from the hand of the Philistines.'**

Samson was an unusual case in that he did not choose to swear a Nazirite vow but was appointed by God to do so from conception. Maybe it is time to consider yourself appointed by God to be a Nazirite for the purpose of being set apart from the culture for God's glory!

If you truly want to make a change in your life, then consider committing to the Lord to abstain from alcoholic beverages or your drug of choice or certain medications for the next six months. A voluntary commitment of this nature is similar to your making a Nazirite vow to the Lord like the Hebrews. You should consider making this type of formal promise unto the Lord. In fact, make this type of commitment to the Lord prior to your attempts to put-off drinking. *It is essential that you seek the help of a trusted Christian medical professional who is aware of your struggles with alcohol and substances* prior to making a Nazirite vow because of the very serious side effects of detoxification from alcohol and other drugs. The commitment will help you to remain clean and sober by focusing upon your oath and promised word to the Lord.

I must warn you sternly, however, before you do this. Deuteronomy 23:21 tells us plainly: **"If you make a vow to the Lord your God, you shall not delay fulfilling it, for the Lord your God will surely require it of you, and you will be guilty of sin."** *Take vows to the Lord seriously and with much prayerful consideration.* Trust in God that He will empower you to fulfill your vow to Him. Then begin putting-on your new thoughts, attitudes, words, and behaviors to pursue and serve God as you begin to see the fruits of a "joyful" lifestyle.

Prayer of Heart Change and Application

Dear Heavenly Father, Give me wisdom to embark upon this plan. I want to make a Nazirite vow to you for the next six months. I do not know how I am going to stay clean and sober, but I know that you will see me through this period of time. Help me find a physician who is wise regarding withdrawal and will point me in the right direction you would have me to take. Fill my mind with your Word and empower me by the Holy Spirit. Thank you for the sacrifice of Jesus Christ and help me to keep my faith in you. Let this vow, if I make it, bring glory to your already glorious Name. Amen.

Chapter 23
Controlled by the Holy Spirit

The Christian addict must begin to allow the Holy Spirit to lead him just as Jesus in the Garden of Gethsemane. In Matthew 26:38-39, Jesus was very troubled about the suffering He was facing:

Then he said to them, "My soul is very sorrowful, even to death; remain here, and watch with me." And going a little farther he fell on his face and prayed, saying, "My Father, if it be possible, let this cup pass from me; nevertheless, not as I will, but as you will."

Understanding Jesus' heart in this prayer will enable you to achieve success in your "transforming" process from addiction.

Jesus never sinned so there is no sin in any of His prayers. It is not a sin to be "sorrowful" as Jesus was about his imminent suffering and death even though He knew it was God's will. In verse 39, Jesus respectfully asks the Father to "let this cup pass from me" meaning that His flesh did not desire to experience the pain and suffering in this way. However, Jesus did not want to obey His flesh but conformed His will to the Father's will by *obeying the leading of the Holy Spirit*. It is no different for you. Later in this same chapter of Scripture, Jesus says in Matthew 26:41: **"Watch and pray that you may not enter into temptation. The spirit indeed is willing, but the flesh is weak."** You cannot give in to your weak flesh but must overcome it and obey the leading of the Holy Spirit just as Jesus did!

What made Jesus conform His will to the Father's will? The answer is the leading of the Holy Spirit. Jesus was always led by the Holy Spirit. He did *not give in* to the will of His own flesh; rather he allowed God's will to be completed. Jesus allowed the Holy Spirit to dominate Him fully. The Christian must allow the Holy Spirit to have control over his will so that he does *not give in* to the temptations of the flesh and its many appetites. The Holy Spirit leads the transforming addict by the written Word of God.

Self-Control: A Fruit of the Spirit

Secular addiction counselors disdain the use of the word, "self-control" because they believe it is condemning to addicts who are victims of the terrible 'disease' of addiction. It is only condemning of addicts if the "self" is trying to "control" itself.

The idea that one's self must be the *source* of the control of "self" is incorrect, not biblical, and indeed is condemning since "self" is not capable of doing the controlling for extended periods of time! That idea of "self" as the source of the control is not what the Bible teaches. In the Bible, "self-control" refers to the idea that the **object** of control is "self." Self is not able to be the *source* of control because the only source of control comes from the Holy Spirit alone. The Holy Spirit controls "self" when one willingly places one's "self" under the Holy Spirit's control just as Jesus did in Matthew 26 above. You must say to yourself and to God, "Not my will, but your will be done, my Heavenly Father." It is willing submission unto God. *The Holy Spirit and each person work together in this process called "sanctification" or growth in Christ.*[149]

Galatians 5:23 lists "self-control" as a fruit of the Holy Spirit that becomes evident in a Christian who is growing and living for Christ alone. I Corinthians 10:31 states: **"So, whether you eat or drink, or whatever you do, do all to the glory of God."** Go back to the earlier chapter ("Redefining the World's Terminology") that dealt with your heart and ask yourself, "Am I doing this for God's glory or is it for self-gratification? Can I do this unto the Lord?" If the answer to both questions is that you are doing it for self and that God will not be glorified by your actions, then do not commit the act.

Self-control has both temporary and eternal value. Remember that I Timothy 4:7-8 states: **"...rather train yourself for godliness; for while bodily training is of some value, godliness is of value in every way, as it holds promise for the present life and also for the life to come."** You need your "self" to be controlled by the Holy Spirit in this life and you will experience its benefits now and in the eternal life to come.

---

[149]Reeder, Harry, "Fruit of the Spirit in Biblical Perspective. Gentleness: The Strength of Truth and the Softness of Grace," sermon series preached at Briarwood Presbyterian Church (PCA), Birmingham, AL, on August 14, 2005. This is just one of an entire sermon series on the fruit of the Spirit by Dr. Reeder and is the most excellent study on it I have ever heard. I urge you to obtain a copy.

Discipline: Training the Body and the Mind to Obey the Holy Spirit

Anything that glorifies God in this life has eternal value, so the Christian addict must seek to glorify God by disciplining himself in all things. The Apostle Paul gave an athletic analogy of "self-control" in I Corinthians 9:24-27:

> Do you not know that in a race all the runners compete, but only one receives the prize? So run that you may obtain it. *Every athlete exercises self-control in all things*. They do it to receive a perishable wreath, but we an imperishable. So I do not run aimlessly; I do not box as one beating the air. But I discipline my body and keep it under control, lest after preaching to others I myself should be disqualified" *(Emphasis mine)*.

The athlete in the above passage exercises self-control in *all things* (verse 25). He carefully watches what he eats and drinks and disciplines his body with physical training and exercise balanced with adequate sleep.

Likewise you must be careful with your body, and with your mind—what you meditate upon. You must have joyful thoughts remembering the character and blessings of God rather than perishing thoughts of *self* and despair. The Holy Spirit is the source of this power. The Holy Spirit works in conjunction with the Word of God. You must memorize, read, study, and meditate upon the Bible allowing your "self" to be fully under the Holy Spirit's control. "Not my will but your will be done, my Lord God" must become the primary thought directing the life of every transforming addict.

Again, the source of the control of self is the Holy Spirit. In active physical addiction, control is lost. Addicts fool themselves and others by thinking they are in control when in reality they are out of control. Proverbs 25:28 states: **"A man without self-control is like a city broken into and left without walls."** In biblical times, a city had walls around it to protect the people from outside invasion, attack, and harm. In this proverb, an addict who lacks self-control is like a city that is unprotected. After the walls of discipline and self-control are broken down, you can easily be tempted, attacked by Satan, and harm will eventually come.

The Bible speaks the truth about addiction. Submission, self-control, and discipline are not concepts you should disdain, but are concepts created by a loving God for your good. God's desire is that you learn how to build up the walls of self-control around your body so that you may be protected from harm. God views self-control and discipline as skills that can be developed and improved upon over time because of His power working in you. As a result of developing these skills, you will become protected from the harm that can devastate your "city"; your family, friends, possessions, and self.

Prayer of Heart Change and Application

Dear Heavenly Father, Control me by the Holy Spirit. Help me to say, "Not my will but your will be done, Lord," just as Jesus prayed in the Garden of Gethsemane. I want to do your will regardless of my feelings, cravings, appetites, and desires. Thank you for being patient with me, Lord. Fulfill your will in and through me. Thank you for the honor of serving you. Amen.

Chapter 24
Focusing Upon Others

An essential element for *remaining* clean and sober for the transforming addict is to focus upon others. Remember that your focus in the past has primarily been upon pleasing yourself and that is why you used your drug of choice. You felt depressed so you drank. You felt lonely so you drank. You felt guilty so you popped pills. You had a successful week at work so you lit up to celebrate. You haven't needed any help devising a reason to drink or use your drug of choice!

The reason for drinking is always rooted in pleasing self rather than thinking of God and others. The majority of our study on addiction has primarily emphasized pleasing God first in all our thoughts, words, and actions. Now, the focus turns to pleasing <u>others</u> before pleasing yourself.

Selfishness vs. Selflessness: Giving to Others

There is a half-truth in the secular realm of counseling that says that the addict "must help himself first" before he can help others. At a basic, theoretical level, it is true that you must become obedient to Christ by being clean and sober prior to becoming a blessing to your loved ones. However, if your primary concern is to help yourself, then your heart has not changed since you are still thinking and acting in a *selfish* manner.

For example, a teenage addict who is now clean and sober demands that her parents forgive her and trust her with the car immediately. She pouts and is cold to her parents when they do not give her the car while they are only trying to encourage her to prove her trustworthiness. She is being selfish and not choosing to see the situation from their perspective.

In the biblical approach to addiction, you must begin looking at the big picture of life and realize that you are not the only person in God's plan. God is using many people to carry out His purposes and you are just one of those people! Your ideas of self-importance fueled by pride are problematic for you whether or not you are clean and sober. *For this reason, the primary goal for the biblical counselor is to counsel and instruct you that your main objective in life is to please God and to love others as much as you already love yourself.*[150]

---

[150]Matthew 22:37-40.

When asked the trick question, "Which of the Ten Commandments is the most important one to keep?" Jesus answered that there are two underlying concepts to the Ten Commandments of God: love God and love others as much as you already love yourself! It is understood that a person *already* loves himself. In Matthew 22:35-40, it states:

> **And one of them, a lawyer, asked him a question to test him. "Teacher, which is the great commandment in the Law?" And he said to him, "You shall love the Lord your God with all your heart and with all your soul and with all your mind. This is the great and first commandment. And a second is like it: You shall love your neighbor as yourself. On these two commandments depend all the Law and the Prophets.**

Jesus cut to the heart of the issue because He knew the sinful heart of mankind!

God has given you responsibilities such as caring for and loving a spouse, children, grandchildren, friends, maintaining a job, house, and car to name a few. You are commanded to be a good steward of those responsibilities and blessings. For example, if you are a husband, then you must begin to love your wife as Ephesians 5:25: **"Husbands, love your wives, as Christ loved the church and gave himself up for her."** Christ gave his life for the church and that is the way a husband is commanded to love his wife! Selfishness must be replaced by *selflessness*.

How do you demonstrate "selflessness"? The answer is that you act in a way that is beneficial to others *without* expecting anything in return. Substance abusers in active physical addiction often manipulate people by lying, misleading by telling half-truths, crying, trying to evoke guilty feelings in others, shifting the blame rather than taking responsibility, and being mired in self-pity. Even when a substance abuser or addict is clean and sober, he or she can still desire to manipulate others. Family members must exercise caution even with a clean and sober substance abuser who has not had a genuine heart change by God.

Two New Slogans to Direct Your Life

If you tend to manipulate others, you probably see other people as a means to an end to achieve some selfish goal. Instead, you need to see how you can minister, serve, or help another person. Rather than *get* from others, you need to *give* to others. Acts 20:35b states: **"It is more blessed to give than to receive,"** and this must become your new slogan for living life! Another great slogan for you is "Not my will but your will be done, Father God." Utilize God's Word to help you develop personal yet meaningful "slogans" for your life's journey.

Secular self-help meetings and modalities understand this concept of helping others as they often say things like, "You've got to give it away to keep it," which means that you have to tell others about this great lifestyle of secular "recovery." These modalities teach their followers to serve others and to tell everyone who suffers from addiction about the great program of "recovering from an addiction." Biblically speaking, this concept is called "evangelism" as converted Christians should *want* to tell others about the goodness of God, how He saved them, and how they are being powerfully "transformed" by Him.

Serving Others

Every Christian needs to be in a position where they are being discipled by someone who is more spiritual, and where they are discipling others who need help. In this way, we are being taught, as well as teaching someone else. This is a balanced, biblical approach to the spiritual relationships necessary for us to successfully overcome an addiction, and live a fruitful Christian life.

The chapter titled, "Responsibility, Gratitude, and Submission," describes the essential elements of the submission relationship. This relationship is one in which you receive instruction, admonition, counsel, encouragement, and blessing from someone who is more spiritual than you. Now we take it a step further and add the opportunity to be teaching someone else the very things you are learning! For a married person, an ideal person to teach is his or her spouse and/or children! For an unmarried person, a younger person or someone who is younger in the Christian faith is an ideal candidate.

Do not underestimate the importance of this biblical truth in your process of "transformation." Mentoring others, (also called discipling), is critical to your spiritual growth for many reasons:

- It allows you to "get out of yourself" and into another person's problems which will make you more grateful for your blessings.

- It will make you a better "people person" and you will thrive in a close spiritual setting with other people.
- This is your purpose in life. Many transforming addicts can be of great service to the church and ultimately to the Lord. Truly transformed addicts make great lay counselors in the church.

If you cannot find that one person to mentor, you can always visit nursing homes, hospitals, and the like to encourage suffering people. Volunteer at a rescue mission for the homeless or a nursing home and be used by God! Visit widows. Give some time to local Boys and Girls Clubs. The possibilities are endless![151]

Do not, however, think you can help old "friends" who are still actively using. There is a warning in Galatians 6:1 that states: **Brothers, if anyone is caught in any transgression, you who are spiritual should restore him in a spirit of gentleness.** *Keep watch on yourself, lest you too be tempted* (Emphasis mine). Certainly, after a significant period of time such as three years, the Christian addict can reach out to help an old "friend" who is active in the addiction but he or she must never attempt to help *alone*. If the Christian addict wants to help an old "friend," take a deacon, elder, or trusted, mature Christian friend along with you, but never go alone! It will cause too much temptation.[152]

Avoiding the Offending of Others

Is there ever a time when someone can drink alcohol or use drugs and not be sinning? Romans 14:20-23 says:

> **Do not, for the sake of food, destroy the work of God. Everything is indeed clean, but it is wrong for anyone to make another stumble by what he eats. It is good not to eat meat or drink wine or do anything that causes your brother to stumble. The faith that you have, keep between yourself and God. Blessed is the one who has no reason to pass judgment on himself for what he approves. But whoever has doubts is condemned if he eats, because the eating is not from faith. For whatever does not proceed from faith is sin.**

---

[151]James 1:27
[152]Mark 6:7.

When the apostle Paul addressed the situation of not eating meat because it might cause your brother to stumble, he was also telling us that there may be situations in which you can drink an alcoholic beverage without sin. Again, the problem for the Christian believer is not the number of fermented microbes that are in the alcoholic beverage. The problem is a heart issue. Ask yourself three key questions to determine if indeed this is a sin matter in your heart:

1. What is the quantity of the beverage and is it excessive?
2. What is my heart's desire for drinking this beverage?
3. Will my drinking of this beverage cause me or my brother or sister in Christ to stumble?

To answer the first question, the quantity of the beverage is easy to measure because it is tangible, but you must be honest. Have you ever said, "I've only had two beers," when in reality, two beers are all you could remember having but you may have had more? Ask yourself: Do I drink too much or use the legal or illegal drug to excess? If the answer is "yes," then you have committed a sin against God the Father. Psalm 51:3-4 states: **"For I know my transgressions, and my sin is ever before me. Against you, you only, have I sinned and done what is evil in your sight…"**

On the other hand, answering the second question is more difficult because it is an issue of the heart. It is not easy to measure because it is intangible and as God reminds you in Jeremiah 17:9-10:

> **The heart is deceitful above all things, and desperately sick; who can understand it? I the Lord search the heart and test the mind, to give every man according to his ways, according to the fruit of his deeds.**

This verse is being mentioned over and over because so many are deceived by thinking that truth comes from within when it really comes from an outside source: God's Word—the Bible.

It often takes another person using God's Word to help you to see the truth. That person may need to confront you with the truth in love so that you turn away from the sin that is causing your relationship with Christ to be hindered.

- Why do you want to drink this alcoholic beverage?
- Are you avoiding emotional pain?

- Are you wanting to "escape" from the troubles of real life?
- Why do you want to take this prescription medication when you are not really in serious physical pain?
- Is it because you want to glorify God or is it because you are looking for a temporary fix?

The third key question to ask yourself pertains to offending others, and it is complex because it has to do with your focus for the well-being of others. In Matthew 22:37-40, Jesus commands you:

> **And he said to him, "You shall love the Lord your God with all your heart and with all your soul and with all your mind. This is the great and first commandment. And a second is like it: You shall love your neighbor as yourself. On these two commandments depend all the Law and the Prophets.**

Jesus does not command you to love yourself. Why is that? Jesus does not have to teach us to love ourselves. Scripture teaches that it is understood that man loves himself already. No one has to teach a child to cry or throw a temper tantrum in order to get what he wants because the child is born with this innate love of self.

Mankind is to love his neighbor and even his enemy as much as he already loves himself. Applying this principle, you must think about your actions in such a way that you are considering how your neighbor will perceive what you are doing and how it will impact your neighbor's view of Christ Jesus. For example, if your neighbor knows that you struggle with addiction and you drink this small amount of alcohol, determine whether your actions will bring glory to God or dishonor to His Holy Name though you are *not* committing any overt sin? You cannot know what someone is thinking but you can determine what the appearance of your actions may be to others.

The Apostle Paul makes it very clear when he teaches this same issue again in I Corinthians 8:7-13:

> **However, not all possess this knowledge. But some, through former association with idols, eat food as really offered to an idol, and their conscience, being weak, is defiled. Food will not commend us to God. We are no worse off if we do not eat, and no better**

> off if we do. But take care that this right of yours does not somehow become a stumbling block to the weak. For if anyone sees you who have knowledge eating in an idol's temple, will he not be encouraged, if his conscience is weak, to eat food offered to idols? And so by your knowledge this weak person is destroyed, the brother for whom Christ died. Thus, sinning against your brothers and wounding their conscience when it is weak, you sin against Christ. Therefore, if food makes my brother stumble, I will never eat meat, lest I make my brother stumble.

Since addiction and drunkenness are really issues of idolatry in one's heart, this teaching of Paul has much relevance. In verse 7, some people through a "former association with idols" are like the former drunkard who is trying to stop drinking now. This former drunkard has a previous association with the idol of drunkenness just as the persons Paul was referring to in this passage of Scripture. The food "really offered to an idol" in these verses is similar to the substance that the modern day drunkard uses. The drunkard is mired in idolatry, too.

To apply this further, the modern day drunkard who purposely drinks this substance (that he once was enslaved to) may be causing his brother to stumble by wounding his brother's conscience. The brother would have to be someone who believes that it is a sin to drink alcohol and could be someone who knows this particular drunkard's past history of idolatry to drunkenness. In this case, drinking the alcohol would be a sin if the drunkard commits the act knowing that a brother may possibly stumble. It is you, the drunkard in this example, whose heart is being examined by the Holy Scriptures in this passage of I Corinthians 8. For this reason, you want to take painstaking measures to consider everything, even the opinions and beliefs of others, when examining your heart anytime that you consider partaking of an intoxicating substance, whether you believe that you are doing it unto the Lord or not.

Will you struggle with sinful thoughts, words, and behaviors related to addiction even after you examine your heart and repent? Yes, again, you will struggle primarily in your thoughts, and it will take your best efforts to work at overcoming the power of your addiction just as it takes work for you to grow in your Christian walk. However, the good news is that your struggles with this sin will lessen in time as you build a sober and obedient lifestyle. It is hard work but worth the spiritual and abundant rewards of God.

Even unbelievers who live obediently to God's laws experience blessings in their lives. For example, a married couple (of two unbelievers) who stay married for fifty years, who do not commit adultery, and who remain sexually pure during the marriage often experience the blessings of family, peace, happiness, and much more due to their obedience to God's laws. They may not even realize that they are obeying God's laws yet they still experience tremendous blessings because it is God's best plan for living. Even their children experience these blessings and avoid the curses of divorce. The general blessings of God are given even to the unrighteous as Matthew 5:44-45 states:

> **But I say to you, Love your enemies and pray for those who persecute you, so that you may be sons of your Father who is in heaven. For he makes his sun rise on the evil and on the good, and sends rain on the just and on the unjust.**

If you are made righteous by God, how much more will you experience His blessings in this life and in the life to come?

Prayer of Heart Change and Application

Dear Heavenly Father, rather than thinking of myself, let me think of others first. Rather than serving myself primarily, enable me to serve others before I serve myself. Do not let me offend others. I want to be a positive ambassador for you, Lord. Help me to know when I am failing to represent you and show me how to honor you publicly and privately. In Christ Jesus' name, I pray. Amen.

Chapter 25

The End of the Matter is Just the Beginning

Idolatry is the proper biblical name in general for substance abuse problems whether you consider yourself a drunkard, binge drinker, binge user, drug addict, substance abuser, "go button pusher," or whatever name you wish to call it. The problem is biblically labeled as the sin of idolatry and it is a heart problem stemming from one's sinful nature. It is a worship problem in that the substance abuser seeks to please himself above pleasing God and others. This worship problem is a universal condition although it is expressed in different ways. The excessive user of alcohol and drugs is his own god; he is actively serving and pleasing the god of Self. Even if you are not using drugs or alcohol, ask yourself: "Am I serving God or seeking to please myself right now?"

In this book, a distinction has been made between two words commonly used regarding the problem of drunkenness: "abuse" and "addiction." Addiction is best defined as the "persistent *habitual* use of a substance known by the user to be harmful." Abuse of an intoxicating substance is defined as the "improper or excessive use, or misuse"[153] of that substance. Do not fool yourself. Abuse, addiction, occasional excessive use of a substance, and drunkenness look different on the outside because of the varying severity of the consequences, but they are all the result of the same inward problem of the heart: idolatry. In the case of drunkenness, idolatry manifests itself by the excessive consumption of alcohol or drugs in order to escape the problems of life and avoid responsibilities—in essence, to feel pleasure and avoid pain or difficulty.

You may belong to either of the following two groups of people who qualify as "idolaters" and "drunkards" under this terminology:

- Those Christians who *occasionally yet excessively abuse* alcohol and drugs but do not consider themselves to be addicted to alcohol and drugs

- Those Christians who are *physically addicted* to alcohol and drugs

---

[153]Merriam-Webster, op. cit.

Both groups are encouraged to read this book and apply the practical instruction to their lives. Excessive use of a substance is a life-dominating and life-devastating sin nature problem; not just a simple sin problem. This sin nature problem requires the Savior's forgiveness and the Holy Spirit's power to overcome, not just your own "will power." It is the "will of God power" that overcomes addiction. The "perishing" mentality fueled by pride, selfishness, and self-pity must be put-off. The mind must be renewed by the Holy Spirit working in conjunction with God's Word under the authority of the local church. A "joyful" and optimistic mentality fueled by serving and pleasing God (and others) must be 'put-on' to replace old attitudes, thoughts, and behaviors. Are you putting off ungodly habits, renewing your mind with Scripture, and putting on new, godly thoughts, words, and behaviors?

It is said in secular circles that the Christian addict has only one thing to change: everything. Changing everything on the outside in terms of behavior and actions **without** renewing the mind and **without** changing the heart attitude (called repentance!) leads to what the world calls an "addictive personality." This "addictive personality" bounces from one addictive object of pleasure to the next, seeking to fill a hole in the heart designed to worship God. While the addictive object may change, the heart attitude of self worship never changes into a proper heart attitude of the worship of and obedience to an Awesome God.

God has "hardwired" all persons to be addicted to worshiping Him alone. In other words, we are created to serve and please Him. God intends for the Christian to be spiritually healthy by having a thriving relationship with the Lord Jesus Christ and healthy relationships with others! By studying the Bible, faithfully attending church, serving in a church ministry, willingly submitting to church leadership, praying regularly, participating in a small group Bible study, and committing oneself to God and serving others, the Christian addict can create godly habits of worship and achieve God's purpose for his life. The Christian addict can begin to **know** his Creator intimately. In turn, he will feel more joyful because he is being used by God to fulfill a divine purpose.

Sometimes humans make life too complicated. God states what life is all about in Ecclesiastes 12:13-14: **The end of the matter; all has been heard. Fear God and keep his commandments, for this is the whole duty of man. For God will bring every deed into judgment, with every secret thing, whether good or evil.** Your addiction or abuse problem starts with your relationship with God. You must fear and respect God in your heart. You must fear God more than you fear what others think and what others may do to you. When you truly commit yourself to understanding God's character as revealed in the Bible, you will learn that:

- He is love
- He is sovereign
- He is the Creator
- He created you
- He knows what is best for you
- He is all-knowing
- He is wise
- He cares for you

Then you will want to keep His commandments because you trust Him more than you trust yourself. Worship God and not yourself.

What must the Christian addict do to maintain a lifestyle that is pleasing to God? In the context of worry and fear, Matthew 6:33-34 gives you the answer:

> **But seek first the kingdom of God and his righteousness, and all these things will be added to you. Therefore do not be anxious about tomorrow, for tomorrow will be anxious for itself. Sufficient for the day is its own trouble.**

The first thing you must do is seek to know more about God's kingdom and His character. Do you know God intimately? How well do you know Him? You are to seek after what is right and do what is right according to God's standards in the Bible. Do not seek after temporary pleasures. When you get to know God intimately, you will begin to develop a trusting relationship with Him. Everything else will take care of itself as your loving Creator will provide all things you truly need. You serve a very good God. Get to know Him more fully today!

The Richness of God's Word

Are you committed to approaching your addiction according to God's Infallible Word? Daily application of biblical principles for overcoming the heart attitude of drunkenness and idolatry pleases God and produces healthy thoughts, motives, words, and actions. The Holy Bible cannot be whittled down into twelve easy steps or ten superb principles for living. It is rich, deep, and meaningful because it reveals a glimpse of the Person of God – His Will, His Son, His Holy Spirit, and His Heart toward us, His creatures.

While mankind offers some nice ideas that can be helpful at times to someone who is a substance abuser, addict, or drunkard, the Christian must turn to the pure Word of God for instruction, rebuke, correction, and disciplined training in righteousness.[154] For the Christian, the primary goal of pleasing God and serving others while maintaining sobriety is essential.

In this book, you have learned about the principles found in God's Word related to the idolatry of drunkenness. You may need to go back over it again so you can absorb more of these concepts and begin applying them to your life. You definitely need to read your Bible over and over because there is so much more in His Word than could ever be written in any book about the Bible. You can utilize the workbook that accompanies this book to help you to dig deeper into properly applying God's Word to your life. I encourage you to do so with a trusted, Christian friend or small group of committed followers of Christ. A Leader's Guide is available.

Why is there such a strong emphasis upon studying and meditating upon God's Word to overcome your addiction? Because many Christians do not take the time to read His Word for themselves but rely upon others to tell them what the Word of God says. Christians must begin the process of renewing their minds on an individual basis so that they can be transformed by truth.

The Most Important Truth

If I have not clearly stated the main point of this entire book, I want to do so right now. This book is *not* primarily about addiction. This book is primarily concerned with Christians having a proper relationship with the Creator of the Universe and with other people. As Christians we must be reminded that we are to serve God rather than thinking of Him as obligated to serve us. God is not a cosmic Santa Claus. God cannot be intimately known by following several man-made steps: "Do this first and this second and this next and

---

[154]II Timothy 3:15-17.

you will know God." This is not true Christianity. True Christian teachings tell us to humble ourselves before God, acknowledging and confessing ourselves to be rebellious sinners desperately in need of God to save us from ourselves by His power and through the Savior He sent, the Lord Jesus Christ.

Addiction is the outward manifestation of the inward problem of the lack of intimate relationship with your Heavenly Father. The drunken behaviors have just been an outflow of that intimacy problem. God graciously wants to have an intimate relationship with you. It is a privilege not a right. God knows that you can best begin to know Him by reading and studying His Word since it best reveals who He is. The Holy Spirit enables you to know Him by opening your eyes when you read and meditate upon Scriptural truths. God wants to reveal Himself to you. Jesus is named "Immanuel" which means "God with us." Jesus reflects God's perfect character in a Man so that God Himself may be known to you.

Take the opportunity to begin knowing the Creator of the universe in a more intimate and meaningful way. You have the rest of your life to cultivate this relationship with Him. You will never know Him completely so it will never get boring, but one day we shall see Him as He is for we shall be like Him. I John 3:2-3 is a promise for all of us who put our hope in Christ Jesus:

> **Beloved, we are God's children now, and what we will be has not yet appeared; but we know that when he appears we will be like him, because we shall see him as he is. And everyone who thus hopes in him purifies himself as he is pure.**

Prayer of Heart Change and Application

Dear Heavenly Father, you are so good, perfect, loving, patient, kind, and faithful to me. You are worthy of my praise. You are worthy of me living my life for you and you alone. Thank you for revealing yourself to me. Thank you for teaching me about the drunkenness and idolatry of addiction. I know the battle has just begun. I know the Holy Spirit is the source of power and will continue to empower me to be victorious over this addiction. I know that my lifelong journey of growing in Christ has just begun, and I am excited because I know it will never be dull or boring. Let me now live to please you and to serve others as much as I already want to please myself. Take my life and transform it into what pleases you, my Creator. Thank you for making me a unique person who can serve you in a special way. Your plan and your purpose are what I live for. Teach me your Word, Lord, so that I may have power and victory over addiction and so that I may know you more deeply. Thank you again for loving me and revealing yourself to me. And let all the people say, Amen. Praise the Lord!

Appendixes

Appendix A
Comparison Chart: The Biblical Church and Self-Help Groups

Self-help groups imitate the Christian church in many ways. Here are some of them:

CHRIST'S CHURCH	SELF-HELP GROUPS
Justification: "born again" of the Holy Spirit (I Corinthians 6:9-11)	Token commemorates the first day of sobriety
Progressive Sanctification-Transformation (never ending process) by the truth of God's Word (Romans 12:1-2)	Recovery (never ending process of growth) by increased self and "spiritual" awareness
Discipleship/Shepherding/Mentoring relationships	Work through recovery materials with a sponsor; sponsor and group relationships.
Accountability; believer speaks the truth in love	Call your sponsor every day (anytime when needed)
Growth in Christ means pray and read the Bible; get wisdom from God and make changes honoring Him	Growth in Recovery means read the self-help books and go to meetings to get wisdom of mankind
Church attendance (Sun. morn/night, Wed. night)	Go to meetings every day if possible
Fellowship with other believers with prayer, biblical principles, encouragement, and truth	Most self-help meetings are called a "fellowship" and often have fun social outings.
Bible Studies with other Christians to learn and grow in the wisdom of God	Secular book studies on recovery principles at self-help meetings to grow in the wisdom of mankind
Ask forgiveness – must be for benefit of others before self and to reconcile the relationship according to Luke 17:3-10	Make amends – often a selfish benefit and motive to clear one's own conscience; sometimes take others into consideration but not a primary motivation

Adoption into the family of Christ; you become a "son" or "daughter" of the Most High God	Acceptance into the fellowship of people of all religions; you become a "label" for life identifying you by your sin forever
Promotes church attendance	Discourages church attendance; promotes self-help
Members are Christian believers and seek to save the lost: unbelievers	Members are "spiritual" people vs. "earth" people who just do not understand the self-help program
Sin nature problem from within; self is problem	Disease from without problem; self is victim
Bible contains many principles to apply to an individual's life with freedom and liberty in Christ	Program is simple with instructions to follow but everyone must work those same principles
Responsibility is key: confess AND hate and forsake your sin because it displeases God	Responsibility is key, but then blame your "disease"- sends a mixed, confusing message
Confess behaviors and thoughts as sin; Jesus died for sin and sinners, not a lifelong "disease," so the power of addiction has been overcome	State that your behaviors and thoughts are caused by a theoretical disease of addiction that you will cope with the rest of your life never to overcome fully
Gospels tell about the life of Jesus and serve as a model for trying to live more like Him everyday	Secular recovery book gives you examples from others who are now living a sober life
Follow Christ for the glory of God	Follow the program, principles, and people for your own good

As you can see, self-help groups mimic the church in many ways. While they claim only to be "spiritual" and not "religious," self-help groups are often "churches for unbelievers." One cannot say that self-help groups have never helped anyone because they have; however, Christians are better served by attending worship services, Bible studies, fellowship meetings, and prayer meetings at their local church. Christians do better to humble themselves and find "accountability partners" in their church, too, rather than outside the local body of believers.

The Gospel is "Good News"

If you are reading this section of the book, there is probably some question in your mind as to whether or not you are a Christian. Where you are going to spend eternity should be a big concern to you. Unfortunately, many people believe there is no afterlife, but that's not what the Bible teaches. The Bible tells us that life on earth is temporary and there is definitely an afterlife. Those who are born again by the Holy Spirit become Christians and will spend their eternal life with the Heavenly Father. Those who do not become Christians will spend their eternal life in an unspeakably horrible place called Hell. Therefore, everyone will inherit one of these two eternal destinations after life on earth.

Although the Gospel message is good news, you must hear the bad news first. The bad news is that apart from Christ you are helpless and sinful. The Bible teaches that everyone is a sinner, in spiritual bondage, and alienated from God because of sin and headed for the eternal destination of hell. Knowledge of sin comes by the law of God which is found in His Word of Truth. God, in his justice, punishes sinners. You cannot save yourself in any way from this punishment. God is serious about sin and He will punish sinners who are not saved by grace through their faith in Jesus Christ.

Jesus alone saves you by grace through faith in Him. His blood was shed to atone for your sins. Eternal life with God is a gracious, free gift from Him. Ephesians 2:8-9 puts it this way: **"For by grace you have been saved through faith. And this is not your own doing; it is the gift of God, not a result of works, so that no one may boast."** Therefore, you cannot come to God in your own strength, with your good deeds, and ask for eternal life unless God draws you to Himself.

Jesus suffered and died for sinners. His blood atones for your sins. The Lord calls sinners like you and me to repent, or turn from sin, and to turn to God. You are given a new heart and a new nature so that you do not have to remain a slave to sin. You are saved to joyfully obey and serve the Lord for His own glory and purposes.[155]

---

[155]Kruis, John G. Quick Scripture Reference for Counseling, Grand Rapids, MI: Baker Books, p. 6.

God's plan and purposes for you may take you in a different direction than you wanted to go, but you can trust His character because He is loving and faithful. God loves His people and no longer sees them as unrepentant sinners, but now sees them as sons who have a relationship with Him.

No one starts out this life in neutral as everyone is born in sin and then commits more sin throughout life. No sin is too big for God to forgive and for you to repent from. No one can earn the gift of eternal life nor does anyone deserve it. Eternal life is a free gift like one you would receive at Christmas. You do not pay for it. Is there any reason why you would not want to pray to receive Jesus Christ as your personal Savior right now? I encourage you to pray right now. A model prayer is the Lord's Prayer in Matthew 6:7-15 but I always recommend that you pray from your heart to God. Do not be concerned about the words you use. In your prayer, confess your sin to God, admit you are a sinner who has lived independently from God, that you have not earned or deserve the free gift of eternal life, and that you desire to have an intimate relationship with God, your Creator, now and forevermore.

When you become a Christian, your new heart and its love for God causes you to want to do whatever pleases God because He deserves it and saved you from the penalty of your sins. Now, you have the Holy Spirit's power living inside you to help you please and obey your new Father God.

Appendix C
Sample Put-off List and Put-on List

You can develop your own list with a blank piece of paper, but this appendix is designed to give you ideas and help you think of things that you may not have considered. You can add anything you want to put-on as long as it is not sinful. Warning: sometimes we make a good thing into an idol which ends up making it a curse rather than a blessing!

THINGS TO PUT-OFF

WHAT:

1. Clothes advertising alcohol and drugs.
2. Cell phones. Too tempting and not needed.
3   Cigarettes. Believe it or not, those who give up smoking improve their ability to stay clean and sober.
4. Coolers used to keep alcoholic drinks cold.
5. Cars. There may be situations in which you need to limit your freedom. No need to drive for a few months. Ask for rides to work. Humble yourself.
6. Secular books and magazines. You know what to read instead (…starts with a "B")
7. Television. Too many beer commercials glamorizing the drunkard's lifestyle.
8. Internet. Too may temptations to do wrong.

WHERE:

1. Bars and restaurants where you used to "hang out" and drink/drug.
2. Houses of old "using buddies," friends, and "drinking buddies."
3. Convenience stores. Too tempting and too easy to pick up a six pack or a cold beer.
4. Grocery store aisles that have liquor and beer only. You can go to the store; just avoid that particular aisle. Do not even look toward the aisle. Look away and focus on other places in the store when you see that aisle.

5. Friends and relatives' houses who drink if only for 6 months or so. Avoid temptation.

6. Places, houses, neighborhoods, and streets where you bought drugs and alcohol. Drive a different route if necessary.

7. Avoid your place of purchase at all costs, and especially if you are alone.

WHO:

1. Some relationships must be put-off permanently while other relationships may only require a temporary put-off.

2. Avoid old "using buddies" and "friends" permanently.

3. Avoid dealers and shady acquaintances at all costs.

4. Avoid meeting new people alone. Have a friend or relative with you.

5. Some relatives may have to be put-off permanently if they drink/drug. Friends, too.

6. Some relatives who drink may be put-off temporarily until you can confide in them and ask them to help you with your struggles.

7. If single, relationships with the opposite sex often need to be put-off.

8. Co-workers who encourage drinking and drugging. Do not associate intimately with them while at work and especially after work hours in a social setting.

WHEN:

1. Put-off being alone for long periods of time (an hour may be too long to some while 30 minutes is too long for others)

2. Put-off feelings of hurt and rejection by going to the person who hurt you directly in order to reconcile the relationship.

3. For the first major holidays when you are sober, consider putting-off where you used to spend your holidays so that you can create a new tradition somewhere else, if necessary.

WHY:

1. Perishing mentality must be put-off as it contributes to depression, hopelessness, anger, self-pity, etc.

2. Do not allow yourself to become a pessimist. You must become balanced.

THINGS TO PUT-ON

WHAT:

1. Clothes advertising Jesus Christ, your church, and Bible verses.

2. Meet in person with an elder, deacon, or mature Christian; coffee or lunch if you like.

3. Chew gum. Put a pocket sized Bible in the exact place where you carried your cigarettes. They are about the same size so it is a great substitute. Read it when you have a physical craving to smoke.

4. Keep a box of Christian CDs, evangelistic tracts, and books in your car where you kept your cooler for cold beer!

5. Walk. Exercise is so good for the transforming Christian addict. Check with your physician first!

6. Christian books and magazines. The Bible.

7. Read a book instead of watching TV. Write your own book based on Scriptures and your life story.

8. Spend the time you would have spent on the internet or watching TV in a real conversation, face-to-face in fellowship with another Christian believer. Have a real relationship with someone and focus upon helping them in some way.

9. Females: Make a meal for someone else and bring it to them.

10. Males: Offer a friend help/service without expecting anything in return.

11. Drink lots of water to replace your physiological thirst and desires for alcohol. Always be drinking something like water, juice, or healthy, non-alcoholic drinks. Experiment and find tasteful, new healthy drinks that you have not tried before.

WHERE:

1. Church, Bible studies, and fellowship meetings with other Christians must be your new "hang out."

2. Invite Christians into your home for fun, fellowship, prayer, or Bible study.

3. Gas up at the pump rather than going into the convenience store. Prepaid credit cards are worth the fees in this situation!

4. Think about the aisles you *can* walk down rather than focusing upon the one aisle that you must avoid. Look at the things you *can* buy and enjoy moderately while at the store.

5. Ask friends and relatives who drink to come over to your house but be clear that they cannot bring alcohol.

6. Plan out a different route to drive home to avoid places, houses, neighborhoods, and streets where you used to buy drugs and alcohol.

WHO:

1. Since some relationships must be put-off permanently while other relationships may only require a temporary put-off, you must put-on relationships that are more healthy and drug free. Be sure to replace a relationship with a new one with the intent for it to be permanent; however, it may only be temporary as time will tell.

2. Get an accountability partner who can speak the truth in love to you.

3. Get a pastor, elder, or deacon who can be your Bible-teaching "dealer" rather than visiting a drug dealer!

4. Meet new people when you have a friend or relative with you.

5. Call relatives that you may have alienated or avoided in the past because you considered them to be "goody two shoes" or "holier than thou" types who did not approve of your partying. These very relatives may become your best relationships.

6. Ask relatives who are Christians to help you by praying for you and calling you and encouraging you to stay sober. Humble yourself and confide in them but use good judgment because not everyone will keep from gossiping.

7. If single, cultivate friendships with the same sex rather than seeking the approval of the opposite sex through romantic relationships.

8. Hang out with co-workers who encourage Christian living and morals. Associate with them while at work and after work hours in a social setting, but only if allowed by your job's rules.

WHEN:

1. Put-on being alone with God for periods of time in prayer and Bible reading.

2. Put-on spending time with other Christian believers for time of fellowship and encouragement.

3. Put-on feelings of love and acceptance by going directly to someone when he hurts you in order to reconcile the relationship. Be meek, humble, and loving.

4. Fill your most tempting time of the day with a special plan to focus upon helping others and studying/worshiping God (i.e. time of day, seasons, holidays, etc.).

WHY:

1. Joyful mentality must be put-on regardless of your circumstances, trials, problems, and adverse situations. Count it all joy (James 1:2). Also, read Romans 8:28-29.

2. Become balanced in your pessimism (or realism as you probably call it) and be an optimist, too! Again, Romans 8:28-29 comes to mind!

3. Develop a gratitude list or a think list based upon Philippians 4:8-9.[156] See Appendix H on how to do this.

---

[156] Adams, Jay, The Christian Counselor's New Testament, Hackettstown, NJ: Timeless Texts, p. 613.

Appendix D
Other Bible Passages Related to Drunkenness and its Consequences

All of the following verses from the Bible pertain to drunkenness and are taken from The Holy Bible: English Standard Version. Wheaton: Good News Publishers, 2001. Spend time looking up each verse and passage of Scripture. Read the verses prior to the reference listed in order to get a better overall perspective of the meaning of these particular passages related to drunkenness. Notice the devastating consequences of drunkenness and how it offends our perfect God. While the world glamorizes and minimizes drunkenness, the Bible tells us the honest and severe consequences of such thinking and behaving.

This is by no means a comprehensive list. There are many more passages of Scripture on drunkenness in the Bible. Take the time and find your own scriptures. If you exhaust all of those verses, research all of the verses related to the topics of idolatry, sorcery, witchcraft, gluttony, lust, adultery, lying, etc. (These are not popular topics because they are brutally honest about the devastation of our sins, but they can serve as reminders for why it is so vital NOT to drink excessively or to abuse drugs.)

Genesis 9:20-23	Genesis 19:30-38	Deuteronomy 21:18-21
I Samuel 1:14-15	I Samuel 25:36-37	Proverbs 31:4-7
Isaiah 19:14	Isaiah 24:20	Jeremiah 25:27
Jeremiah 51:7	Habakkuk 2:15	Luke 12:45-46
Isaiah 28:1-4 & verses 7-8	Jeremiah 23:9	Joel 3:3
Hosea 4:10-11	Proverbs 20:1	Proverbs 21:17
Proverbs 23:20-21	Proverbs 23:29-35	Luke 21:34
Ephesians 5:15-21	I Corinthians 6:9-11	I Corinthians 5:11
I Thessalonians 5:7	I Peter 4:3	Revelation 18:3

The Extent of My Problem

How devastating have the consequences been from your addiction? Use this worksheet to determine the life-devastating consequences you now must face as a result of your problem of addiction.

1. **Marital:** If you are married, list the ways that your addiction has affected your intimacy with your spouse. Be sure to include lying, manipulation, control, poor communication, secrets, sexual problems, finances, in-law problems, and other hindrances to being "one flesh" according to biblical standards.

2. **Economic/Financial:** Figure out how much money you spent on your addiction in a typical day. Be sure to include gas, hotel rooms, phone bills, paying for others to use drugs, overdrawn bank accounts, and other related expenses.

Homework Assignment:

Now, estimate how much you spent on your addiction in a typical week by multiplying your above dollar figure for one day by the number of days you used in a typical week? For example, some people use 3-4 days a week so they would multiply 4 days by the number for one day reached above. Some use all 7 days so they would multiply it by 7. Now, estimate how much you spent on your addiction during this past 12 months. For example, 52 weeks multiplied by the amount in the weekly estimate above.

Example is in the chart that follows on the next page:

NAME OF EXPENSE	ESTIMATE COST PER 1 DAY	COST PER WEEK (Last column x 7 days usually)	TOTAL YEARLY COST (Last column x 52 weeks)
Buying Alcohol	$5.00	$35.00 ($5 x 7 days)	$1,820.00 ($35 x 52 weeks)
Buying Drugs	$100.00	$300.00 (only used 3 days so $100 x 3 days)	$15,600.00 ($300 x 52 weeks)
Hotel Rooms	$40.00	$80.00 (only used 2 days so $40 x 2 days)	$4,160.00 ($80 x 52 weeks)
Gas/Cell Phone	$5.00	$15.00 (only used 3 days so $5 x 3 days)	$780.00 ($15 x 52 weeks)
Overdrawn Bank	$20.00	$20.00 (1x per month)	$240.00 ($20 x 12 months)
		YEARLY TOTAL:	**$22,600.00**

Obviously, this is just an example but it is staggering to think how much money is wasted on drugs and alcohol per year. How else has your addiction cost you money?

3. **Social:**
  • How has your addiction affected your relationships with friends? How has it affected your relationships with church family and friends?

- How close are you to your pastor and church leaders?
- How has your addiction affected your relationships with co-workers?
- How have you treated people in general at the grocery store, gas station, etc.?

4. **Physical:** Rate your health on a scale from 1 to 10 (10 being in great health). How has your addiction caused your health to deteriorate? Name the ways.
   - If you smoke cigarettes or drugs, now or in the past, go to a pulmonary doctor to assess the condition of your lungs.
   - What exercise did you give up for your addiction? What eating habits did you develop that are not good for your health?
   - Do you drink water? Did you take care of your personal hygiene when using drugs?

5. **Emotional:**
   - What emotions do you struggle with the most: depression, self-pity, anger, worry, fear, etc.?
     - ➢ In what ways did your addiction *help* you to manage those emotions?
     - ➢ In what ways did your addiction *hurt* you in managing those emotions?
   - Are you a "feelings-oriented" person who must do what he/she feels?
     - ➢ Do you give into your feelings too much so that they tend to control you or lead you, rather than you controlling them?

6. **Familial:**
   - In what ways has your addiction affected relationships with family members (parents, siblings, children, extended family, etc.)?
   - What things have you done to hurt those relationships (steal, lie, cheat, manipulate, control)?

7. **Occupational:**
    - In what ways have you cheated your employer? Be specific. Not getting to work on time, being "hung-over" and not your best at work, and having your mind focused upon craving the drug rather than work are examples of cheating your employer.
    - Have you stolen from your employer in any other way?

8. **Legal:** Whether or not you have gotten caught, how have you broken the law? For example, breaking the law can be as simple as speeding in your vehicle or dealing drugs. Be specific.

9. **Spiritual:**
    - In what ways has your addiction been more of a priority to you than being obedient to God?
    - How much have you attended church this past year?
    - Have you been active in your church participation beyond just showing up every Sunday for a worship service?

10. **When was the first time you drank alcohol/used drugs?**
    - Describe the circumstances around that first time of drinking/drug usage.
    - How many years have you drank/used drugs since that first time?
    - Have you had periods of sobriety?
    - If so, for how long and what were the circumstances around your ability to refrain from alcohol and drugs during that time?
    - How often did you drink alcohol/use drugs this past week? _____ List number of days
    - In the past, when you were drinking/using drugs regularly, how many days out of the week did you use on average?

    _____
    - What is your drug of choice?
        ➤ Second choice?
        ➤ Third choice?

    Estimate: How much time did you spend thinking about your drug of choice yesterday? How much time did you spend thinking about it already today?

- List the things that you have done in the past that you now regret because of your love for drugs and the bad choices you made? (Ask God to forgive you for these things. Keep this list of people you've hurt because you now need to pray and find a way to ask forgiveness of them for your selfishness.)

What have I DONE?	Who was affected by my actions (or inaction)?	Plan for FORGIVENESS:

Appendix F

Contract For
Restructuring One's Life

**"Whoever keeps the commandment keeps his life;
he who despises his ways will die." Proverbs 19:16**

I cannot stress enough the importance of an hourly schedule for each day of the week for the first 3 months of sobriety. Write out as much detail as possible beginning from the "Awake" time, eat breakfast, etc. to the end: "Lights out." Do one for each day and take into account differences between weekday and weekend days. Be specific and structure it as it should be. Then, log your actual times each day to see how closely you kept to your original schedule. Adjust it as needed, but try to keep it as closely as possible. Do not allow yourself too much wiggle room.

Here is a sample contract to use for structuring one's life:

1. Will be home by 6:00 pm Monday - Friday.
2. Will be home by 8:00 pm Saturday - Sunday. (I Thessalonians 5:5-8)
3. Will not drink alcohol or use drugs for six months. (II Timothy 2:21 & I Corinthians 6:19)
4. Will provide weekly drug test results.
5. Will be on time to work and maintain my job responsibilities.
6. Will attend regular biblical counseling, at intervals recommended by my counselor.
7. Will provide finances for house and car payment by the 10th of each month.
8. Will not sneak out of the house at night.
9. Will not use the telephone without permission and without writing down who I am calling and the time of call in the telephone log.
10. Will not use profanity. (James 3:9-11)

11. Will attend worship service on Sunday mornings, evenings, and Wednesday evenings.

12. Will attend one other church-sponsored activity once a week (i.e. Bible study / fellowship).

13. Will have dinner with the family each weeknight.

14. Will take part in a family devotional meeting once per week.

15. Will not meet with anyone without a Christian friend or loved one present.

16. Will not have any guests in the house unless permission is obtained 24 hours in advance.

17. Will not smoke cigarettes. (More success at overcoming an addiction to alcohol and drugs is reported when addicts stop smoking cigarettes- believe it or not!)

18. Will not play inappropriate music or watch inappropriate television shows or movies.

19. Will not burn incense or candles in the house.

20. Will not lie or be dishonest in any way with loved ones.

Again, this is a sample contract. Tweak it as you see fit. For all of these restrictions (or put-offs), you can write a positive alternative (put-on) to put in place of the restriction so that you do not view these negatively. Look at all the Christian liberties and freedoms that God has allowed you to experience. Be joyful and not resentful at these things.

Appendix G
Renewing the Mind

Here's a trick question: How do you renew your mind? You don't do it alone, but God does it when you place the Word of God inside your heart. Colossians 3:16 states: **"Let the word of Christ dwell in you richly, teaching and admonishing one another in all wisdom, singing psalms and hymns and spiritual songs, with thankfulness in your hearts to God."** You must let "the word of Christ dwell in you richly." Let God's Word take up residence inside of you so much that it permeates all that you do. Now, here are some Scripture passages to read, study, meditate, and memorize so that your mind may be renewed by the Holy Spirit.

1. Before reading the passage, pray that God would open your eyes so that you can see clearly the lies you have believed and the truth that you must believe.

2. Read the passage one time through without stopping.

3. Read the passage again slowly and break it up into smaller phrases/words/pieces so that you can gain an understanding of each piece separately.

4. Think about what God's message is communicating to you in each separate piece. Usually, God's Word tells us something we are thinking or doing incorrectly as well as telling us the truth we must begin thinking and doing correctly. I like to think of this stage as renouncing the lies I believed and announcing God's truth about the issue.

5. Meditate upon each phrase until you have a better understanding of that section.

6. Memorize the verse by writing down the piece of Scripture and stating it out loud over and over.

7. Close your eyes and see if you can recite it without looking.

8. Now, move to the next piece of the Scripture verse and repeat the process.

9. At the end, recite the entire verse together and practice it three times each day (breakfast, lunch, and dinner) so that you have it down perfectly, smoothly, and quickly.

10. State it to a trusted Christian friend or loved one. Tell them what it means and how it helped you.

Here's a very simplistic example on how to do the above with Ephesians 4:22-24:

> ...to put off your old self, which belongs to your former manner of life and is corrupt through deceitful desires, and to be renewed in the spirit of your minds, and to put on the new self, created after the likeness of God in true righteousness and holiness.

1. Pray: "Lord, please open my eyes so that I might see what I need to do to change and how you are going to change me at the same time. I want to see wonderful things in your law, today."

2. Read it one time through (look at it above).

3. Now, read it slowly. Although I would break it up in this manner, you can break it up into even more pieces than this: Ephesians 4:22-24:

   a. to put off your old self

   b. which belongs to your former manner of life

   c. and is corrupt through deceitful desires

   d. and to be renewed in the spirit of your minds

   e. and to put on the new self

   f. created after the likeness of God in true righteousness and holiness.

4. God is stating:

   • I must change. The lie I believed is that I could go on living irresponsibly and keep drinking and "drugging" without consequences. The truth is that I must put off my old way of doing things.

   • My old self is that person who is selfish and lives like the unbeliever I used to be. The lie I believed is that I can live like an addict and still claim to be living like a Christian. The truth is that my lifestyle as an addict is not glorifying to God because it reflects the life of an unbeliever rather than the life of a Christian.

   • My old self is corrupt with desires that even deceive me. In other words, my addicted lifestyle tricks me in that I believe I am pleasing to God when I am not. That is the lie I have believed but the truth is that I am corrupt and selfish when I live according to my old nature to fulfill my desires and lusts for drugs and alcohol.

- I need to be renewed in the spirit of my mind. I need to think biblically. The lie I believed is that I can stop doing drugs on my own (put-off) without having to do anything else. The truth is that I must have my mind renewed about God, addiction, others, and myself. The battle begins in my mind and my thinking leads to emotions and actions.

- I must also put-on a new self. I must become a new person. If I stop doing drugs and do nothing else, then I am still a drug addict and drunkard even though I am not using (called a "dry drunk" in secular world). Therefore, the truth is that I must begin to think and act like a new creation in Christ by glorifying God in my actions. I must do things for others and consider others more important than myself.

- Wow. I have been created by God after His likeness, so how did I get into this sinful mess of addiction? I do not act righteously or holy when I am in the midst of my addiction. The lie that I believed is that I am a piece of junk God created by mistake. The truth is that I am His creation, I sin and choose to push the "go" button, and I can act rightly by the power of the Holy Spirit.

5. Christian meditation is different from secular meditation (i.e. yoga, etc.). Christians actively think about a specific verse/passage of Scripture and how it applies to their lives. Secular meditation is passive. One may allow anything and everything to come into one's mind. There is no direction or focus. "Freedom" is encouraged but what comes into one's mind is often not "freeing" at all! Christians must be purposeful and active in their thought life; therefore, meditation is upon the pure truths of God found in the Word. Meditate upon the verse or passage of Scripture each day for a week.

6. Memorize each piece of the above verse and slowly join it together as a cohesive unit (see steps 7 & 8 above). For this particular verse, I would take my time and spend at least a week on it.

7. Close your eyes and recite it piece by piece at first. Then try to do the entire passage. Take your time. This is not a race!

8. Practice the piece that you are working on before each meal. Or speak the piece during the prayer for your meal. Be creative!

9. Ask your spouse, friend, or family member if you can recite it for them. This will encourage them as well as you. Do not be afraid of failing or "looking foolish." Honor God.

Appendix H
Gratitude List and Thankfulness Verses

You must plan ahead in anticipation of the temptations you will face in overcoming a physical addiction. One practical tool that can help you is a "think list" or "gratitude list." When preparing a gratitude list, there are two verses from the Bible that are really helpful in developing your list. Philippians 4:8-9 states:

Finally, brothers, whatever is true, whatever is honorable, whatever is just, whatever is pure, whatever is lovely, whatever is commendable, if there is any excellence, if there is anything worthy of praise, think about these things. What you have learned and received and heard and seen in me—practice these things, and the God of peace will be with you.

Utilize this passage to help you develop a list of things that are "true, honorable, just, pure, lovely, commendable, excellent, and worthy of praise" for which you can be grateful. Then, follow the command to practice these things by reading this list aloud every morning to start your day and throughout the day when you are tempted to feed your "perishing mentality." Make multiple copies of it to keep in your pocket, in your car, in your nightstand, in your Bible, and anywhere else for quick access. Read it anytime you begin to have "perishing" thoughts.

Take a sheet of paper, turn it sideways, and use the chart below to help you visualize how to make a gratitude list so that you can create your own!

True	Honorable	Just	Pure	Lovely	Commendable	Excellent	Praiseworthy

THANKFULNESS VERSES TO MEMORIZE AND MEDITATE UPON

All of the following verses pertain to thankfulness and gratitude toward the Lord and are taken from The Holy Bible: English Standard Version. Wheaton: Good News Publishers, 2001. Spend time thinking about one verse per week. Meditate upon it and try to memorize it. You will be able to memorize it as you "practice" it more and more. Then, you will have a powerful weapon to use against the lies of the enemy and the attacks on your values from the world.

This is not a comprehensive list as there are many, many more passages of Scripture in the Bible. Take the time and find Scriptures that remind you about how good God is and how thankful we should be.

> **Therefore let us be grateful for receiving a kingdom that cannot be shaken, and thus let us offer to God acceptable worship, with reverence and awe, for our God is a consuming fire (Hebrews 12:28-29).**

> **Through him then let us continually offer up a sacrifice of praise to God, that is, the fruit of lips that acknowledge his name (Hebrews 13:14-15).**

> **I will give to the Lord the thanks due to his righteousness, and I will sing praise to the name of the Lord, the Most High (Psalm 7:17).**

> **Oh give thanks to the Lord, for he is good, for his steadfast love endures forever! Let the redeemed of the Lord say so, whom he has redeemed from trouble (Psalm 107:1-2).**

> **Oh give thanks to the Lord; call upon his name; make known his deeds among the peoples! Sing to him, sing praises to him; tell of all his wondrous works! Glory in his holy name; let the hearts of those who seek the Lord rejoice! (Psalm 105:1-3).**

And be thankful. Let the word of Christ dwell in you richly, teaching and admonishing one another in all wisdom, singing psalms and hymns and spiritual songs, with thankfulness in your hearts to God. And whatever you do, in word or deed, do everything in the name of the Lord Jesus, giving thanks to God the Father through him (Colossians 3:15-17).

Therefore, as you received Christ Jesus the Lord, so walk in him, rooted and built up in him and established in the faith, just as you were taught, abounding in thanksgiving (Colossians 2:6-7).

I will give thanks to the Lord with my whole heart; I will recount all of your wonderful deeds. I will be glad and exult in you; I will sing praise to your name, O Most High (Psalm 9:1-2).

Preserve me, O God, for in you I take refuge. I say to the Lord, "You are my Lord; I have no good apart from you" (Psalm 16:1-2).

Therefore my heart is glad, and my whole being rejoices; my flesh also dwells secure (Psalm 16:9).

Who delivered me from my enemies; yes, you exalted me above those who rose against me; you rescued me from the man of violence (Psalm 18:48).

The Lord is my strength and my shield; in him my heart trusts, and I am helped; my heart exults, and with my song I give thanks to him (Psalm 28:7).

I will thank you forever, because you have done it. I will wait for your name, for it is good, in the presence of the godly (Psalm 52:9).

I will give thanks to you, O Lord, among the peoples; I will sing praises to you among the nations. For your steadfast love is great to the heavens, your faithfulness to the clouds (Psalm 57:9-10).

But we your people, the sheep of your pasture, will give thanks to you forever; from generation to generation we will recount your praise (Psalm 79:13).

Oh give thanks to the Lord, for he is good, for his steadfast love endures forever! (Psalm 107:1).

Let them thank the Lord for his steadfast love, for his wondrous works to the children of men! (Psalm 107:8). These same exact words are used as a refrain in Psalm 107:15, 107:21, and 107:31.

I will give thanks to you, O Lord, among the peoples; I will sing praises to you among the nations (Psalm 108:3).

With my mouth I will give great thanks to the Lord; I will praise him in the midst of the throng (Psalm 109:30).

Praise the Lord, all nations! Extol him, all peoples! For great is his steadfast love toward us, and the faithfulness of the Lord endures forever. Praise the Lord! (Psalm 117:1-2).

Oh give thanks to the Lord, for he is good; for his steadfast love endures forever! (Psalm 118:1).

I was glad when they said to me, "Let us go to the house of the Lord!" (Psalm 122:1).

Praise the Lord! Praise the name of the Lord, give praise, O servants of the Lord, who stand in the house of the Lord, in the courts of the house of our God! Praise the Lord, for the Lord is good; sing to his name, for it is pleasant! For the Lord has chosen Jacob for himself, Israel as his own possession. For I know that the Lord is great, and that our Lord is above all gods. Whatever the Lord pleases, he does, in heaven and on earth, in the seas and all deeps. He it is who makes the clouds rise at the end of the earth, who makes lightnings for the rain and brings forth the wind from his storehouses (Psalm 135:1-7).

Give thanks to the Lord, for he is good, for his steadfast love endures forever. Give thanks to the God of gods, for his steadfast love endures forever. Give thanks to the Lord of lords, for his steadfast love endures forever (Psalm 136:1-3).

I give you thanks, O Lord, with my whole heart; before the gods I sing your praise; I bow down toward your holy temple and give thanks to your name for your steadfast love and your faithfulness, for you have exalted above all things your name and your word. On the day I called, you answered me; my strength of soul you increased. All the kings of the earth shall give you thanks, O Lord, for they have heard the words of your mouth, and they shall sing of the ways of the Lord, for great is the glory of the Lord. For though the Lord is high, he regards the lowly, but the haughty he knows from afar. Though I walk in the midst of trouble, you preserve my life; you stretch out your hand against the wrath of my enemies, and your right hand delivers me. The Lord will fulfill his purpose for me; your steadfast love, O Lord, endures forever. Do not forsake the work of your hands (Psalm 138:1-8).

Praise the Lord! Praise God in his sanctuary; praise him in his mighty heavens! Praise him for his mighty deeds; praise him according to his excellent greatness! Praise him with trumpet sound; praise him with lute and harp! Praise him with tambourine and dance; praise him with strings and pipe! Praise him with sounding cymbals; praise him with loud clashing cymbals! Let everything that has breath praise the Lord! Praise the Lord! (Psalm 150:1-6).

Saying, "We give thanks to you, Lord God Almighty, who is and who was, for you have taken your great power and begun to reign" (Revelation 11:16-17).

And they were to stand every morning, thanking and praising the Lord, and likewise at evening (I Chronicles 23:30).

For although they knew God, they did not honor him as God or give thanks to him, but they became futile in their thinking, and their foolish hearts were darkened (Romans 1:21).

Appendix I

Quick Reference for Biblical Approach to Addiction

If you are counseling or trying to help a loved one trapped in an addiction, you may use the following steps to guide you. Remember these are only guides you may utilize. Since every situation is different, you may need to vary the steps, but always let biblical principles guide you in your approach to helping an addict.

Seek a medical doctor's advice first. Depending on how much bondage the addict is in, you have to get them into a controlled, safe, and drug-free environment so they can "put-off" any temptations to drink alcohol or use drugs. Detoxification is one option, but not always necessary. Follow the doctor's advice.

The addict is usually not willing or compliant at first. Here are three (3) typical responses:

1. The addict wants to go back to substance abuse, is non-compliant with the authority over them, and finds a way to get back to drinking and doing drugs as quickly as possible.

2. The addict decides to rest awhile from drugs and alcohol so they comply with most of the rules until they decide to go back to their addiction. The addict "fools" everybody into thinking he is repentant by using the right words; however, an astute Christian will often discern the false repentance by observing that what is really in the heart of an addict is still selfishness, pride, and self-centeredness. The addict is really only "fooling" himself.

3. A Christian addict who really wants to change shows genuine signs of remorse, humility, gratitude, and REPENTANCE early in the process. Although not entirely willing at first, he becomes willing and works hard to become more obedient to God. Listen for the acceptance of RESPONSIBILITY for their actions as that is key. They are not afraid to do chores and tasks that are dirty and unglamorous because they are grateful to be out of the awful situation they were in while using drugs and alcohol. Plan on giving the Christian addict at least 40 days until you begin

to witness some real changes, but you will see evidence of a changed, willing heart from day one!

Create a safe structured environment for the Christian addict and do not allow him/her to be alone if at all possible. Set up consequences for violations of rules but always use those violations as an opportunity to examine the addict's heart. Teach forgiveness and repentance in that teachable moment, and allow the Christian addict to practice these biblical principles. The Bible says in Proverbs 29:15, that both the "rod and reproof" are required to give a child wisdom. Likewise, the Christian addict needs the rod (or consequence for his violation) AND a reproof (verbal, teaching instruction explaining what he did wrong, what God says about it, and what to do right the next time).

Slowly ease more responsibilities to the Christian addict as he/she demonstrates trustworthiness and faithfulness. Hold the Christian accountable for Bible studies, daily devotions, etc. so that you can better assess faithfulness and willingness.

Allow the Christian addict to live independently when sufficient changes have been made and the transformation process is solidly in place. At some point, the Christian addict is to become responsible for his/her own life while always recognizing his/her dependence upon God, the church, and others when appropriate. The primary goal is to allow the Holy Spirit to transform an irresponsible victim into a responsible person who can now help others and worship God everyday.

The heart attitude of humility and a servant's mindset is what God desires from a repentant addict. In Luke 15:11-32, the prodigal son became humble. The prodigal son did not return to his father and say, "Hey, Dad, I need to borrow a hundred bucks to fix my car. I need rent money, too. Oh, and by the way, can you get someone to wash my car while I eat dinner?" Instead, he returned to his father and said, "I am not worthy to be your son. I will be a slave for you. I want to serve you now. What can I do for you, Dad?" Can you see the difference in the heart attitudes in these two examples? When this renewing of the mind occurs, it is truly a beautiful sight to behold. To God be the glory for repentant sinners saved by grace (Ephesians 2:8-9).

Appendix J
Life Story

Writing your life story has several purposes and many benefits. One purpose for writing a life story is that it serves as a "memorial stone" for you and your children about what great things the Lord has done in your life. After the Israelites crossed over the Jordan River in a miraculous event ordained by God, the Lord commanded them to get large memorial stones to commemorate the event and use as an opportunity to teach future generations about what God had done in their lives. Joshua 4:6-7 states:

> **...that this may be a sign among you. When your children ask in time to come, 'What do those stones mean to you?' then you shall tell them that the waters of the Jordan were cut off before the ark of the covenant of the Lord. When it passed over the Jordan, the waters of the Jordan were cut off. So these stones shall be to the people of Israel a memorial forever.**

Before writing your life story, take a large piece of poster board, write out a time line from birth to the present. It will look something like this across your poster board:

Birth   Present

Now, use pictures and symbols to identify those people, events, and life circumstances that had an impact upon your life: positive or negative. Use symbols to depict the progression of your life's journey. Take 4 to 6 hours to do this one phase of preparing for your life history. You can do it alone and then ask a loved one for input in case you have forgotten anything, but I urge you to do it alone first before asking for help. It may be best to do it alone completely.

After you finish the time line of your life's journey, then spend a little time reflecting upon how God used key people, events, and life circumstances for your growth. Now, identify on the poster board the various phases of development in your life. Look at these seasons of growth and capture the periods of time and key people who impacted your life. Notice how the time line gives you a big picture perspective and provides new insights and encouragement about God's faithfulness in your life.[157]

Now, write out your life story utilizing the time line you just completed. Write it out as though you are writing a novel and make it as detailed and interesting as you can without embellishing or lying! As you author your own book about your life, remember to include life lessons, biblical principles, new insights, and God's Sovereign, loving, and guiding Hand. One of the main points of this exercise is for you to create a "memorial stone" to remind you and your children and your grandchildren about the goodness and sovereignty of your Creator and Heavenly Father. Do not leave God out of your life story as He is the most important character!

---

[157]Wailing, Terry, Focusing Leaders, CRM, 1998, page 35.

Appendix K
Words of Instruction and Caution

1. You must possess and understand three foundational principles in order to experience the transforming power and hope that is offered by Christ.

    a) You must be a Christian to understand God's perspective on addiction and gain insights to bring lasting change into your life. If you are not a Christian, do not quit reading this book! Keep reading and read Appendix B daily.

    b) You must believe in the supremacy of Scripture, the Holy Bible.

    c) You must believe that it is through the partnership of the Holy Spirit, the Holy Scriptures, and your obedience to them that lasting change is made available to you. This is called sanctification and it is a lifelong process.

2. Are you willing to dispose of the world's definitions of your problems and embrace what God says about your life? Using the non-biblical terms "substance abuser" and "addict" and "alcoholic" suggests that one is less responsible before God and that is not true. The substance abuser and addict are responsible before God for the thoughts, words, and behaviors that led to becoming physically addicted to alcohol and drugs. Christians are capable of being *physically* addicted to a drug; therefore, the words "substance abuser" and "addict" will be utilized in this book with caution and with the understanding that God's answers for addiction are spiritual, powerful, practical, and hopeful for believers. Be conformed to God's ways and transformed by the renewing of your mind. Do not attempt to make God's ways conform to your desires. God is your sovereign, infinitely wise Creator.

3. Do not read this book without prayer support. Is there someone in your life right now (a Christian friend, pastor, family member or loved one) who can commit to praying for you while you read and work through the concepts and instructions in this book? It may even be the person who gave you this book. Tell that person

you are reading this book and ask them to commit to praying for you daily until you finish it. This may be a year-long commitment (or more) so choose wisely whom to ask.

4. Do not read this book alone. Is there someone in your life right now (a Christian friend, pastor, family member or loved one) who can commit to walking with you through this period of time in your life as you seek God's answers for your addiction? This may or may not be the same person described in #3 above. You might even need more than one person to fulfill this responsibility for the commitment will be even greater for this task. This person needs to be a strong Christian person who has a deep love for God, and is willing to walk with you through this struggle. Prayerfully find this person before you go any further. You cannot be isolated, and you cannot do this alone. You need God and His mighty resources. Because the information in this book may be new and unfamiliar to you, you may need someone like a church leader or biblical counselor to read it with you who will be able to answer spiritual questions that arise.

5. You must have a Bible on hand every time you read *The Heart of Addiction*. In addition, I recommend purchasing *The Heart of Addiction Workbook*, a separate prayer notebook, and pen to help you and your trusted Christian friend look at the matters of your heart in light of your particular struggles.

6. Your primary goal for changing your ways must be to please God and glorify Him in all your thoughts, words, and behaviors – not just to sober up and get your circumstances fixed. If your circumstances at this time have driven you to look for help and you do not think your goal right now is to please God, then know that our journey together will ultimately bring you to the place where all there is to life is this – fearing God and honoring Him by keeping His commandments.

7. Are you currently planted and active in an evangelical, Bible-teaching church? If your answer is 'yes', then ask your pastor for help (or ask him for help in finding someone who can help you) as you work through the concepts in this book. If your

answer to this question is 'no', then begin to actively search for a Bible-teaching evangelical church today. Once again, you cannot isolate during this transformation process. Jesus had disciples and He commanded His followers to make disciples and to teach others.[158] You and I need teachers in life.

Use these 7 principles to sit down with a mentor and devise a customized "program" to follow to overcome your addiction. Appendix F will help you to add structure to your daily routine.

---

[158]Matthew 28:19-20

ABOUT THE AUTHOR

Mark E. Shaw, D.Min., is the Founder of Truth in Love Ministries. He and his wife, Mary, have four children and reside in Indianapolis, IN. As a prolific author, a certified addictions counselor since 1999, and a networking leader across the nation, Dr. Shaw has been a sought-after speaker on the topics of local church counseling and addictions. Internationally, he has joyfully accepted speaking and teaching opportunities in Russia, Romania, Dominican Republic, Egypt, and Albania. Here in the U.S., his most recent assignment was serving as the Executive Director and Pastor at Faith Church's Vision of Hope, a program for at-risk girls in Lafayette, IN. He holds CADAC II certification with the state of Indiana (ICAADA) and maintains biblical counseling certificates with ACBC and IABC.

Starting his career in the secular counseling arena in the 90's at various outpatient and residential programs, including a medication-assisted addiction treatment facility, Mark soon developed a burning desire to be able to freely offer the hope of the Gospel of Jesus Christ to all the hurting people that came across his path. He then went to pursue his desire to serve the Kingdom in full-time ministry. His Doctor of Ministry in Biblical Counseling was obtained from Birmingham Theological Seminary, which is where he first began writing practical, easy-to-read, and hopeful resources to offer help for anyone who is struggling. *The Heart of Addiction: A Biblical Perspective;* and *Divine Intervention: Hope and Help for Families of Addicts,* are among his most popular publications. Others include *Relapse,* a workbook style resource for those who return to their addictive struggles again; *Addiction-Proof Parenting: Biblical Prevention Strategies;* and *Strength in Numbers: The Team Approach to Biblical Counseling.* Browse all 20 of his resources at www.focuspublishing.com for more information.

Mark has also founded a new initiative, The Addiction Connection, www.theaddictionconnection.com as a network that facilitates training, addiction resourcing, and commissioning for those interested in utilizing a genuinely biblical approach to serve people with addictions. As an outreach arm of Truth in Love Ministries that seeks to connect and equip those on the front lines of addictions counseling, The Addiction Connection allows Mark to utilize his giftedness in relationally encouraging other like-minded biblical addictions counselors, while being a source of valuable information for those seeking biblical hope and help for themselves or loved ones.

Mark's passion is to glorify God through making disciple-makers by speaking the truth in love, seeing God fulfill Ephesians 4:11-16 in churches locally to globally.

Other publications by Mark E. Shaw:

BOOKS:

Divine Intervention: Hope and
Help for Families of Addicts

The Heart of Addiction Workbook

The Heart of Addiction Leader's Guide

Relapse: Biblical Prevention Strategies

Cross Talking: A Daily Gospel
for Transforming Addicts

Addiction-Proof Parenting:
Biblical Prevention Strategies

Strength in Numbers: The Team
Approach to Biblical Counseling

Eating Disorders: Hope for Hungering Souls

BOOKLETS:

Hope and Help through Biblical Counseling

Hope and Help for Marriage

Hope and Help for Men
as Husbands and Fathers

Hope and Help for Self-Injurers and Cutters

Hope and Help for Gambling

Hope and Help for Video Game,
TV and Internet "Addiction"

Hope and Help for Sexual Temptation

Hope and Help for Chronic Illness

How Not to Raise an Addict

Understanding Temptation

The Pursuit of Perfection (with Bill Hines)

All of Mark Shaw's resources are available from
Focus Publishing
www.focuspublishing.com